DARK HORSE

Also by Todd Rose

The End of Average

DARK HORSE

Achieving Success

Through the Pursuit

of Fulfillment

TODD ROSE

and OGI OGAS

HarperOne
An Imprint of HarperCollins*Publishers*

HarperOne

Photograph of Michelle Carter, page 196, courtesy PCN Photography/Alamy Stock Photo.
Photograph of Heidi Krieger, page 196, courtesy Wolfgang Thieme/German Federal Archives.

HarperCollins books may be purchased for educational, business, or sales promotional use. For information, please email the Special Markets Department at SPsales@harpercollins.com.

FIRST EDITION

Designed by Bill Ruoto

Library of Congress Cataloging-in-Publication Data

Names: Rose, Todd, author. | Ogas, Ogi, author.
Title: Dark horse : achieving success through the pursuit of fulfillment /
    by Todd Rose and Ogi Ogas.
Description: San Francisco : HarperOne, 2018
Identifiers: LCCN 2018014673 (print) | LCCN 2018017336 (ebook) | ISBN
    9780062683649 (E-book) | ISBN 9780062683632 (hardcover)
Subjects: LCSH: Success—Psychological aspects. | Excellence. | Satisfaction. |
    Individuality.
Classification: LCC BF637.S8 (ebook) | LCC BF637.S8 R5875 2018 (print) | DDC
    158.1—dc23
LC record available at https://lccn.loc.gov/2018014673

18 19 20 21 22 LSC 10 9 8 7 6 5 4 3 2 1

For my father, Larry

For my son, Zain

We hold these truths to be self-evident, that all men are created equal, that they are endowed by their Creator with certain unalienable Rights, that among these are Life, Liberty and the pursuit of Happiness.

—Thomas Jefferson, the American Declaration of Independence

contents

breaking the mold

Behind it all is surely an idea so simple, so beautiful, so compelling
that when—in a decade, a century, or a millennium—we grasp it, we
will all say to each other, how could it have been otherwise?
—Physicist John Archibald Wheeler

1.

It's safe to say nobody saw Jennie coming.

In 2005, using the ten-inch reflecting telescope at Farm Cove
Observatory in Auckland, New Zealand, Jennie McCormick
discovered an unknown planet in a solar system fifteen thousand
light-years away. A few years later she pulled off another uncommon feat when she discovered a new asteroid, which she patriot-
ically christened "New Zealand." She has coauthored more than
twenty papers in academic journals, including the prestigious
Science. The actress Gates McFadden, who played Dr. Beverly

Crusher on *Star Trek: The Next Generation*, sought out Jennie at a science fiction expo to request her autograph. Yet one of Jennie's lesser known accomplishments might be her most impressive of all: she became an internationally respected astronomer without obtaining a college diploma of any kind.

In fact, she never even graduated from high school.

Jennie was raised by a single mother in the river city of Wanganui. "I never fitted in well at school," she recalls. "I was a teenage girl with hormones, I didn't like the way I looked, I didn't like my shoes. I was headstrong and didn't have a lot of parental guidance. I just wanted to get out of there."

At the age of fifteen, she dropped out of school and took a job cleaning out horse stables. Not long after, Jennie's mother left her. Compelled to make her way on her own, Jennie attempted to pass the high school equivalency exam. She was not successful. By the time she was twenty-one, Jennie had become a single mother herself, supporting her infant son by serving chicken combo meals at a fast-food joint. Her future, to put it mildly, looked bleak.

Then came her turning point.

One night in her midtwenties, Jennie was visiting relatives who lived on the edge of an extinct volcano caldera, far from city lights. A family member handed her a pair of binoculars and urged her to peer up at the Milky Way, saying it was a sight that could only be seen in the backcountry. "I can still see myself lying down in the wet grass and looking through the binoculars at the sky and just, *Oh my God! Wow!*," Jennie recounts. "All those stars, it was just *awesome*. I was hooked! I knew nothing about them at all, nothing, but after that I just had to know more."

Jennie's stellar epiphany motivated her to learn everything she could about astronomy. Though she had little knowledge of science and few educational resources, she patiently trained herself to make precise observations with increasingly larger telescopes. In 1999, after eleven years of independent study and practice, Jennie cobbled together a domed observatory on her patio out of cast-off equipment and rusty parts. Five years after she completed her backyard "Farm Cove Observatory," Jennie employed a sophisticated observational technique known as gravitational lensing—harnessing the gravity of intervening stars to bend and focus distant light—to behold an exoplanet with a mass three times that of Jupiter. She became the first amateur to discover a new planet since 1781, when William Herschel discovered Uranus.

Another person nobody saw coming was Alan Rouleau. Named one of the top tailors in the country by *Town & Country* magazine, he designs handcrafted wardrobes for corporate titans, celebrities, and professional athletes. His boutique, Alan Rouleau Couture, resides on the swankiest stretch of Newbury Street in Boston, where he serves as the VIP tailor for the Taj, the Ritz-Carlton, the Four Seasons, and the Mandarin Oriental. He has been called a "virtuoso of exclusive fabric"—Piacenza cashmere, Drago super 180s, and Loro Piana super 200s all make their way into his modish creations. Alan's unique expertise blends mathematical precision, an exceptionally deep knowledge of the qualities of different cloth, and one of the most unappreciated aspects of bespoke tailoring—understanding each individual client on his own terms.

"You have to take into account their personality, their age, their skin tone, their career, their lifestyle—and especially their aspirations," explains Alan. "You've got to recognize not just who they are, but who they want to be." Alan's easygoing confidence and roguish charm invites clients to open up and reveal themselves, even those accustomed to the most attentive service and possessing the most discriminating taste.

You might guess that attaining such an elite level of mastery would require a lifetime of devotion to one's craft. And indeed, in the United States, most upscale tailors are raised in families who have been fashioning custom apparel for generations, or else are genteel imports from Europe where it's not unusual for tailors to be apprenticed in the art from boyhood.

Alan followed neither path.

He grew up in Leominster, a hardscrabble town in central Massachusetts, as one of six children. After he graduated from high school, Alan enrolled in Southeastern Massachusetts University, an inexpensive regional college, but given the number of siblings, his parents could not afford his tuition. Alan tried to pay his way through college by taking on multiple part-time jobs, attending classes during the day, pumping gas in the evenings, and loading UPS trucks before dawn. It didn't work out. Alan's exhausting hours prevented him from keeping up with his schoolwork, so he took a leave of absence in the hope of earning enough money to one day return to college. He wound up working as a bartender in the mill town of Gardner, serving fifty-cent drafts to college kids and blue-collar workers. It was not a very promising foundation for professional advancement.

But what Alan lacked in resources and connections, he made up for with savvy people skills and canny business instincts. When Alan's boss was unexpectedly forced to sell the bar where he worked, Alan seized the opportunity to purchase the business. Even though he had no assets and was only twenty years old, Alan managed to persuade a bank to loan him the money to buy the bar by arguing that his people skills would ensure his success as the new owner. Alan was right. He increased both customers and profits and eventually paid the loan off. But he didn't stop there. He also bought the building the bar was in, then opened a real estate company. He bought a four-decker apartment building. Then he bought another building and converted it into a restaurant. He purchased another bar at a racquetball and tennis club in the nearby town of Fitchburg—then bought the entire club. By the time he was twenty-eight, Alan had parlayed a night gig intended to pay for college into a small-town business empire.

Despite his enviable success, he felt that something important was missing from his life. A few years later, Alan looked in the mirror one morning and realized, "This is not who I truly am. There is more to me than this." In a move that shocked everyone around him, Alan sold off all his businesses and relocated to Boston, where he tried his hand at something that even those who knew him best would never have predicted: making men's suits.

It was a radical career pivot—but one that so thoroughly filled the void inside Alan that he immersed himself completely in the art of crafting custom apparel. After two years of diligent training and practice, at the age of thirty-five, he won his first national fashion award. Many more would follow. Soon Alan Rouleau Couture was holding its own against the most established and prominent tailors in the country.

Alan's and Jennie's journeys break the mold for how we think about the development of talent. To become a successful astronomer, the prescribed sequence is to obtain your PhD, complete a postdoc at a respectable university, and settle into a tenure-track professorship—not drop out of school, then teach yourself astronomy in your backyard. To become a successful bespoke tailor, the conventional route is to follow a youthful passion for fashion and slowly and steadily hone your skills over many years of apprenticeship at the feet of a master—not perform a mid-life swivel from an entirely unrelated profession. Jennie and Alan seemed to come out of nowhere, bursting onto the scene with their own signature version of excellence.

There is a term for those who triumph against the odds—for winners nobody saw coming.

They are called dark horses.

2.

The expression "dark horse" first entered common parlance after the publication of *The Young Duke* in 1831. In this British novel, the title character bets on a horse race and loses big after the race is won by an unknown "*dark* horse, which had never been thought of." The phrase quickly caught on. "Dark horse" came to denote an unexpected victor who had been overlooked because she did not fit the standard notion of a champion.

Ever since the term was coined, society has enjoyed a peculiar relationship with dark horses. By definition, we ignore them until they attain their success, at which point we are entertained and inspired by tales of their unconventional ascent. Even so, we rarely feel there is much to learn from them that we might profitably apply to our own lives, since their achievements often seem to rely upon haphazard spurts of luck.

We applaud the tenacity and pluck of a dark horse like Jennie or Alan, but the very improbability of their transformation—from fast-food server to planet-hunting astronomer, from blue-collar barkeep to upscale couturier—makes their journeys seem too exceptional to emulate. Instead, when we seek a dependable formula for success, we turn to the Mozarts, Warren Buffetts, and Tiger Woodses of the world. The ones everybody saw coming.

Mozart was composing symphonies at age eight, Buffett was buying stock at eleven, and Woods was winning golf tournaments at six. Early in life, they knew where they wanted to go and put in the long hours to get there. These conventional grandmasters seem to offer a more easily reproducible strategy for success: know your destination, work hard (very, very hard), and stay the course in the face of all obstacles until you reach your goal. This "Standard Formula" is confidently touted by educators, employers, parents, and scientists as the most reliable recipe for developing individual excellence. In contrast, the convoluted trajectories of dark horses like Jennie and Alan seem like curious one-offs rather than replicable blueprints for success.

But what if we have it exactly backward?

3.

Humans have been offering each other advice about success for a very long time. Precepts for the good life—what scholars often call "success literature" but which is more popularly characterized as "self-help"—are as old as philosophy. Aristotle, Confucius, and St. Augustine all authored tip sheets for prosperity. We might imagine that most of the counsel dispensed by these ancient gurus has endured as timeless words of wisdom, but that's not quite true. Success literature has a shelf life.

The most useful kind of advice is actionable and specific, and therefore tightly bound to the time and place where it originated. The recipe for success in third-century Polynesian society (learn to build and pilot canoes) was different from that in the thirteenth-century Mongol Empire (learn to ride and care for horses). The formula in the fifteenth-century Aztec Empire (avoid becoming a human sacrifice) was different from that in the eighteenth-century Russian Empire (avoid becoming a serf).

The general tropes of success literature are fairly consistent within any given epoch, but they frequently go through dramatic shifts whenever society transitions into a new era. One such inflection point is illustrated in the 1775 pamphlet *The Way to Be Rich and Respectable: Addressed to Men of Small Fortune*. Author John Trusler was writing during the final stages of England's conversion from a feudal economy into a merchant economy. He observed that in the emerging epoch, opportunities for wealth and status were no longer limited to hereditary dukes and barons: "Men were [previously] happy to be the vassals or dependants of their Lord, and prided themselves in little but their submission and allegiance . . . but as on the increase of trade, riches increased; men began to feel new wants . . . and sighed for indulgences they never dreamed of before." What was the formula for achieving success in this new era? Trusler suggested a strategy that at first seemed fanciful and impractical but that eventually came to define the new age: "independency." Not the tried-and-true practice of obedient allegiance to an aristocratic patron, but the unprecedented pursuit of personal autonomy.

The epoch that you yourself were born into commenced in the early twentieth century, as Western society transitioned into a factory-based manufacturing economy. That epoch is often dubbed the Industrial Age, but it would be more apt to call it the Age of Standardization. The assembly line, mass production, organizational hierarchies, and compulsory education became commonplace, leading to the standardization of most fixtures of everyday life, including consumer products, jobs, and diplomas.

As with every epoch, the Age of Standardization spawned its own definition of success: attaining wealth and status by climbing the institutional ladder. This new conception gave rise to modern self-help books, including such perennial bestsellers as Dale Carnegie's *How to Win Friends and Influence People* (1936), Napoleon Hill's *Think and Grow Rich* (1937), and Norman Vincent Peale's *The Power of Positive Thinking* (1952). This upward-looking generation of success literature emphasized habits and techniques designed to help individuals ascend the organizational hierarchy. As Hill advised, "The better way is by making yourself so useful and efficient in what you are now doing that you will attract the favorable attention of those who have the power to promote you into more responsible work that is more to your liking."

The Age of Standardization also marked the first time that self-help and mainstream science converged into the same recipe for obtaining success. As the twenty-first century rolled in, *New York Times* bestsellers and blue-ribbon social scientists were touting variants of the Standard Formula. For generations, the message "know your destination, work hard, and stay the course" has been impressed upon us as the most dependable stratagem for securing a prosperous life. This advice appears so unassailable that disregarding it seems perilous and foolish. Indeed, many recent books even go so far as to claim that the Standard Formula rises to the level of timeless human wisdom.

Not this book. *Dark Horse* is premised upon the conviction that we are entering a new epoch demanding a very different formula for success.

4.

We now inhabit a world where, with uncanny accuracy, Netflix recommends movies you might enjoy and Amazon suggests books you might like to read. It's a world of YouTube and on-demand television, individualized Google search results and customized news feeds, Facebook and Twitter. All these unprecedented technologies share the same defining quality: they are *personalized*. Yet this heady eruption of personalization technology is merely the peak of a mountain of changes upheaving society and heralding the dawning of an Age of Personalization.

We are experiencing this shift to the personal in our healthcare. Physicians increasingly prescribe the cancer treatment that will work best for *you*, given your unique physiology, health, and DNA, instead of prescribing the generic treatment that works best on average. More and more nutritionists are providing dietary recommendations tailored to your own metabolism and health goals, instead of offering one-size-fits-all recommendations, such as the US Food and Drug Administration's recommended daily allowances or the myriad food pyramids promoted by health organizations around the world. The growing push to monitor our individual well-being has given rise to Fitbit watches, 23andMe at-home DNA testing kits, and health apps like MyFitnessPal and Samsung Health.

We are experiencing this shift to the personal in our workplaces. Society is transitioning from an industrial economy dominated by large, stable, hierarchical organizations to an increasingly diverse and decentralized knowledge-and-service economy populated by freelancers, independent contractors, and free agents. You can no longer expect to work for the same firm your whole career; instead, most of us will switch jobs twelve or

more times before we retire and will outlive most of the organizations we work for.

Even our most rigidly standardized institution—education—is
experiencing the birth pangs of this pivot to the personal. Philan-
thropic organizations are investing billions of dollars in personalized learning programs that can be adapted to each student's
needs and abilities. The Bill and Melinda Gates Foundation and
the Chan Zuckerberg Initiative are funding the implementation of personalized education technologies in schools across the
country. Even colleges are beginning to embrace personalized
learning. In 2013, Southern New Hampshire University became
the first university to jettison grades and credit hours and win
Department of Education approval for a degree program that is
100 percent self-paced and competency-based.

These epochal changes in the way we learn, work, and live
might seem to be unrelated, but they are all rooted in a single
idea that animates the emerging Age of Personalization.

Individuality matters.

5.

The growing conviction that individuality matters is also transforming the way we think about success. In 2018, the nonprofit
think tank Populace conducted a national survey through Luntz
Global that questioned a demographically representative sample
of nearly three thousand men and women about their perspectives
on success. When the participants were asked what constituted
society's definition of success, the two most common responses by
far were wealth and status. But when asked if they agreed with this
definition, only 18 percent reported completely or mostly sharing society's view, with 40 percent asserting that they had moved

away from society's view over the course of their life. Instead, a large majority of respondents asserted that their own *personal* definition of success prioritized happiness and achievement.

This discrepancy between public and private views of success manifested most clearly when participants were asked about what kind of person was considered most successful: though 74 percent declared that according to *society's* definition it was "someone who is powerful," 91 percent said that for them *personally*, it was "someone who is purpose-driven." In other words, most of us tend to think that everyone else believes you must be rich and powerful to be successful, while at the same time feeling that we ourselves need personal fulfillment and a sense of self-determined accomplishment to consider ourselves successful.

But just because we now desire a new kind of success doesn't mean we know how to get it. This rising demand for a life of personalized success has run ahead of what science can deliver because the academic study of success remains stubbornly marooned in the Age of Standardization. For nearly a century, researchers have almost exclusively investigated one-size-fits-all notions of success, persistently posing the straightforward-seeming question: "What is the *best* way to achieve success?"

We took a different approach.

As scientists, the two of us were brought together by our shared conviction that individuality matters. We believe that to build a great and thriving society, we must get the best out of everyone, no matter who you are or where you are starting from. All our research is fueled by the proposition that the best way to help every human being live up to their full potential is by understanding and empowering individuals. In the spirit of this credo, we asked a slightly different question: "What is the best way for *you* to achieve success?"

To find the answer, we turned to dark horses.

6.

We did not choose dark horses as subjects because of some kind of academic tradition of using them in success research. There is no such tradition. In fact, when we surveyed the scientific literature, we could not find any major investigations of experts who pursued unconventional pathways to success. No, the reason we decided to study dark horses was personal.

We had both struggled through life, always swimming upstream. Todd dropped out of high school at age seventeen, married his teenage girlfriend, and had two children before his twentieth birthday. He supported his family by selling chain-link fence across rural Utah. Ogi dropped out of four different colleges five different times and could not hold down a nine-to-five job, at one point supporting himself by selling used books out of the trunk of his car. We both had a long rap sheet from our transgressions during the Age of Standardization, languishing through long stretches when we tried our best to conform to the standardized institutions of work and school, yet were never able to fit in.

Maybe we only managed to claw our way to professional proficiency through dumb luck, but one thing we knew for sure was that whatever success we had scraped together was the result of breaking the rules of the game. Not out of defiance or hubris. Out of grim necessity. All of our attempts at following the Standard Formula resulted in failure.

That realization provided us with our hunch that dark horses might present a special opportunity for investigating how to achieve excellence on your own terms. If there were in fact principles for attaining mastery that could be adapted to any person—no matter who you are or where you are starting from—we thought the best place to look for them was in the lives of experts who succeeded outside the system.

That's why we launched the Dark Horse Project.

We began interviewing experts from a wild menagerie of disciplines, including opera singers, dog trainers, hair stylists, florists, diplomats, sommeliers, carpenters, puppeteers, architects, embalmers, chess grandmasters, and midwives—not to mention astronomers and tailors. We did not try to impose any preconceived notions about self-improvement or the nature of talent on our subjects. Instead, we listened. We let each expert describe their journey to professional excellence in their own words.

It turns out that you can learn a lot by listening. We quickly discovered that many experts had done poorly in school or dropped out entirely (like Jennie McCormick). We interviewed an executive at Apple who quit an elite graduate program in computer science, a record-setting pilot who never went to college, and the owner of an international marine-mammal-training organization—who also happens to be Disney's longest-working voiceover artist—who spent his childhood getting home-tutored by a stranger.

Other dark horses did quite well in school or business but abruptly switched their careers to something entirely different (like Alan Rouleau). We talked to a man who obtained a PhD in literature before trekking to the frozen north and returning as an expert on exotic fungi, a construction company executive who became the first vice chancellor for Oxford University in nine hundred years who didn't come out of the academic ranks, and a woman who studied cognitive linguistics in an Ivy League graduate program until she abandoned academia to become a world-class poker wizard.

Every dark horse we interviewed followed an unorthodox route to excellence, by definition. But the question we needed to answer was this: Did Jennie and Alan and the other mold-breaking experts share anything else in common, some essential quality that explained *how* they achieved their improbable mastery?

7.

You might guess, as we did at the outset, that all dark horses share some defining character trait, such as an urge to buck the system. Maybe most dark horses would turn out to be mavericks with outsized personalities, like Richard Branson—rebels driven by a fierce ambition to make their mark and prove the world wrong.

That's not what we found at all.

Instead, we discovered that the personalities of dark horses are just as diverse and unpredictable as you would find in any random sampling of human beings. Some are bold and aggressive; others are shy and deferential. Some enjoy being disruptive; others prefer being conciliatory. Dark horses are not defined by their character. Nor are they defined by a particular motive, socioeconomic background, or approach to training, study, or practice. There *is* a common thread that binds them all together, however, and it was hard to miss.

Dark horses are *fulfilled*.

8.

When we first set the Dark Horse Project in motion, fulfillment was the last thing on our minds. We were hoping to uncover specific and possibly idiosyncratic study methods, learning techniques, and rehearsal regimes that dark horses used to attain excellence. Our training made us resistant to ambiguous variables that were difficult to quantify, and personal fulfillment seemed downright foggy. But our training also taught us never to ignore the evidence, no matter how much it violated our expectations.

Many dark horses explicitly mentioned "fulfillment." Others talked about their strong sense of "purpose." Some described their "passion" for their work or their "sense of pride" in their achievements. A few spoke of living a "life of authenticity." Several dark horses volunteered "this is my calling," and one informed us in hushed and reverent tones, "I am living the dream." No matter how they described it, every dark horse we conversed with was confident in who they were and deeply engaged with what they were doing. Simply put, their lives are meaningful and rewarding.

Like the rest of us, they struggled with getting the kids to bed and paying down the car loan, and there was invariably more they hoped to accomplish in their careers, but they woke up most mornings excited to get to work and went to bed most nights feeling good about their lives. This discovery led us to the most important revelation of all.

As we dug deeper, we realized that their sense of fulfillment was not a coincidence. It was a choice. And this all-important decision to pursue fulfillment is what ultimately defines a dark horse.

9.

The fact that dark horses were *choosing* to prioritize fulfillment stands in stark contrast to the way we usually think about how we come by it. We tend to believe that we are granted happiness as a *consequence* of mastering our vocation—that fulfillment is the *payoff* for attaining excellence. But how many people do you know who are excellent at their jobs, yet unhappy all the same?

One of our friends is a highly paid corporate lawyer, but she never ceases complaining about how disengaged she feels from the daily grind, bitterly voicing her wish that she had chosen a different path. Another of our friends is a physician with a thriving practice, yet he remains bored by his work, finding solace in travel and hobbies instead.

The fact that excellence is no guarantee of fulfillment should not surprise us. After all, fulfillment does not appear anywhere in the Standard Formula. Instead, institutions and scholars who earnestly trumpet the Standard Formula *imply* that if you know your destination, work hard, and stay the course, fulfillment will be bestowed upon you once you reach your destination. Earn your diplomas, land a good job, and happiness will ensue . . . somehow.

The Age of Standardization has enforced the dictum that if you strive for excellence, you will obtain fulfillment. Yet even though this maxim has been impressed upon us for generations, we are finally starting to abandon it en masse as we realize just how hollow its promise rings in the emerging Age of Personalization. Dark horses are helping drive this epochal transition because their lives embody an antithetical truth that flips the script. The most important headline about Jennie and Alan and the other unlikely luminaries from the Dark Horse Project is not that their pursuit of excellence led them to fulfillment.

It is that their pursuit of fulfillment led them to excellence.

10.

At first, we were puzzled. How on earth could prioritizing fulfillment consistently enable dark horses to attain excellence? But as
we continued our interviews, we began to realize that the answer
lay within the very reason we decided to recruit dark horses in
the first place.

Their individuality.

The circumstances that provide fulfillment are different for
each person, because each person's interests, needs, and desires
are different. Dark horses were not fulfilled by being excellent
at *some*thing but by being deeply engaged with their *own* thing.
Jennie McCormick is fulfilled by gazing through telescopes at
distant worlds. Alan Rouleau is fulfilled by fashioning stylish apparel. Swap their jobs, though, and neither one would be very
happy.

Even within a single profession, different dark horses find
purpose and pride in different aspects of their work. Some architects derive pleasure from designing the biggest and most
provocative buildings, others from figuring out how to minimize the environmental impact of buildings. Some athletes prefer solitary sports where winning or losing rests entirely on their
own shoulders; others prefer the camaraderie and shared responsibility of team sports. There is no such thing as one-size-fits-all
fulfillment.

People often believe that when it comes to earning a living,
you must choose between doing what you like and doing what
you must. Dark horses teach us that this is a false choice. By
harnessing their individuality, dark horses attained both prowess
and joy. By choosing situations that seemed to offer the best fit
for their authentic self, dark horses secured the most effective cir-

cumstances for developing excellence at their craft, since engaging in fulfilling work maximizes your ability to learn, grow, and perform. Thus, dark horses provide a new definition of success suited for the Age of Personalization, one that recognizes that individuality truly matters:

Personalized success is living a life of fulfillment and excellence.

11.

For all its dazzling promise, the looming Age of Personalization can be disorienting and frightening. When confronted with such sweeping social upheaval, our instinct is often to return to the reassuring safety of the old ways, the cookie-cutter promises of the Age of Standardization. Even if the old ways don't fit us perfectly, at least they are familiar and predictable. But following the same old formula is no longer the safe strategy. It is now a sure way to get left behind.

The world around us is changing so rapidly that it can often seem unrecognizable. Institutions, attitudes, and norms are in a state of flux, leaving people anxious and confused. But concealed inside this chaotic upheaval lies immense promise. Opportunities that not so long ago were mere wishful thinking have become possible. And what was once merely possible, dark horses have shown to be practical. And soon, as personalization spreads throughout the entire breadth of society, the merely practical will become essential.

Fortunately, you don't need to wait for the Age of Personalization to save you. You can start advancing toward fulfillment and excellence right now. The successes of dark horses demonstrate not only how to triumph when thrust into this chaotic new world, but also how to prevail when you must buck the rigid

old system that confines you still. Stereotype-shattering stars like
Jennie and Alan demonstrate that personalized success does not
depend on who you know, how much money you have, or what
you score on the SAT. It is not reserved for those perched at the
top of the ladder. By its very nature, personalized success is available to everyone.

The key to attaining fulfillment and excellence is a mindset
that empowers you to fit your circumstances to your unique interests and abilities. This mindset can be rendered in plain English:

Harness your individuality in the pursuit of fulfillment to achieve
excellence.

Prioritizing fulfillment is hardly a new idea. A long line of
philosophers and gurus have exhorted us to chase our passion or
put happiness first. But what is almost always lacking in these ser-
mons are actionable instructions. "Follow Your Bliss" is a bumper
sticker, not a road map. "Do What Feels Good" can often be a
surefire prescription for feeling bad. What is really needed is a set
of practical guidelines that can help *you* figure out what *you* truly
want and how to attain it, given *your* unique circumstances. That
is why we wrote this book.

Dark Horse is first and foremost a user manual for the dark
horse mindset. In the chapters that follow, we share lessons from
the Dark Horse Project that demonstrate *how* to harness your
individuality to achieve fulfillment and excellence on your own
terms. Our aim is not to help you become the best in the world—
often a counterproductive proposition. Instead, we want to help
you become the best version of yourself.

We will show you how the four elements of the dark horse
mindset have been road tested by a wide array of women and
men nurturing every manner of aspiration. Their journeys reveal

a counterintuitive approach to success that has been hidden in plain sight. As you may have guessed by now, these dark horses are not the kind of celebrity superstars who usually adorn the pages of books about success. You will not find Steven Spielberg or Serena Williams or Steve Jobs deconstructed in the chapters ahead. Instead, you will meet Spielberg's assistant director, an Olympic shot-putter, and one of Steve Jobs's first hires, along with a White House political operative turned professional closet organizer, a management consultant who quit her lucrative job to start a supper club, and a US Marine who built one of the nation's most successful dog-training companies.

The Dark Horse Project reveals that we can learn as much from their stories as we can from those of their more celebrated counterparts—often much more. Their overlooked triumphs illustrate how personalized success is truly achievable by everyone, not just the privileged or the elite. They demonstrate that the pursuit of fulfillment does not resign you to a vow of poverty or a life of hardship.

It maximizes your chances for living your very best life.

Whether you feel trapped in a dead-end job or are taking the first steps on your journey, whether you think you already know your true calling or feel directionless and adrift, the dark horse mindset can guide you to a life of passion, purpose, and achievement.

chapter 1

the standardization covenant

Men in control of vast organisations have tended to be too abstract in their outlook, to forget what actual human beings are like, and to try to fit men to systems rather than systems to men.

—Bertrand Russell

1.

Ingrid Carozzi is one of the most acclaimed floral artists in New York City. She crafts sumptuous, one-of-a-kind arrangements for high-society weddings, the Burberry flagship store, and the royal court of Sweden. Some might call Ingrid a late bloomer, though. For most of her life, nobody expected her to achieve such success—least of all Ingrid.

When she was in her midthirties, Ingrid was working as a low-level associate for a Manhattan public relations firm, the latest in a string of jobs that did not particularly suit her. She had previously served stints as an airline attendant, an English teacher, a croupier, and a waitress. She had started out as a social anthropology major before drifting in and out of five different college programs. Despite her earnest career gyrations, professional success eluded Ingrid.

More than one person voiced the opinion that Ingrid's problem was a lack of discipline. If she wanted to make something of herself, they advised, she needed to pick one thing and work hard at it. But Ingrid always worked hard. By the time she took the public relations gig, she had come to believe that the real problem was something other than a simple question of industriousness. That in some elementary way she could not find her place in the world. "I was always trying to stick to the straight path, because I thought that's how you learned where you were supposed to fit in," Ingrid says. "But whenever I took the straight path, things never seemed to work out."

Most dark horses confided feelings similar to Ingrid's. Such confessions did not come easy. Nobody wants to talk about dropping out of college. Nobody wants to talk about getting fired or trudging through jobs they hate. Nobody wants to own up to feeling inadequate or inconsequential. When it comes right down to it, nobody ever wants to admit feeling out of place in their own life. And yet, most dark horses went through at least one mirthless period when they felt exactly that.

John Couch, for one, gained admission to the University of California, Berkeley's highly selective PhD program in computer science but soon felt his instructors' mathematical and abstract approach to programming was at odds with his own creative, human-focused impulses. John felt so out of place that he decided to abandon his graduate studies altogether.

Another example is Doug Hoerr. For ten years, he had been working for his relatives' landscaping company in Peoria, Illinois, designing and building suburban gardens, lamppost plantings, and residential patios. Though he enjoyed the planning of projects and always looked forward to working outside with his hands, Doug felt limited by the constraints of his job. Instead of obeying the standard blueprints of conventional landscape design, he yearned to use plants in new and inventive ways—to convert horticulture into a living palette that could express his own creative vision. Realizing he needed to make a change, Doug abruptly quit his job, sold almost everything he owned, and ventured overseas.

Time and again, we encountered a common theme in the journeys of dark horses: a period when they did not fit into their lives—when they felt like a round peg in a square hole. Some were stuck in tedious jobs that required little in the way of acumen. Others developed enviable expertise in a field they believed they *should* be mastering because it was respectable, stable, or lucrative, yet they felt little satisfaction. Despite feeling bored or frustrated, underutilized or overwhelmed, most dark horses reluctantly plodded along for years before finally coming to the realization that they were not living a fulfilling life.

Then came the turning point.

As Ingrid puts it, "I didn't feel pride in myself until I embraced the winding path."

2.

For Jennie McCormick, the turning point was lying in the wet grass gazing up at a celestial curtain of light and vowing to fathom the whirling mystery of the stars. For Alan Rouleau it was disposing of his small-town enterprise and venturing to the big city.

Before arriving at their crossroads, dark horses tried to adhere to the track laid out for them by society, often unthinkingly. Afterward, their decisions were motivated by a new premise. They made their choices based on what seemed most likely to lead them to fulfillment.

Thus, fulfillment manifested in our conversations with dark horses in two key ways. First, as a self-reported description of their state of mind. They *told* us they "loved their life." Second, and more revealing, fulfillment consistently burst forth as a distinctive narrative element.

When we probed critical junctures in dark horses' progression toward excellence, instead of focusing on training techniques or the acquisition of new skills, they described choosing opportunities that fit their truest self. Even in the face of all the mundane struggles of everyday life, such as bills, babies, family tragedies, and economic downturns, they strived for authenticity. For a sense that their individuality mattered.

Dark horses frequently encounter forks in the road that prompt them to forsake the straight path for a winding path. But that invites the question: What, exactly, is provoking these turning points?

3.

You might suspect that the agent provocateur is different for each dark horse. Strictly speaking, that's true. Fulfillment is always personal. But if personal fulfillment varies from dark horse to dark horse, this fact alone provides a clue about the type of agent that could repeatedly incite dark horses to believe they need to change the direction of their life: it must be a pervasive social force that suppresses individuality. For her part, Ingrid knew exactly where to cast the blame: "The biggest reason I felt like I never fit in was the Law of Jante."

In Scandinavia, where Ingrid grew up, the Law of Jante is a set of deeply rooted cultural beliefs concerning the relationship between individuality and success. As Ingrid explains, "According to the Law of Jante, everybody is supposed to be treated the same, everybody is supposed to act the same, you are not supposed to think that you're special in any way, and you're definitely not supposed to just go off and do your own thing."

Around here, there is a more familiar term for this mindset. *Standardization.*

4.

By the 1890s, the E. R. Squibb Company of Brooklyn had become the leading manufacturer of ether, mineral salt laxatives, and disinfectant toothpaste in the United States and enjoyed a large share of the market for quinine, opium, and chloroform. The company's unprecedented commercial success marked the birth of American Big Pharma, an achievement entirely attributable to its founder's uncompromising commitment to standardization.

Dr. Edward Robinson Squibb originally worked as a physician for the US Navy, where he was tasked with evaluating the quality of medications the navy procured. Squibb quickly discovered that the purity of virtually every drug not only varied from supplier to supplier, it often varied from batch to batch— and sometimes from bottle to bottle. Fed up, Squibb decided he would build a company whose guiding mission would be to manufacture drugs that were meticulously identical. The long-abiding motto of the E. R. Squibb Company was "Reliability. Uniformity. Purity. Efficacy."

Its unshakable dedication to standardization propelled the organization all the way forward into the twenty-first century, where it endures today as Bristol-Myers Squibb. At the dawn of the Age of Standardization, many other American corporations also became modern titans of industry by standardizing their products, including Exxon (originally Standard Oil, the first company to standardize kerosene), Kellogg's (originally Battle Creek Toasted Flakes Company, the first company to standardize breakfast cereal), and the Ford Motor Company ("Any customer can have a car painted any color that he wants so long as it is black").

The goal of all standardization is to maximize the efficiency of a system of production. The prime mechanism by which standardization accomplishes this is through the elimination of individual variation. Standardization establishes fixed processes that convert fixed inputs into identical outputs, without deviation or fluctuation.

In other words, the standardization mindset is committed to the principle that *individuality is a problem*.

5.

It certainly made good sense to apply the standardization mindset to the manufacture of products. If you have a headache, you want every pill in a bottle of aspirin to be the same as every other. If you are driving across the country, you want a gallon of gas to be the same whether you buy it in Maryland or Missouri. And even though we might want our car customized to suit our personal taste, Henry Ford's standardization of automobiles underscored the greatest consumer benefit from standardized products: lower costs. In Ford's era, the choice for most Americans was not between a standardized car and a customized car—it was between being able to afford an inexpensive black-painted Model T or having no car at all.

In fairness, if you are standardizing a system of production, then individuality truly is a problem. It's a problem for reliability, uniformity, purity, and efficacy, which means it's a problem for productivity. That's why individuality was systematically eliminated from industry at the dawn of the Age of Standardization.

If we had limited ourselves to standardizing products, there might not have been any need for the book in your hands. But our collective notion of success—and our individual ability to attain it—was utterly transformed once we decided to standardize human beings the same way we standardize aspirin.

There was nothing sinister about this development. It was merely the natural extension into the workplace of an extraordinarily successful manufacturing philosophy. In the old nineteenth-century system of custom craftsmanship that was eventually supplanted by standardization, a company's workplace was frequently reorganized to suit the sensibilities of each new crop of laborers. But the "father of standardization," American industrialist Frederick Taylor, realized that in a system of factory production where machines were expensive and heavy but humans were cheap and malleable, it was more efficient to arrange the workers around the machines than to arrange the machines around the workers.

Thus, the first unfortunate souls to get standardized were the factory workers. They were assigned new roles that were fixed and unvarying, requiring little or no independent thought. Tighten that screw. Tote that bale. Cut that wire. By the time Charlie Chaplin wrote and directed the 1936 movie *Modern Times*, depicting his Little Tramp character haplessly battling a world of mechanized factories, almost every American worker had been transmuted into a cog in the great supermachine of industrial efficiency.

Ray Kroc, one of standardization's most devoted acolytes and the founder of a franchise that continues to manufacture billions of identical Big Macs each year, justified this conversion of human beings into widgets by appealing to the wisdom of the standardization mindset: "We have found out as you have that we cannot trust some people who are nonconformists. We will make conformists out of them in a hurry. . . . You can't give them an inch. The organization cannot trust the individual; the individual must trust the organization."

6.

In this spirit, the early standardizers of the workplace devised a new form of business organization composed of a rigid hierarchy of two classes of employees. On the bottom were the *workers*, whose obedient duty (according to Frederick Taylor) was "to obey the orders we give them, do what we say, and do it quick." On the top were the *managers*, who told the workers what to do and henceforth were granted full authority to make all decisions within an organization.

That sounds like a sweet deal for the managers. But even though they annexed most of the workers' previous power and autonomy, the managers, too, swiftly found themselves treated as interchangeable parts rather than distinct talents. In a standardized organizational hierarchy, every manager fills a fixed and predefined role. The duties of the comptroller and the director of marketing do not vary depending on the person who occupies the post. In a standardized workplace, no position is exempt from the dictum that individuality is a problem.

Next, standardization spread to our children. Admiring the astonishingly successful standardization of the business world, education reformers were inspired to redesign schools and the classroom experience around the same guiding principle of ruthless efficiency. In the early twentieth century, the entire American educational system was transformed through standardized curricula, standardized textbooks, standardized grades, standardized tests, standardized semesters, and standardized diplomas. Replicating the industrial division of workers and managers, professional educators were henceforth divided into a rigid hierarchy of teachers and administrators. Classrooms were redesigned to emulate factories, all the way down to school bells announcing class changes in imitation of factory bells announcing shift changes. "Our schools are, in a sense, factories, in which the raw products (children) are to be shaped and fashioned into products to meet the various demands of life," wrote Ellwood Cubberley in his highly influential 1916 guide to educational standardization, *Public School Administration.*

First we standardized work. Then we standardized learning. Then we integrated our standardized workplace with our standardized educational system, establishing standardized careers. And once the full passage of our experience was standardized from our first day of kindergarten until the morning of our retirement, it marked the complete standardization of a human life.

7.

Since the 1950s, standardized life paths have been perhaps most apparent in the career tracks for lawyers, doctors, and engineers.

In these fields there is precious little chance of becoming a working professional without proceeding through all the prescribed stages of training in the prescribed order and in the prescribed manner. High school, college premed, medical school, medical licensing exam, medical internship, medical residency, attending physician—success! Over the course of the twentieth century, standardization has insinuated itself into just about every vocation so that today there are ordained routes for becoming an airline pilot, executive chef, nuclear physicist, corporate accountant, cinematographer, high school principal, pharmacist, and department store manager.

The establishment of standardized career tracks to professional excellence inaugurated the Age of Standardization's definition of success: attaining wealth and status by climbing the institutional ladder. And once the route to prosperity and competence became well-defined, fixed, and predictable, every member of society could see exactly what they needed to do to achieve professional success: pick your career goal, then march resolutely down the appropriate training track to its appointed end. It should come as no surprise that fulfillment appears nowhere in the Standard Formula. Fulfillment depends on individuality, and individuality was expunged from the straight path at the very onset of the Age of Standardization.

Thus, the uniformizing values of standardization spread throughout the industrialized world on the heels of factories and schools. The reason we all came to accept this dehumanizing system so wholeheartedly is because society made an implicit promise to its citizens in the Age of Standardization: if you can follow the straight path to its destination, you will be granted employment, social status, and financial security. This promise eventually became so firmly entrenched in American society (and calcified into an even more rigid form in Europe, and petrified into an utterly inflexible form in Asia) that it assumed the form of a fundamental social contract.

According to the terms of this Standardization Covenant, society will bestow its rewards upon you as long as you abandon the individual pursuit of personal fulfillment for the standardized pursuit of professional excellence.

8.

Why would anyone agree to such self-negating terms? Because on the face of it, the Standardization Covenant seems both egalitarian and fair—especially compared to what came before. In the nineteenth century, genuine opportunity was limited to those privileged with the right family, right ethnicity, right religion, right gender, or right bank account. In contrast, the Standardization Covenant appeared to establish a bona fide meritocracy.

Under the covenant, not *everyone* could attain success—you still needed to work hard and demonstrate talent—but for the first time, the ladder of opportunity became accessible to *anyone*. That remains its ostensible promise: whoever proves to exhibit the most merit as judged by our standardized institutions will be granted access to society's best opportunities. The covenant pledges that by hewing to the straight path, anyone has a fair chance to become a radiologist, patent lawyer, management consultant, Fortune 500 executive, or Ivy League professor. All you need to do to claim your prize are the same things everyone else is required to do—you just need to do them better than your peers.

Take the same classes, but get better grades. Take the same tests, but get better scores. Pursue the same diplomas, but attend better universities. The chief commandment for achieving success within the Standardization Covenant can be summed up in eight simple words:

Be the same as everyone else, only better.

9.

The flip side of this commandment also happens to constitute the covenant's fatal flaw: *our standardized institutions of opportunity were never designed for personal fulfillment.*

The Standardization Covenant demands, with apparent prudence, that we suppress our yearnings and delay our happiness in the name of a long, dutiful march toward professional proficiency. Under the covenant, happiness is the *reward* for working hard and staying the course. The prospect of abandoning the straight path for your own quirky hunt for fulfillment strikes most people as self-indulgent and foolhardy. If you expect happiness before you've paid your dues, you're scorned as a special snowflake or spoiled brat—or worst of all, a millennial.

This is the explicit sentiment of the Law of Jante, as well as the implicit judgment of the Standardization Covenant, a judgment almost universally embraced throughout the Age of Standardization. Most moms and dads sign off on the covenant after concluding that the waiving of some unknowable measure of near-term happiness is a small price to pay for a recognizable guarantee of future security. Of course every parent wants their child to be happy—but they take it as an article of faith that the promised rewards of the straight path will offer their child the freedom to indulge whatever needs and passions might arise later in life, thereby compensating for any hypothetical joys that were renounced along the way.

It's certainly a rational calculation. If success consists of ascending the institutional ladder of opportunity—of scaling the gleaming rungs of school and work—then you will do what you can to prevent your child from getting marooned at the bottom. As any college admissions officer or high school counselor can tell you, most parents don't want to hear about philosophical prescriptions for a fulfilling life—at least, not until their child has been admitted to Stanford. They just want to know how to boost their kid's chances of getting in.

The covenant compels us to measure individual success through a simple linear reckoning: How high did you climb? Such an interpretation of success also runs the other way—if people *do* manage to hoist themselves to the topmost rungs, we expect that they damn well better be happy. What is the point of scaling the ladder if not to grasp the ultimate prize of personal fulfillment? When we hear an NFL player or Hollywood actor complain about their lot in life, we have little sympathy. You're a famous millionaire and depressed? What's wrong with you? In the same peremptory manner, we shrug off the misery of those who end up in menial jobs. Happiness is for winners, after all! Under the Standardization Covenant, it makes perfect sense that if you failed to stay the course, you should not expect the same benefits as those who exerted the sweat and toil to reach the summit.

Even though most parents know in their heart that taking an SAT prep course or exaggerating on a college admission essay is not going to help their kid become a happier or more purposeful human being, they vigorously defend such activities as essential for attaining the covenant-promised good life—and avoiding the fearful mire of the covenant-transgressing bad life. That's why when choosing where to raise their children, parents with the means often evaluate neighborhoods on the basis of the average GPA and college admission rates of students in the local school district, even paying a premium to live in communities with higher average SAT scores.

But the unquestioning obedience to a system of talent development that ignores personal fulfillment has profound consequences for all of us. Most notably, it compels you to experience a crisis of soul-searching doubt when you realize you are not living a life of authenticity.

It compels you to experience a turning point.

10.

The fact that the Standardization Covenant does not prioritize personal fulfillment explains why the feelings of disaffection, restlessness, and uncertainty experienced by dark horses are so frequently devalued by those in charge of the straight path. Students and employees who complain of unrewarding experiences are often dismissed as possessing an unjustified sense of entitlement, or ridiculed for their presumption that institutions should accommodate their individuality.

There's no avoiding such cynicism if you choose to travel the winding path, even from those who care about you the most. Not because your family and friends want you to be a conformist, but because your choice is contradicting their basic sense of how the world works. They want you to be successful, and the only way they can conceive of that happening is by heeding the Standard Formula: knowing your destination, working hard, and staying the course.

Thus, anyone who experiences their own turning point must make a momentous decision. You can continue to pretend that if you *just work harder,* you will finally break through to success . . .

. . . or you can break the covenant.

11.

For most of her life, Ingrid Carozzi tried to be the same as everyone else, only better—except she always seemed to end up different and worse. She enjoyed art and considered applying to design schools in Sweden, but her family made it clear that art was not a legitimate pursuit, while others told her that she didn't have enough technical skill to be an artist, anyway. Ingrid still recalls one of her friends' fathers asking her, "Why do you want to be a designer when you can't even draw?"

Ingrid usually responded to these disappointments by blaming herself. Like any good citizen of the industrialized world, she had internalized the values of the Standardization Covenant—or, in her case, the Law of Jante. "When I was younger, I was doubting myself all the time," Ingrid remembers. "Back then, I thought that to be happy you had to pick something that you were good at, and that's what I kept trying to do, except I never seemed to be very good at anything. And since I never was very good at anything, I was never very happy."

Ingrid moved to New York in her midthirties, hoping that America might provide her with new opportunities. She loved the bustle and diversity of Manhattan immediately, so different from the straitlaced Scandinavian lifestyle. To secure a work visa to allow her to stay in the States, she took a job as a public relations associate, pitching luxury brands to journalists. She also took on freelancing work doing branding and design work for businesses. It was stable employment that provided just enough to survive in Manhattan, but she still yearned for a role that fit her better.

Ten years passed. Ingrid had all but resigned herself to making the best of her public relations career when, out of the blue, a former client offered her an unusual side gig. The Swedish-American Chamber of Commerce asked Ingrid to create the floral arrangements for an upcoming fete being thrown by the chamber at the Mandarin Oriental hotel.

"I had never done anything with flowers before," Ingrid explains. "The head of the Swedish-American Chamber of Commerce chose me because I was raised in Sweden, and because she thought I had a great eye for colors from the previous design work I did for them."

The Standardization Covenant demands that we follow the Standard Formula to attain excellence, which will then lead to fulfillment—somehow. Dark horses, meanwhile, harness their individuality in the pursuit of fulfillment, which creates the optimal conditions for attaining excellence. To do this effectively requires a commitment to knowing yourself as thoroughly as possible. Only by understanding the details of your interests and desires can you recognize and embrace opportunities that suit your authentic self. And after almost two decades of professional mishaps and educational dead ends, Ingrid finally had a pretty good understanding of who she was.

She knew she enjoyed making people happy by creating things "that make someone's little moment more beautiful." She hated repetition and lengthy commitments; she preferred short-term projects with clear start and end dates. She preferred deadlines, which inspired her to do her best work. Similarly, she enjoyed working within a budget, since the constraints fomented creative solutions. She knew that she was very visual and instinctively understood color. She enjoyed conveying a message through design. She liked physical, heavy work, like lifting, hammering, and cutting. She liked getting client feedback immediately after finishing a project, which she calls "instant gratification." She enjoyed cooking, and it turned out that crafting floral arrangements involved many of the same elements that appealed to her about cooking: "You put together all these ingredients to make a product that you serve on a table to guests." Finally, she understood how to make things look regal and expensive but not too showy, "which is how you make money with corporate clients."

When she was younger, Ingrid didn't know all these details about herself, and because of the Law of Jante she didn't believe the details mattered much anyway. But now she realized that crafting flower arrangements for a public event might be a great match for her unique constellation of interests and abilities. Ingrid threw herself into the project with enthusiasm. She hunted for salvaged wood with a rustic feel and, entirely on her own, hammered together pastoral wooden crates that she filled not only with flowers, but with potted herbs popular in Sweden such as crown dill and thyme. Ingrid used her keen eye for color to make sure the hues of the flowers, herbs, and crates all worked together and complemented the decor of the event. Ingrid's final product was like staring into a portrait of a farm stand painted by Peter Paul Rubens. And it was a smash hit.

One guest was so overwhelmed by Ingrid's flowers that she was in tears, telling Ingrid that the sight of them transported her back to her childhood. The woman who hired Ingrid—the president of the Swedish-American Chamber of Commerce— was also elated. Afterward, she regularly hired Ingrid to design flowers for other events, where she proudly told guests how she had "discovered" Ingrid. The chef for the event, who runs a two-Michelin-star restaurant, pulled her aside to compliment her and to tell her how delighted he was that the herbs in her arrangements matched the cuisine he had prepared. All night long, guest after guest sought out the unknown woman responsible for the remarkable floral design.

"It was a eureka moment," Ingrid tells us. "It finally gave me a sense of worth."

Though she had no savings to speak of, Ingrid launched her own floral design company, Tin Can Studios, in Brooklyn. At first, her entire business consisted of a website with photographs of her floral arrangements. But word of mouth spread quickly, and soon she could devote herself full-time to floral design. "In the early days, I didn't have any overhead, because it was just me," Ingrid says. "And I didn't need to pay for inventory, because the clients paid me up front, and I used that payment to buy all the flowers and anything else I needed for the job."

Here is the crucial point you should register about Ingrid's mindset when she decided to stop her public relations work and go all-in on an unproven business idea. At the time, she did not "know her destination"—she had no idea how much money she would make from her new venture and had no clear sense of what her business might ultimately look like. Nor did she suddenly buckle down and "work hard"; she always worked hard. And she certainly wasn't "staying the course" on some long-suppressed professional dream; she had never contemplated a career in floristry before. Nor was it an act of defiance against the system. Her clients were generally conservative in their tastes—corporate customers seeking reliability rather than rebellion.

Instead, Ingrid made the decision to reject the Standard Formula—and the Law of Jante—once and for all and blaze her own winding path.

Rather than developing her craft by taking conventional classes on floristry, she learned about the qualities of flowers through trial and error and by asking vendors for help. Instead of following the standard templates of floristry when creating a new floral arrangement, Ingrid applied the basic rules of good visual design as she understood them. In other words, she began to take seriously the proposition that her individuality truly mattered.

"I didn't really care how other florists made carnation balls or tied flowers together. Sometimes I want to do the exact opposite," Ingrid explains. "I think of my flowers as a class of schoolchildren, and I treat each one like its own individual person. One is stronger, one should be hiding in the corner, one should be looking at me and smiling at the camera." The result is a unique approach to floristry featuring hand-crafted containers, found objects, lush textures, strong contrasts, expectation-violating compositions, and a painterly sense of color.

She didn't just become a floral designer. She became an Ingrid Carozzi floral designer.

12.

Ingrid's exact journey to personalized success is unlikely to be replicated because it's unlikely that anyone else will share her precise pattern of interests, abilities, and opportunities. But if we look beyond the unique details of her narrative, we can discern a deeper pattern common to every story of dark horse success.

Recall John Couch, who felt out of place in the highly theoretical computer science doctoral program at Berkeley. "I was experiencing an impedance mismatch," John explains, using an electrical engineering term. "One of my professors, seeing my lack of interest, asked me, 'Don't you want to be famous?' But what he meant by 'fame' was writing up an esoteric paper in a journal that maybe a dozen people would read. But there are many other ways to be famous, including through teaching or creating." In his second year, the mismatch between John's personality and the department's arid approach to coding drove him to reluctantly drop out.

He believed his once-promising computer career was over. "I felt like a failure," John says. "For years, I couldn't go near the Berkeley campus without getting sick to my stomach." But not long after he left school, John was interviewed by the young CEO of a Silicon Valley startup who wanted to design a new kind of personal computer. John shared his unorthodox belief that innovations in human-facing software—not hardware, as most believed—would soon have the greatest impact on the future of the computer industry. Steve Jobs agreed. He hired John to be the first vice president of software at Apple.

Soon, John found personal fulfillment by designing the innovative strategic software plans for the Apple II and III computers as well as the first commercial graphical user interface. "It was software that had never been done before, a completely different kind of coding than what they were teaching at Berkeley. It was one of the best times of my life."

Like Ingrid, John decided to pursue personal fulfillment by harnessing his individuality, and thereby achieved professional excellence. So did Doug Hoerr. In his early thirties, he trekked from Peoria, Illinois, to the famed country gardens of rural England in order to learn about horticulture from the most skillful plantsmen and plantswomen in the world. "I guess it's like if I had wanted to learn to play the blues from the very best, I would have gone to Chicago and tracked down Buddy Guy," Doug explains. "I wanted to become a world-class landscape architect and expert plantsman, and the very best mentors to learn horticulture from were in England." Doug's time there wasn't easy. He worked as a common laborer, spending his days weeding, double digging, and wheelbarrowing for almost no pay—and, eventually, after he earned their trust, discussing horticulture with master garden designers over dinner.

Two years later, after his money ran out, Doug flew back to Illinois and opened a one-man landscape architecture firm in the alcove of his Evanston apartment. "You could say I left England with a master's degree in horticulture," Doug says. Eager to apply his newly acquired skills, he persuaded the CEO of Crate and Barrel to hire him to design and build a garden planter in front of its flagship store in Chicago. Doug's audacious planter wasn't like anything Chicagoans had seen before, drawing praise from customers, architectural critics, and even Richard M. Daley, then mayor of Chicago. By adopting English principles and expressing them in his own voice, Doug had redefined the notion of urban curb appeal in one bold stroke. His creation was so impressive that the city invited Doug to design similar plantings down the medians of Michigan Avenue, the main shopping thoroughfare in the city.

It was exactly the kind of challenge Doug was yearning for.

The spectacle that Doug conjured along the streets of Chicago braided together contrasting annuals, perennials, bulbs, and ornamental grasses in a dynamic tapestry of color that transformed with the seasons—an effect unknown in American urban landscaping. Doug also employed plants that were complete novelties, such as bright acid-green sweet potato vines, bronze-colored castor bean plants that slowly shaded into crimson, and, most provocatively of all, the humble kale. All the plants were selected according to their ability to withstand car exhaust and city pollution and according to each planter's microclimate, reflecting

its specific sunlight, wind, and moisture conditions, which often
varied drastically from block to block—yet another technique he
had picked up in England.

Doug's horticultural tour de force was immediately embraced by tourists and jaded locals alike as a signature element
of the city. For the next twenty years, Doug designed all the
celebrated "Michigan Avenue Medians." His concept was du-
plicated throughout Chicago—which now overlooks more than
a hundred miles of planters—and adopted by dozens of other
cities around the world. Today, one of the basic elements of any
twenty-first century urban beautification project is the incorpo-
ration of dynamic living designs, a fact that is entirely traceable
to Doug's trailblazing creations.

Though the precise twists and twirls of every dark horse journey are unique, the first step of the journey is always the same:
the decision to prioritize fulfillment. When dark horses make
that choice, they do not focus on the potential wealth to be had or
how masterful they might one day become. Instead, they recognize that an opportunity exists that fits their individuality—and
they seize it. From that point forward, they make their decisions
based upon who they are, rather than who others tell them they
should be. And by continuing to make decisions in this manner,
dark horses inexorably develop excellence.

That's not to say that those who follow conventional career
tracks are in some way foolish or misguided. They aren't. Those
who choose to follow the straight path to its destination deserve
respect and support. Their journey may be rigid and preordained,
but they have earned their success. We don't mean to criticize any
particular path a person takes to reach success, but to open up
a vast atlas of undiscovered trails—an atlas obscured by blindly
adhering to the standard formula.

Our standardized institutions of opportunity were never designed for fulfillment—and they never can be. A system built upon the principle that individuality is a problem can never be tweaked to embrace individuality, any more than a battleship can be tweaked into a fighter jet. We can't standardize our way out of standardization. But dark horses teach us that you can *personalize* your way out of standardization.

Though we end this book by showing how we can mend our social contract and build a better system of opportunity based upon fulfillment, you don't need to wait for an overhaul to the system before taking action. You can start pursuing personalized success right now.

Whether you are considering marching down the straight path or blazing your own winding one, the next four chapters explain how to move forward. Each chapter describes one element of the dark horse mindset. These practical and actionable elements rest upon a powerful set of conceptual principles from the twenty-first-century science fueling the emerging Age of Personalization, an interdisciplinary field known, appropriately enough, as the science of individuality. As you make your way through the pages ahead, these four elements will gradually come together to provide you with a new understanding of the world and your place within it. They will reveal *how* you can engineer fulfillment in your own life, right here, right now.

This dark horse mindset may sound too good to be true. As much as you might wish to believe that prioritizing fulfillment will somehow guide you safely to success, you may still harbor lingering doubts about this book's counterintuitive advice. *Maybe its prescriptions work for some people in certain circumstances—but not for everyone. Not for me.*

The main reason it can be so difficult to believe in the four elements of the dark horse mindset—the reason it can be so difficult to believe these elements will work for *you*—is because all our lives we have been conditioned to view success through the lens of the standardization mindset. Even our understanding of basic concepts like "passion," "purpose," "perseverance," and "achievement" are wholly colored by the aging values of the Standardization Covenant. That's why the hardest part of the journey to personalized success isn't adopting the new mindset . . .

. . . it's letting go of the old one.

13.

One of the most transformative moments in the history of *Homo sapiens* was when our perception of the relationship between two celestial entities was completely reversed. For eons, people believed that the Earth was the center of the universe, while the Sun, quite appropriately, was its obedient satellite. Then one day Copernicus proposed the opposite: that the Sun was the true hub and the Earth a mere subsidiary.

It was a clash of assumptions, between what was obvious to everyone and what made no intuitive sense at all. After all, the Sun sure *seems* to be circling the Earth. Moreover, the upstart heliocentric mindset rested upon a strange kind of unproven math, while the mathematics supporting the geocentric mindset had been providing dependable results for more than a thousand years. In the second century CE, the Greek astronomer Ptolemy articulated complex formulas that described the movements of the celestial bodies around the Earth, performing a reliable job of forecasting the appearance of Mercury, Venus, Mars, Jupiter, and Saturn.

If you were ever curious about what it was like to live during a time when everyone blindly assumed the Sun revolved around the Earth—when everyone clung to a false assumption ingrained so deeply they didn't think of it as an assumption at all—you don't need to rely on your imagination. You're living in such an epoch right now.

For more than a century we have embraced the obvious and self-evident fact that the *institution* is the rightful hub of society, a supreme entity governing the lives of obedient individuals. It's extremely difficult to imagine our social universe operating any other way. So when someone declares that we can reshape our understanding of excellence and achievement around strange new principles appointing human beings as the center of our social universe, it's understandably difficult to swallow.

We might like to think that the moment Copernicus set forth his new heliocentric mindset, society's views changed rapidly in response to his superior logic and evidence. But that's not what happened. Assumptions are very stubborn things, particularly when they are stitched into the fabric of everyday reality. It's little wonder, then, that a century after Copernicus published his new model of the universe, most people remained unconvinced that the Earth could be orbiting the Sun. Even after Galileo discovered the four moons of Jupiter, proving incontrovertibly that the Earth was not the center of all orbits, when he invited his geocentric-minded colleagues to peer through his telescope to see the moons for themselves, many insisted they could not see what Galileo claimed they should see. Some declared it hurt their head just to look.

The Standardization Covenant is holding all of us back. Though its views of talent and success are easy to grasp and reassuringly familiar, there is no future for a society devoted to the proposition that the pursuit of standardized excellence leads to fulfillment. The dark horse mindset, meanwhile, opens onto an unbounded social universe of achievement and joy. It offers a view of human potential where a farm boy from Peoria can turn cities into gardens, a Swedish vagabond can invent a new form of efflorescent art, and a high school dropout can discover new worlds a million lifetimes away.

To see this new universe for yourself, just peer into the glass.

chapter 2

know your
Micro-Motives

I think it all comes down to motivation. If you really want to do something, you will work hard for it.

—Edmund Hillary

1.

Korinne Belock was raised in East Bernard, a small town in rural
Texas. For as long as she can remember, she always felt a strong
desire to help people. As a freshman at the University of Texas
she thought that getting involved in local politics might offer
her the chance to serve her neighbors, so she became an intern
for a state senator. She liked the people she worked with and the
feeling that she was contributing something positive to the world,
so after she graduated Korinne parlayed her Austin statehouse

experience into a job in Washington, DC, serving as an assistant to the former political director for Bob Dole's presidential campaign. From there, she was hired by Michael Bloomberg and worked on his first campaign for mayor of New York City. After he won, she stayed on as a member of his staff, serving as a director of government affairs at City Hall. She earned a reputation as someone who could be relied upon to get things done, attracting the attention of Republicans at the federal level. She was soon plucked from City Hall and offered a position in the office of political affairs for the George W. Bush White House.

At the age of twenty-eight, Korinne had secured a meaningful role in national governance. It was an enviable career start in the tough world of professional politics. Yet in 2009, when Bloomberg opened the door to Korinne to rejoin him at City Hall, she found herself at an unexpected crossroads. Even though Korinne could choose from a range of plum roles in New York politics, for the first time in her career she hesitated.

The truth was, Korinne felt burned out. She had been charging full-speed ahead for so long, she understandably thought she needed some time off. But the more she reflected on her state of mind, she realized that her hesitation wasn't a simple matter of needing a vacation. To her surprise, Korinne realized she did not want to work in politics anymore.

She had always looked forward to the bustle and excitement of working around people who were trying to make a difference. But after toiling at every level of government for more than a decade, she was beginning to realize that the true nature of her motivation might be different from what she had once assumed.

She still wanted to help people. She was sure of that. But when it came right down to it, she simply wasn't all that excited by campaigning or governing—the two mainstays of American politics.

Most of her colleagues were energized by the adrenaline-pounding competition of elections, the privileged access to power, the give and take of deal-making—but such activities never held the same luster for her. Even though Korinne had greatly enjoyed a few of her political jobs, if she was completely honest with herself, what she had liked most about those roles was not the voter research or the policy debates or the public outreach initiatives. It was something much simpler.

Korinne liked organizing things.

She was the kind of person who affixed colored tabs to all her books as a way of visually categorizing them on her shelf. Whenever she saw something cluttered or unkempt, she felt a gnawing compulsion to reassemble it into a tidy arrangement. She could take a rambling scrawl of ideas from her boss and quickly convert it into a brisk list of talking points. Her brain was like a high-speed centrifuge, taking in information and swiftly separating the vital from the irrelevant.

Her favorite political assignment was setting up public rallies for Bloomberg's campaigns. That empowered her to organize people, publicity, and events on an expansive scale. Her political affairs position in DC, meanwhile, had been a mixed bag. She enjoyed serving as a trip director and organizing the details of the president's travel, but she wasn't particularly enthused when she was assigned policy research or had to write a briefing paper.

Her least favorite position had been working in City Hall after Bloomberg won his first campaign. She had been tasked with coordinating government affairs with city agencies. An important role, true, but not only did the job not involve much organizing, it often required waiting around for other people to get things done. That drove Korinne crazy.

She gradually recognized that whenever she thought about leaving politics to exclusively spend her time organizing things—even something as mundane as cleaning messy closets or tidying up unkempt kitchens—it lifted her spirits. It felt *right*.

Her awareness of the mismatch between what she wanted to do most and what politics actually offered her drove Korinne to her turning point. "I realized, I can do all the things I would need to do to start working for myself," she says. "When you see you can build a successful multimillion-dollar campaign, it doesn't seem that hard to take five grand and start an organizing business."

She sat down in a coffee shop and made a four-page "punch list" of all the things she needed to become a professional organizer and established a firm timeline for setting up her business. In late 2010, she officially closed out her political career and launched Urban Simplicity. Working out of her small apartment in Manhattan, she began devoting herself to helping people simplify their lives. From the start, most of her clients have been women. Some are professionals who want to maximize the efficiency of their home office or improve their work-life balance. Other clients experienced a major life change, like a move, a new job, a new baby, a marriage, or a divorce that caused their organizing systems to break down, leaving them overwhelmed. Korinne redesigns their physical spaces (such as offices, kitchens, closets, pantries, basements, or garages) and establishes new scheduling systems to manage their workflow, helping transform their daily experience from intense and stressful to easy and manageable.

Korinne quickly earned a reputation as a lifesaver. One client from Brooklyn raved: "Korinne came to my shop to revamp my cluttered, overrun office desk. She is super easy to work with, realistic on project timing, and brilliant in her suggestions for creating procedures that can easily be maintained. What good is a clean desk, after all, if it's just going to get messy again?" The referrals started pouring in. Before long, Korinne needed to hire people to help her keep up. She recently opened a new office in 2018 in Palm Beach, Florida.

It's true that many of her friends and former colleagues were left scratching their heads by Korinne's abrupt change in direction. "I sometimes heard things like, well, you know, organizing closets is not the same as working in the White House." But that never bothered Korinne because today she is happier than she ever thought possible. She is her own boss, running a thriving company and improving her clients' quality of life. She spends every day accomplishing one of her most ardent aspirations: creating harmony out of discord.

Korinne achieved personalized success by knowing what mattered most to her.

2.

Your motives comprise the emotional core of your individuality. What you desire—and what you do not desire—defines who you are in a unique and deeply personal manner.

The only way to ensure that your individuality truly matters is by honoring your most heartfelt yearnings and aspirations. When you engage in activities that are congruent with your true motives, your journey will be compelling and satisfying. If you misjudge or ignore your motives, your progress will be plodding and dreary—or you may abandon the road altogether.

Understanding the genuine nature of your motivation is

essential for you to attain fulfillment, because only by tapping your own unique motives will you feel a sense of authenticity, meaning, and completeness. The cardinal task of the dark horse mindset is to harness your individuality, and this mission commences the moment you set out to discern your true motives.

Identifying what inspires you might seem like a no-brainer. What could be easier than recognizing what fires you up? Unfortunately, surveying the landscape of your motivation is harder than it looks because the Standardization Covenant is always kicking sand in your eyes.

3.

Our institutions of opportunity are not interested in the messy details of your personal desires. Our schools and jobs were never designed to help you figure out what whets your appetite. Such information is irrelevant under the Standardization Covenant. The motivational concerns of institutions are impersonal and procedural: they want to motivate as many individuals as possible to attain standardized excellence with the least effort and cost.

In the name of efficiency, institutions usually collapse the entire variety of human passion into a single featureless "generic motivation," a simple one-dimensional metric ranging from high to low. Generic motivation goes by many different names, including self-discipline, resolve, tenacity, perseverance, fire in the belly, and grit. But in the final analysis, all these labels are merely shorthand for "Your individuality does not matter."

Under the Standardization Covenant, you are either motivated to traverse the full length of the straight path, or you are not. If you feel bored, distracted, or frustrated, institutions rarely try to adjust their offerings to make them more engaging or relevant. Instead, their usual response is that you should simply buckle down and gut it out. Stiffen that upper lip! Dig deep and show some get-up-and-go!

But the fact of the matter is that ignoring someone's personal motives is not a particularly effective way to motivate her. This is borne out by the fact that the longer anybody stays within a standardized system, the less motivated she becomes. For most people, their motivational intensity peaks in kindergarten and steadily diminishes thereafter. A 2016 Gallup study found that while only 26 percent of fifth-graders are disengaged from school, 55 percent of eighth-graders are disengaged, rising to 66 percent of high school seniors. You might expect that motivation starts climbing again once you graduate and obtain gainful employment, but Gallup found that a staggering 67 percent of employees feel disengaged from their jobs.

The failure to motivate students certainly hasn't gone unnoticed by those on the front lines of standardized education. A 2014 survey by *Education Week* found that 60 percent of teachers and administrators agreed that most of their students were not highly motivated. You might expect that this fact would prompt our educational institutions to try to understand each student's unique interests and aspirations. Instead, many institutions have simply shifted from one-dimensional generic motives to a small set of "universal motives" that they hope can be leveraged to motivate a majority of students to work hard and stay the course.

For example, one parenting website asserts that you should motivate kids by "encouraging healthy competition. Cheer on your child to beat another runner in a race or to take home the trophy from the spelling bee." A midwestern university advises that to motivate pupils, "Set your room in a U-shape to encourage interaction among students." An online community of educators aims for the stomach, insisting, "Kids really like to eat. For fifth graders or seniors in high school, pizza goes a long way. Food is a great way to give kids a pat on the back and continue motivating them."

This short list of universal motives—competition, interaction, hunger—are certainly directly actionable, and on the face of it they might seem like an improvement over generic motives. But they are all still attempts at boosting motivation *on average* while ignoring everything important about the individual students themselves. Like generic motives, universal motives are institutional rather than personal, general rather than specific, top-down rather than bottom-up.

Scientists also have a long history of jockeying to identify the supreme "universal motive" that can be safely relied upon to stimulate anyone and everyone. Freud notoriously contended that the desire for sex lay at the root of all human action. His disciple Alfred Adler, on the other hand, emphasized the universal desire for power, whereas Freud's most famous acolyte, Carl Jung, argued for the preeminence of the universal desire for life. The psychiatrist Victor Frankl declared that the desire for meaning was universal to the human heart, while the psychologist Erik Erikson believed it was the desire for growth. These are all genuine and widespread motives, sure. They're just not universally invigorating.

Though many people find competition rousing, others find it demoralizing. Some kids will be stimulated by the forced interactivity of a U-shaped classroom, though others feel uncomfortable if they are subjected to the collective gaze of others. Pizza undoubtedly motivates many students to study harder, but for others a bribe of greasy, semiburnt dough can be a turnoff. The absence of a purported universal motive in someone's character is neither a biological aberration nor a moral shortcoming. It's simply a reflection of the astonishing variety of human motivation.

It's easy to understand why institutions want to reduce motivation to a simple one-dimensional scale or a small set of universal motives. It makes life much easier for the authorities because in a standardized system individuality is a problem. It's much less of a hassle to rearrange the chairs or to assign someone a "grit score" ranging from 1 to 10 than to attempt to understand each student's unique motivational profile.

Every standardized institution, by definition and design, is focused on efficiency above all else, and generic motives and universal motives are efficient ways of moving the needle—on average, at least. But they're horrible for your own fulfillment. Not only do standardized views of motivation ignore everything that is important about who you are, but by incessantly focusing all of our attention on a small set of institutionally ordained motives, the Standardization Covenant constrains our thinking about what a personal motive can even be.

Fortunately, dark horses reveal the hidden truth about motivation.

4.

Korinne is motivated by the desire to organize. That is already a fairly specific motive. But if we dig deeper, her true motivation is even more specific than that. What really gets Korinne's blood pumping is organizing *physical space*. "I most enjoy decluttering an apartment or an office, or making a kitchen or pantry clean and functional," Korinne says. "I do like setting up systems and processes and the visual aspects of organizing, finding products that match the interior design of a place. But organizing physical

spaces is my favorite. When I go into my own closet and rearrange things, I just feel better about my life."

The desire to organize closets might seem too quirky and
trivial to dignify it by calling it a motive at all, let alone a fundamental human motive. And yet, for Korinne this highly
personal *micro-motive* guided her to a life of authenticity and
achievement.

The lives of dark horses demonstrate the remarkable specificity of micro-motives. For example, Dianna Smith is motivated
by the desire to recognize and classify living things. Today, she is
a highly regarded mycologist and the chief identifier for the Pioneer Valley Mycological Association and is frequently contacted
for assistance in identifying unusual specimens of fungi. "The
mushrooms of the Northeast are my specialty," Dianna explains.
"I can recognize and tell someone a lot about a mushroom, its
favored habitat, what it is doing underground or on wood."

Pamela Hatchfield feels drawn to form a personal relationship with cultural artifacts. Today, she is an art conservator. As
the head of Objects Conservation at the Museum of Fine Arts
in Boston, she recently had the pleasure of opening one of the
oldest time capsules in the country, buried under the Massachusetts State House by Paul Revere and Samuel Adams. "Treating
artifacts is at some point a very solitary individual relationship,"
Pamela explains. "You talk to your colleagues and look at other
people's research to help you develop an understanding of what
that thing is made of and how it was made and how those materials might have deteriorated over time. But then you interact in
a very intimate way with that object. And that's very meaningful
to me and very important."

Yet even this brief survey fails to capture the true distinctiveness of micro-motives. Dianna enjoys recognizing and classify-

ing living things that she can pick up, handle, and share with others, which is why she was drawn to fungi.

Alvaro Jamarillo also shares Dianna's desire to recognize and classify living things—but he is driven to classify creatures that are mobile, colorful, and elusive. Today, he is a professional birder. "I've always liked birds, but when I entered my PhD program in biology, I was told to stay away from birds, they are not interesting. Instead, I was assigned by my biology professor to study leaf-cutting ants in Ecuador," Alvaro recounts. "I got to the jungle and realized I was not excited by the ants. I was spending all of my time trying not to look at all the tropical birds around me, and then I finally realized—I loved birds. I was getting more fulfillment out of looking at birds and talking about them with nonacademics than I was getting in my academic program." Eventually, Alvaro followed what mattered most to him and dropped out of his doctoral program. He started his own successful company, Alvaro's Adventures, taking guests on birding tours around the world.

Conservator Pamela Hatchfield's micro-motive is also quite particular: she is motivated to form relationships with *three-dimensional* artifacts, such as ceramics, figurines, and masks; she has little interest in *two-dimensional* artifacts such as paper and photographs. "Flat on paper seems more like reproduction to me, while three-dimensions seems more like creating," she explains. But another elite art conservator, Margaret Holben Ellis, holds a complementary micro-motive. Her own special interest is reflected in her academic title: Eugene Thaw Professor of *Paper* Conservation at the Institute of Fine Arts at New York University. "I'm a 2-D person," Margaret explains. She relishes the high stakes involved in preserving and restoring seventeenth-century etchings, medieval manuscripts, and ancient Egyptian papyri. Every decision matters, because modifications to paper are usually irreversible. Being an effective paper conservator requires focus and an obsessive attention to detail, as well as a deep knowledge of the underlying materials. But there is another reason why Margaret has such an affinity for paper, one that perhaps represents her most personal connection of all. "For me, when I think of great art, I think in two dimensions: the etchings of Rembrandt, the engravings of Dürer, the watercolors of Winslow Homer. Even a blank sheet of paper calls out to me."

But micro-motives run deeper still. Alvaro, the birder, enjoys identifying birds *visually* by glimpsing the briefest flash of color. But fellow birder Ted Floyd—the editor of *Birding*, the flagship magazine of the American Birding Association—is highly motivated to identify birds *auditorily*, by hearing the songs they sing. His ability to mentally analyze the qualities of birdsong is so highly refined that he can sketch the audio waveform of any birdsong he hears; his sketches consistently match up with the actual waveforms recorded by sonogram equipment. For Ted, recognizing birds by their songs takes on an existential significance. "I don't consider the sound of a bird any less real than the sight of a bird," he says. "Whether it's photons in our eye or air molecules jostling in our cochlea, they are filtered representations of reality and that's fascinating to me."

Paul Messier is another art conservator who prefers working with two-dimensional artifacts—namely, photographs. He is the head of the Lens Media Lab at Yale University and the codirector of the Photograph Conservation Initiative at the Hermitage Museum in St. Petersburg, Russia. However, unlike paper conservator Margaret or object conservator Pamela, Paul is not primarily driven by the desire for a relationship with the artifact. He is most motivated by the thrill of detective work. Paul is one of the foremost authorities on the authenticity of photographs, winning international acclaim for his ability to expose forgeries. He has accumulated the world's largest reference collection of photographic papers to help satisfy his desire to be the very best at ferreting out photographic fakes.

Yet another expert who is motivated by flat artifacts is Keith Clarke. Since he was a young boy, he was attracted to a very particular kind of two-dimensional object: maps. He liked some of the same things that appeal to conservators about flat artifacts, such as their aesthetic colors, clean lines, and interesting visual structure. But what captivated him the most was their *informational* qualities: the fact that they were compact, high-density representations of ideas and data. Today, Keith is one of the world's most renowned cartographers and a pioneer of digital mapmaking, leaving behind paper for more sophisticated and abstract informational representations. He has conducted important research on Cold War satellite imagery, the movements of glaciers, the discovery of hidden archaeological sites, the depletion of Brazilian forestlands, and the identification of the oldest map in the world.

Dark horses demonstrate the stark contrast between frequently touted universal motives such as "the desire for competition" or "the desire to be creative" and the finely tuned specifics of your own cravings, predilections, and fascinations. And if you want to attain fulfillment, it's essential to know *exactly* what puts the wind in your sails—not what someone else thinks should get you going. That's why *Know Your Micro-Motives* is the first and most crucial element of the dark horse mindset. When you devalue your own interests in favor of what the Standardization Covenant thinks you should want, bad things happen.

Just ask Saul Shapiro.

5.

Saul is wired with a seemingly unusual micro-motive: he likes aligning physical objects with his hands. Whenever he encounters something that is awry, like a wobbly wheel on a shopping cart or a tilted picture frame, his mind is drawn by an invisible pulley to manipulate the out-of-synch components until they are square and right. You will not find the urge to align physical things on any list of universal motives, yet for Saul, this desire is genuine, potent, and deeply personal.

One of Saul's most fulfilling memories from college was when his studio woodworking design professor instructed the class to carve a sphere out of a block of wood by hand. Saul became obsessed with the assignment. After chiseling the cube into a rough sphere, he placed the ball in a bag that he carried with him wherever he went. All day long, he put his hand inside the bag to feel for uneven spots, then used sandpaper to smooth them down. The act of eliminating any and all imperfections filled him with gratification. When Saul turned the sphere in, his teacher was astonished. After carefully measuring its curvature, the teacher refused to believe that Saul had not used machine tools. After Saul convinced him that he had achieved the result through assiduous effort, the teacher informed him that he had never seen anything like it. Saul's sphere was perfect.

You might be thinking, *That's nice . . . but, erm, what profession could harness such an odd source of motivation?* You'd be surprised. One possibility is orthodontics, where the central task is aligning patients' crooked teeth. Another possibility is the job that Saul chose. He was hired as an engineer in the 1980s by a company that was attempting to tackle a tough technical problem: creating a physical interface that would convert an electrical signal on an old-style copper wire into a laser signal on a fiber-optic cable. The reason this engineering problem was so difficult was because it required precisely aligning a semiconductor chip the size of a grain of sand with a fiber the width of a human hair. The alignment needed to be precise within a fraction of a micron. When Saul was hired, nobody at his company or anywhere else had been able to get the crucial pieces to stay aligned. For Saul, however, it was the kind of problem that appealed to one of his most potent micro-motives, and he solved it single-handedly (well, double-handedly).

Saul's interface was widely adopted throughout the telecommunications industry. "There was a time when if you were talking on Sprint's network, you were probably talking through one of my devices," Saul asserts.

His device made his employer a fortune. Saul, however, received only a small bonus. Up until this point, Saul was happy in his engineering job. Yet for the first time, he began to question his role. "I would see guys with MBAs making presentations, and they were making much more money than me and getting to run the company, too," Saul explains. "I started to think to myself, maybe I should be one of those guys."

So Saul abandoned his fulfilling engineering career and moved into middle management. Truth be told, Saul's collection of micro-motives was not especially compatible with a management role. He did not enjoy supervising others or relying upon them in order to get things done. Though quite congenial and personable, Saul was never particularly interested in networking, office politics, presenting his ideas to others, or persuading them to come around to his point of view. Some of his most potent micro-motives—such as working with his hands, tinkering with gadgets and mechanisms, doing mathematical calculations, working alone, and of course aligning objects—were almost entirely neglected when he served as a manager. Saul traded in this rich collection of personal micro-motives for two: his desire for greater income and his desire to have a greater say in company strategy.

After obtaining an MBA equivalent from the MIT Sloan School of Management, Saul spent the next sixteen years going through a series of ups and downs as a middle manager at several media and technology organizations. When he turned fifty, his bumpy and not very satisfying run as a corporate manager came to an end. For the first time, he struggled to get hired.

Unfortunately, Saul couldn't return to his previous career track. Since more than two decades had passed since he had worked as an engineer—a period during which the rapid development of the internet had transformed the field—his engineering skills were woefully outdated. In his early fifties, Saul was working as a tax preparer for H&R Block and as a recruiter of new subscribers for a small online tax preparation company. Not only did he have little control over his life, but he was not making much money, which was the entire reason he had switched careers in the first place.

That's when Saul experienced his turning point.

He knew that one thing that meant a lot to him was being his own boss. But he didn't want to start a whole new business from scratch, since he wasn't very interested in marketing and promotion. This led him to wonder whether perhaps there was some kind of franchise that he might be able to buy, where he could simply step into a proven business model.

He met with a franchise broker who shared with Saul a range of affordable franchises that were available to purchase around New York City. One was a servicing company for the elderly.

That didn't appeal to him at all. One was an employment agency. But the last thing Saul wanted was to recruit people and deal with employees. There was one surprising franchise, however, that caught Saul's eye.

Upholstery repair.

Even though he had little experience with the craft, Saul immediately recognized that success in upholstery repair depends on one's ability to precisely match repairs to existing fabrics, textures, and colors. That was a process Saul knew he would enjoy.

He would not need to oversee any employees, so he could be a "one-man band." He could work with his hands and immediately see the fruits of his labor, which was important to him. He could run the business from his home without the need for a brick-and-mortar shop, since he would be going to clients' residences or offices to make repairs. And because he would be traveling around the city, he could ride his bike, which he greatly enjoyed.

In 2013, at the age of fifty-seven, Saul opened his own Fibrenew Upholstery Repair franchise in Manhattan. If you've ever needed to mend the frayed corners of a family-heirloom armchair, remove a stain from a leather sofa, or patch torn vinyl on a car seat, you know how difficult it can be to hide the repair. But Saul quickly developed excellence at these tasks, because he was able to harness an entire platoon of his most fervent motivations.

Saul performs masterful work and has a steady supply of customers who give him great reviews. He does repairs for Broadway shows, TV personalities, Times Square hotels, and captains of industry. In 2015, he was named the Best Leather-Couch Repairman in the city by *New York* magazine.

"People who know me best would agree that I'm happier now

than with anything else I have done with my career," Saul says. "I enjoy what I do almost every day and I'm financially secure. In the end, I figured out how to align my livelihood to my nature."

6.

Even if you accept the value of Knowing Your Micro-Motives, figuring out what they are can often seem like an impossible task. Needless to say, they do not come with printed labels. Fortunately, you can take advantage of an instinctive activity that you perform every day to grab hold of the micro-motives concealed inside you and hold them up to the light.

We call it "the game of judgment."

How many times over the past week have you judged someone—a colleague, a talking head on cable news, a stranger in the checkout line? We're used to thinking that these spontaneous judgments are telling us something about others, but now you're going to use these unfiltered reactions to learn something about yourself.

Your micro-motives are composed of strong and abiding feelings rooted deep within your unconscious self. They include subtle preferences, frank desires, and private longings. Your goal in playing the game of judgment is to use your instinctive reaction to others to zero in on these live emotional wires and attempt to trace them to their source.

There are three steps to the game of judgment. First, become aware of the moments when you are judging someone. This is something we all do all the time. It's human nature to react to others, whether it's a mail carrier, police officer, massage therapist, neighbor, store clerk, or someone tweeting about politics.

Only now you need to develop an awareness of *when* you are doing it so you can consciously attend to your reaction.

Second, identify the feelings that emerge as you reflexively judge someone. How do you know when you are on the scent of a micro-motive? When you have a vivid reaction. It doesn't matter whether it's positive or negative, celebratory or condemnatory, as long as the feeling is pronounced. Remember, you're trying to get in touch with your authentic emotional core.

And third, ask yourself *why* you are experiencing those feelings. Be honest with yourself. The physicist Richard Feynman said it best when he warned, "You must not fool yourself—and you are the easiest person to fool." Focus on what you would like if you had their life, and what you would hate. For example, if you watch a celebrity interview and find yourself thinking, *How can anyone be truly happy when they are chasing riches or fame?* then you know that money and acclaim are probably not strong motivators for you. On the other hand, if you reacted to the story of Saul Shapiro by thinking, *Come on, now . . . the guy's an upholstery repairman. Let's not pretend he's successful!*— you've just learned something valuable about yourself. Status and acclaim matter greatly to you. That's fine; own it. To attain fulfillment, you must be true to what lights your fire—whatever that may be.

Keep in mind, the purpose of the game of judgment isn't to coolly assess the merits and deficiencies of other people. It's not about *them* at all. You should have no pretense to objectivity or else you're doing it wrong. The goal is to use your intense emotional response to ferret out the hidden contours of your own desires.

The Standardization Covenant is so pervasive and entrenched

that the most difficult part of the game of judgment is resisting the sense that we *should* be motivated by certain supposedly universal motives, causing us to overlook or downplay our own desires. But the game of judgment can help break the spell—as long as you are attentive and specific. If you are judging a park ranger, you might initially think, *Being outside and around nature all day would sure be great!* Or judging a debt collector, your first reaction might be, *Oh boy, I would really love tracking down deadbeats and forcing them to pay up!* Don't stop there. Keep sifting through your feelings until you've gone as far as you can. When judging the park ranger, you might also realize, *Even though being outside would be great, it does seem like a lonely job. I don't think I could handle the daily isolation.* Now you've identified two potential micro-motives: the desire to be around nature, and the desire for steady social engagement. When judging the debt collector, try to determine which gets your heart thumping faster: the process of tracking down deadbeats, or the act of making them pay. Is there something about catching people who are trying to avoid being caught that energizes you? Or is it something about being an agent of fair play, administering justice when nobody else can?

When it comes to Knowing Your Micro-Motives, the details always matter.

It's usually easier to start off judging people rather than situations because other humans provide your brain an automatic and prominent emotional trigger, while situations (especially familiar ones) require you to consciously intervene and prod yourself to pay attention even when you're not having a conspicuous reaction. But once you get the hang of exploiting your spontaneous reactions to others, you can expand the game of judgment to encompass all of your experiences.

Whether you find yourself in novel circumstances or in a situation you encounter almost every day, try to pay attention to *exactly* what you like or dislike about it. If you are a student and feel bored or annoyed in math class, focus on the precise source of your feelings. It's almost never as simple as "I don't like math." Are you having trouble listening to the droning spoken words of the teacher—would you rather be reading words in a book? Are you uncomfortable having other students so close to you—do you need more physical space? Do you have trouble staying quiet for so long—do you feel the urge to interact with others? Do you want to hear stories rather than facts and equations? Each of these reactions reflects a very different micro-motive.

By cultivating awareness of your emotional responses, all of life can become a laboratory for self-understanding.

The game of judgment takes some time to get the hang of, but it's far more reliable and effective than what the Standardization Covenant offers as its official alternative: standardized tests. There are hundreds of "career tests" endorsed by blue-ribbon social scientists that employers and guidance counselors use to evaluate the motives of tens of millions of employees and students each year. Despite what the test makers may insist, these tests are in no way designed to help you identify your unique pattern of motivations, but rather to determine how closely your responses resemble those of the "average professional" in a given field. Career tests are evaluating universal motives at best and generic motives at worst.

Moreover, standardized assessments of motivation are always doomed to misinterpret or ignore one of the most important facets of your motivational profile: the presence of contradictory motives, such as simultaneously wanting to be around other people and wanting to be alone.

If you believe in one-dimensional metrics of motivation like tenacity, grit, or fortitude, then contradictory motives make no sense at all. How do you evaluate grit if you want to conform just as much as you want to rebel? But when you embrace the true diversity of your micro-motives, even the most antithetical of aspirations can be harnessed and consolidated into a unified sense of purpose.

7.

Kim Dau grew up in the Atlanta suburb of Roswell. Her father was a Vietnamese refugee who immigrated to the USA in 1975 after the fall of Saigon. Her American-born mother came from a staunch Catholic family. Both parents were relatively strict and believed that academic success was the surest way to financial security. "It was very important for me to do well in school. I listened to my teachers, completed my homework, and followed the rules," Kim says. She maintained an A average and won praise for her studiousness, diligence, and respect for authority.

Kim found biology especially fascinating. "One class really stuck out. I was captivated by the lesson on the digestive system. It was this complicated system with these processes and subprocesses that all fit together in a complex way. I liked thinking about all those moving parts, the beauty and the puzzle of this elaborate system." Her interest in biology drove her toward a conventional career as a physician, a path that her parents happily supported.

Kim was a model student who rarely questioned authority figures until her freshman year of high school. That's when she heard music that awakened her to a new perception of the world. "When I was fourteen, I responded emotionally to the big vocals and raw lyrics of Tori Amos. I also began to listen to Ani DiFranco and Courtney Love, women with strong identities who communicated their pain and humanity through powerful songs. It was my first real consciousness of politics."

Kim's friends in high school were mostly high-achieving bookworms like herself. After her music-driven awakening, however, she felt drawn to another group of kids: the burnouts, a coterie of rebellious underachievers who played in a band and often skipped school to smoke marijuana. Some of them would not finish high school. "I never did drugs. I never played hooky," asserts Kim. "But I spent a lot of time with them. There was something that attracted me to the idea of being able to walk in two completely different worlds."

This notion of inhabiting two divergent worlds soon crept into her attitude toward medicine. Even though Kim had a sincere faith in the illuminating power of science, she had also developed a personal curiosity about her Vietnamese roots. Her father had never talked much about his homeland while she was growing up, but as she approached her high school graduation she learned that her grandfather, who died before Kim was born, had been a healer who used herbs and acupuncture. She also discovered that her uncle, who lived in France, was an acupuncturist. She began to read about alternative medicine with great interest, conscious of the fact that it was a very different view of health and well-being than Western medicine.

Nevertheless, her nascent appreciation for alternative medicine did not sway her from her professional plans. Kim applied to Duke University and was accepted. "I majored in biology on the premed track with a clear intention of going to medical school and becoming a doctor. But by the end of my freshman year, other interests had begun to tug me in new directions."

In her sophomore year, Kim took a medical course that

featured Amy McDonald as one of the guest speakers. Amy was a nurse on the faculty of the Duke School of Medicine, but she was also a midwife—formally, a certified nurse-midwife (CNM). "Amy immediately opened up this new view of medicine for me," Kim says. "She was part of the system—she was a highly respected professional in a highly respected academic institution, she had a good salary and retirement benefits—but she was also pushing back against the system. She was trying to change things. I went to the library and started reading about midwifery, and it immediately connected with me, my desire to be part of the system but also wanting to transform the system."

Though Amy was part of the mainstream medical establishment, there was not yet consensus that midwifery represented a legitimate and necessary role within medicine, and many doctors looked askance at midwives as interlopers in the serious business of delivering babies. Midwives—including Amy—were working hard to change such attitudes, believing they were restoring to expectant mothers some of the dignity and self-determination that had been eroded by a paternalistic medical establishment.

Kim cites a scene from the Monty Python comedy *The Meaning of Life* that captures her awakened perspective on the modern birth process. It depicts the actors John Cleese and Graham Chapman portraying two obstetricians at a hospital. They are summoned to the delivery room to deliver a baby. The room contains a variety of large machines, but Chapman complains, "It looks rather barren in here," and then demands, "More apparatus in here please, nurse!" The nurses swiftly cart in so many beeping and flashing pieces of equipment that the delivery room resembles the cramped cockpit of a space shuttle.

"Jolly good, that's much, much better," says Cleese approvingly. "Still something missing though, eh?" The doctors look around, and then say together, "Patient!"

A nurse finds the pregnant woman behind the towering wall of machines. The doctors boot the husband from the room ("Only people involved are allowed in here!") and shush the mother when she asks what she should do ("Nothing, dear, you're not qualified!"). Then, as a crowd of staff look on, Chapman hurriedly extracts the baby and briefly shakes the newborn in front of the mother's face before yelling, "Sedate her!" Nurses wheel the baby away and Chapman promises the slumberous mother that she will be able to watch the birth at home on video.

Kim realized that she wanted to help provide women with greater freedom to control their own bodies and determine their own birth experience, delivering their children surrounded by people who care about them. Several of Kim's micro-motives were harnessed in her newfound aim of becoming a nurse-midwife. The process of birth was a kind of complex physiological system of the sort that Kim's mind was naturally drawn to exploring and mastering. Her desire to be part of a rule-abiding institution was also fulfilled, since she still very much wanted to be part of the medical establishment and academia. But her seemingly contradictory desire to reform the establishment, a desire first evoked by the intensely political lyrics of artists like Tori Amos and directed into her curiosity about alternative medicine practices, was also fulfilled. "I really viewed becoming a nurse-midwife as a way to make a difference, to bring about meaningful change."

After she graduated from Duke, Kim was accepted to a nursing program at the University of California, San Francisco, the first step to becoming a CNM. She delayed enrolling for a year so that she could travel and serve as an apprentice at various midwife facilities around North America. But in an echo of her adolescent friendship with the "rebels," she spent much of the year learning from certified professional midwives—CPMs instead of CNMs. CPMs are not recognized by many states and usually operate outside of mainstream medical establishments. They exhibit a more antiestablishment mentality than CNMs, and during her travels Kim soaked in their independent culture and autonomous way of life.

Kim spent time at facilities in Mexico, New Mexico, Texas, Oregon, and Washington before finally attending nursing school in San Francisco, graduating with a master's degree specializing in nurse-midwifery and women's health. Now a CNM, Kim returned to Duke University Medical Center where she took a staff position working for her former mentor, Amy. As she began regularly "catching babies"—the act of attending births—she came to better understand some of the unexpected nuances of her micromotives. Though Kim speaks with authentic reverence for catching babies, she soon realized that she was more passionate about creating large-scale changes to the medical system so that it was more respectful of expectant mothers' autonomy—so that it focused on the health, wellness, and dignity of families. Her mind was still drawn to complicated systems—and she found that the best way to make use of this interest was by immersing herself in the American legislative process.

"I spent time in Sacramento trying to pass healthcare bills related to childbirth and midwifery," Kim says. "One bill failed, one bill is still being debated, and one got passed and signed into law."

Today, Kim is the director of the Nurse-Midwifery Education Program at the University of California, San Francisco. It is the most fulfilling role of her life, since she is responsible for educating a new generation of midwives who will go forth into the medical establishment and drive their own change. She also serves as the chair of the health policy committee for the California Nurse-Midwives Association, a position that allows her to continue to work on midwifery legislation. She was awarded the Public Policy Award from the American College of Nurse-Midwives in 2013 and the Healthy Policy Award in 2014 from the California association for her legislative efforts in that state.

Kim is living a life of authenticity and achievement. She is highly respected by the marginalized and by the mainstream, by ivory-tower academics and by those toiling in the trenches. Though a standardized view of motivation would see Kim as indecisive and waffling, ping-ponging between two opposite goals, her personalized success demonstrates that it is possible to harness conflicting micro-motives and convert them into high-octane fuel.

8.

In Western society, we are frequently urged to *follow your passion*. In this prescription, passion is conceived as a unidirectional force arising from a source of energy deep inside us, like the magnetic force generated by the churning core of the Earth that always points north. We cannot subdue or redirect our passion, in this view; we can only divert the direction of our life so that it aligns with passion's unwavering arrow.

This prescription fits perfectly within the Standardization Covenant, which prefers its aspiring professionals to heed simple one-dimensional motives. The Standard Formula commands you to know your destination, and if your motivational profile can be reduced to a single white-hot force, then all you need to do is pick a distant career destination that lines up with the fixed vector of your passion. If you have a passion for medicine, for instance, you are urged to start climbing the ladder toward medical school. If you have a passion for computers, you are instructed to chart an educational trajectory that leads to a job in Silicon Valley.

The dark horse mindset rejects this view. For dark horses, passion is multidimensional and dynamic—and, crucially, under your intentional control. Dark horses reveal that passion is not something to be followed, but something you can *engineer*.

The key to engineering passion does not lie in following the one motive that burns hottest inside you, but rather in deliberately leveraging as many different motives as possible. The more distinct micro-motives you can identify and harness, the greater your engagement will be with your life. You could say that Korinne has a passion for being a professional organizer, and while that's not wrong, it neglects the rich spectrum of her motivational profile. Korinne feels passion for her work because it fulfills several personal yearnings: her desire to organize physical space, her desire to help people (Korinne especially enjoys helping professional moms who work from home), her desire to do something different every day, her desire to be her own boss, and her desire to build her own enterprise that can grow and change. It is the synergistic sum of all these varied micro-motives that contributes to her incendiary blaze of passion.

For dark horses, passion is a blowtorch. You can aim it by choosing which micro-motives to activate. And you can always induce it to burn even brighter, because you can always find new micro-motives to use as fuel.

Following your passion takes little effort. Engineering your passion, on the other hand, is a more serious undertaking. It requires that you diligently pursue a deeper understanding of yourself. Engineering passion is hard work—but the benefits are enormous.

When you Know Your Micro-Motives, passion becomes infinitely flexible since different opportunities will activate different sets of your micro-motives. This adaptability imbues your passion with something it lacks in the standardization mindset—*sustainability*.

Though your motives are deep and enduring, they do evolve over time. Your hottest micro-motives when you are twenty may not burn so brightly when you are fifty. The adaptability of engineered passion allows you to adjust to changes in your motivational profile by seeking out new opportunities that harness new combinations of your micro-motives. There might seem to be little connection between upholstery repair and electrical engineering, but for Saul, they are united by the shared micro-motives of physical alignment, working with his hands, and working alone, even though each vocation activates different sets of alternate motives. In contrast, if you've fixed your life upon a passion for, say, computers—dutifully scaling the ladder toward standardized success in the computer industry—and one day you discover that the appeal of sitting in front of a computer screen has faded, the Standardization Covenant offers no easy remedies.

But there is a more fundamental benefit from self-engineered passion. It is not only a reliable source of the energy to act, it is a wellspring of personal authenticity. When you embrace the full range of your micro-motives, you are putting a stake in the ground that announces to the world, "This is who I truly am."

chapter 3

know your Choices

Destiny is not a matter of chance; it is a matter of choice. It is not a thing to be waited for; it is a thing to be achieved.

—William Jennings Bryan

1.

Susan Rogers is a full professor at Berklee College of Music in Boston, where she serves as the director of the Music Perception and Cognition Laboratory. She particularly enjoys working with the students at Berklee, who Susan rightly calls "some of the brightest and most talented young musical artists in the world." The feeling is mutual, as she is one of the most popular members of the Berklee faculty, winning the Distinguished Faculty Award in 2012. It's easy to see why. Her generosity, optimism, and self-deprecating frankness infuse any conversation with an engaging sense of authenticity.

Susan has carved out an enviable position for herself as a university scientist, the kind of job that many STEM students hope to land one day. There is a standard career track for attaining success in academia, but that was not the route Susan traveled. Instead, her life followed a winding path.

Susan's mother died from cancer when Susan was fourteen. She and her three brothers were raised by their father, a pest exterminator, in Anaheim, California, and she assumed responsibility for managing the household, cooking, and cleaning. Eager to escape from the perpetual drudgery of housework—as well as the tension and quarreling that became her daily state of affairs after her father remarried—Susan dropped out of high school and married her twenty-one-year-old boyfriend. "I just wanted to get out," Susan recounts. "I thought marriage would allow me to take responsibility for myself, while remaining under the protection of an older man. At the time, I didn't see how naïve that was."

Her husband was prone to outbursts of jealous fury. If he suspected her of looking at another man, he would become enraged and cruel. Unfortunately, he experienced such suspicions frequently. Seeking relief from the unrelenting abuse, Susan found solace and grace in music.

From her earliest memories, Susan always felt a thrilling reverence for turntable melodies. She enjoyed a broad range of rock and blues artists, but her favorites were performers like James Brown, Marvin Gaye, Stevie Wonder, and Sly Stone. "Soul was the musical street I lived on," Susan explains. "Soul was my resonant frequency."

Perhaps not surprisingly, her husband became jealous of her interest in music. He would hide her records or simply smash them. His resentful denigration of her musical affections extended outside their home. One night Susan was attending a Led Zeppelin concert at the Forum in Los Angeles. "I was there with a bunch of friends from work, and I had organized the whole thing. Though my husband had reluctantly given me permission to go, he told me I had to be home by ten thirty. Zeppelin didn't even start playing until nine, and by ten I realized the show was one of the greatest things I had ever seen in my life. If I left, I'd miss this incredible experience, and it would be embarrassing, like I'm a child. But if I stayed, I feared I might get punched in the face." Susan sighs deeply before continuing. "I chose not to get punched in the face."

But as Susan was departing the Forum, in a sudden burst of emotion, she made an impetuous promise. "I know this sounds so Scarlett O'Hara, but it really happened: I looked up at the rafters and swore before God Almighty that one day I would come back to the Forum and mix live sound."

It was a wholly implausible vow. Susan had no connection to the music industry and knew nothing at all about mixing sound. Her only relationship with music was as an enthusiastic fan, attending concerts and listening to records. She worked in a biomedical manufacturing plant where she painstakingly stitched heart valves into stents to be implanted into cardiac patients. She did not play an instrument and had never touched any musical equipment. Not only was she clueless about how to become a sound mixer, she possessed only the vaguest idea of what a sound mixer actually did.

And of course, she was married to a man who belittled her interest in music every day. Not long after the Zeppelin concert, she was sitting at a table doodling, drawing nothing in particular.

Suddenly her husband walked by and spat out, "Why don't you draw a rock star's big fat cock to suck on."

It was Susan's turning point.

Her husband had certainly said far worse to her, but this time all the pain and rage that she had been bottling up inside boiled over. "It was so foul," she explains. "So uncalled for. So hateful. And then he just turned around and walked out. That's when I thought, *You know what—I really do have a choice here.*"

She stood up, picked up her purse, and walked out the front door. She kept on walking and walking through the streets of Long Beach, California. Finally, she checked into a motel. She did not return home again. A week later she filed for divorce.

"I chose to find out who I truly was," Susan says. "I chose to make my own choices."

2.

Choice puts your individuality into action. It is the means by which you convert passion into purpose.

As the Age of Personalization gathers strength, we are entering a time of exploding choice—when it comes to consumerism, at least. Barely thirty years ago, most TVs in the United States carried just four commercial networks: ABC, NBC, CBS, and Fox. Today, Comcast offers more than six hundred channels. Back then, the so-called soda wars consisted of just two adversaries: Coke and Pepsi. Nowadays, it seems like every visit to the convenience store finds a new brand of ordinary drinking water. But all of this pales to the supernova of consumer choices billowing out of the internet. Amazon alone offers more than five hundred million products—dwarfing the number of items available to purchase by even the wealthiest of consumers who once needed to hop in the car to buy products from brick-and-mortar stores.

We're living in a golden age of consumer choice. Yet, when it comes to making important choices about your life—when it comes to school and careers—things have hardly budged in more than a century. That's because the Standardization Covenant took *meaningful* choice away from you and placed it firmly in the hands of institutions. This is one of the driving premises of standardization, after all: increase the efficiency of a system by taking all decision-making authority away from workers and students and reallocating it to managers and administrators.

"Be the same as everyone else, only better," is not a petition for individual choice. Just the opposite, in fact. Our standardized educational system does not allow you to choose the length of your courses, the method of instruction, the textbooks you read, the pace of learning, or even which courses you take. In most cases, you cannot choose your instructors, the size of your classes, the time of your classes, or how much money you spend on a required course. Most professions—including all of the most lucrative ones, such as medicine, science, engineering, and law—demand that you complete a fixed and compulsory set of educational milestones before they will even begin to consider hiring you. The business world isn't much better. It isn't called a corporate ladder for nothing! Your only choice in most large companies is to move up—or move out. In fact, "up or out" is formal policy in many industries, including academia, accounting, management consulting, the military, the Foreign Service, and much of Silicon Valley.

This is the most quietly effective way that standardization extinguishes your individuality—by depriving you of the opportunity to choose.

3.

When our institutions of opportunity are challenged about the dearth of individual choice on the straight path, they often counter by pointing to the handful of choices you do possess. Look: You can choose which college to attend! You can choose what to major in! And it's up to you to choose what to do with that diploma!

Under the Standardization Covenant, these are certainly some of the most important decisions you will ever make. But it's a bit of a stretch to call them *choices*. Instead, our standardized institutions replace *choosing* with *picking*.

Even though you purportedly have the freedom to decide between attending, say, the University of Michigan or the University of North Carolina, this decision is entirely dependent on which colleges actually admit you. You are not *choosing* which college to attend. You are *picking* a college from the list of schools that admitted you. It's the difference between picking an entrée from a restaurant menu and choosing what you want to cook for dinner using any of the available groceries in the supermarket.

Choosing is an *active* process. When you have the freedom to choose, you can create your own opportunities, including ones that nobody else might consider. Picking is a *passive* process. When you pick a proffered option, someone else has already made the real choices and you are merely selecting a piece of candy from their proffered box of chocolates.

Many authorities even try to convince you that this reduction of autonomy is for your own good by denigrating choice. Recently, when we gave a talk to an academic audience about personalized learning, an administrator at a major university stood up and protested that providing students with more choice was overly idealistic. "Do you actually work with undergrads?" he asked. "You can't give them the freedom to choose their educational path, or they will just choose to do nothing!"

To support his critique, this gentleman cited a phenomenon known as "the paradox of choice" but which we might refer to as "the shampoo problem." He pointed out, correctly, that research has demonstrated that when people must pick from a large and diverse set of options, they often become overwhelmed and paralyzed, making their decision at random, picking the most salient option or declining to make a decision at all. "Asking students to make educational choices without significant constraints would be akin to asking them to select a bottle of shampoo from a hundred different brands on a crowded shelf," the administrator asserted. "Most simply grab the shampoo with the lowest price. But more informed consumers pick the one that *Consumer Reports* said was best, because when you have so many options to pick from, the wisest thing to do is let an authoritative curator tell you which ones are good."

Was he right? Or might there be another solution to the "shampoo problem"?

4.

If you were a bird, what habitat would you choose to live in? The tropical rainforest of the Amazon Basin? The high altitudes of the Tibetan Plateau? The chilly lakes of Minnesota? With so many habitats available, choosing one might seem like an overwhelming burden. But if you were a bird, the choice wouldn't be difficult at all. You'd simply choose the habitat that fit the *kind* of bird you were.

If you were a penguin, you'd choose a cold shore next to a part of the ocean filled with delicious little fish. If you were a hummingbird, you'd choose a warm climate with abundant flowers brimming with nectar. If you were a peregrine falcon, you'd choose a mountainous region with high craggy spots where you could build your nest and plenty of small birds living below that you could swoop down upon. When it comes to choosing a habitat, each type of bird—like all creatures great and small—selects one that fulfills its unique constellation of needs and preferences.

This is an example of a concept from the science of individuality known as *fit*: the match between your individuality and your circumstances. Fit is also the solution to the shampoo problem.

Sure, choosing from one hundred different shampoo products can be daunting . . . if you have no idea who you are or what you want. But the better you know your needs and preferences with regard to your hair, the easier it becomes to choose the shampoo that fits you best. If you have oily, color-treated hair with an itchy scalp, want only natural ingredients, and don't want a product that was tested on animals, then you might select Maple Holistics' Degrease Shampoo. If you have dry, damaged, curly hair and need a moisturizer with omega vitamins, then you might try SheaMoisture's Rescue + Repair Clarifying Shampoo. If you've got dandruff and just want a cheap and effective shampoo that doesn't have any floral or fruity scent, then you can grab Head & Shoulders Classic Clean. Even when it comes to something as simple as choosing a shampoo, your individuality matters.

The institutions' solution to the shampoo problem, in contrast, is letting administrators decide which shampoo works best on average—or, perhaps, which shampoo is easiest and cheapest to provide—and then demanding that you use that institutionally endorsed brand. Even if institutions offer you a handful of options to choose from, it's not much better. At the end of the day, this top-down system is designed to benefit institutions, not you.

The true power of choice is the power to find and select opportunities that activate the greatest number of your own micromotives. The power of choice is the power to engineer your *purpose*—and thus the power to achieve fulfillment. If you are free to search for choices that fit your individuality, you might discover opportunities that nobody else would even notice.

Many different habitats fit the peregrine falcon, including the coastal cliffs in California, the Hindu Kush in Central Asia, and the Southern Tablelands in Australia. But peregrine falcons also flourish in a rather surprising habitat. The island of Manhattan. New York City has very tall buildings where the falcon can safely make its nest and survey the parks and streets below. There are swarms of fat pigeons, starlings, blackbirds, and blue jays flying all over the city without any other predators for the falcons to compete with. Even the experts were surprised when the falcons moved in, but the reason the peregrine falcon chooses to live within a glass-and-steel cityscape is that there is a great fit between the falcon's preferences and the urban environment of Manhattan.

When you have the ability to make your own choices for how you will learn, work, and live, you are a peregrine falcon questing for the right habitat. Maybe you'll be suited for the Himalayas. Maybe you'll be suited for Wall Street. Maybe both. But the only way to know for sure is to make your own active choices. If you rely on others to tell you what you are suited for, if you blindly follow the straight path, you may very well end up at the wrong destination. That's why the second element of the dark horse mindset is *Know Your Choices*.

Sure, institutions may know more about astronomy or land-scape design or music than you. But you know more about *you* than any institution does, and dark horses demonstrate that this knowledge is far more powerful.

5.

After Susan Rogers left her husband, she was presented with her first real opportunity to make a career choice that fit her indi-viduality. At this point in her life, she knew she did not want to return to school. Nor did she want to continue with her manu-facturing job. Those picks would be right for some people, but the most salient motive driving Susan was her interest in music. Was there some kind of musical path open to her?

To figure this out, she considered the full spectrum of her micro-motives. A youthful passion for music often prompts fan-tasies of becoming a rock star. This was never a serious consid-eration for Susan. She was not interested in singing, nor was she enthused about learning to play an instrument. The idea of per-forming on a stage in front of a large audience did not appeal to her at all. On the other hand, after all those years taking care of her family and husband, Susan knew that she enjoyed providing support to others; she only disliked service roles when nobody seemed to value her efforts. When others noticed and appreciated her support, it gave her great satisfaction.

Susan was also interested in tasks that involved "engineering." She liked tinkering with gadgets and appliances and trying to puzzle out whether they could still operate without each part. When she was younger, she took apart her Chatty Cathy doll to see the little record player and crude stylus housed inside. She loved the flexible records that came in cereal boxes, fascinated by the fact that a coded pattern was "written" onto the plastic. She had been promoted to lead her assembly team at the biomedical manufacturing plant because of her competence with the intricate handiwork required to properly stitch stents. Even though she had dropped out of high school, she had always been drawn to science because of its emphasis on figuring out how things worked.

The main reason that she had blurted out her vow about mixing sound at the L.A. Forum was because of one of her albums. On the back cover of Sonny and Cher's *Look at Us* was a photograph of a man sitting in front of a studio recording console. The photo was labeled "sound engineer."

"When I first saw that picture I remember thinking, *That could be me*. I could imagine myself managing all that gear, even though I had no idea what any of it was for," Susan says, describing her own version of the game of judgment. "And now, as I was trying to figure out what to do, I realized that if I was the person in charge of the equipment in a recording studio, I might really enjoy it, because I could provide service to musicians and manage the gear."

In 1978, Susan decided to look for a way to become a professional sound engineer. Unfortunately, the standard path presented a problem. She could go to school for a year and get a degree, then serve as an apprentice for an existing engineer. The good news about this option was that the best program, at the University of Sound Arts, was right in Susan's backyard on Sunset Boulevard in Hollywood. Its faculty consisted of working engineers who served major bands and labels in L.A., the world capital of the recording industry, and who moonlighted at the university for extra cash. The bad news was that Susan didn't have the three thousand dollars she needed for tuition.

The even worse news was that in the music industry, engineering was almost exclusively a boy's club. Susan lacked any personal connections in the industry who might introduce her to a working engineer and help bridge the gender gap, nor was there an obvious female role model for Susan to emulate or contact.

With the straight path for becoming a musical engineer seemingly closed off to her, Susan looked past the standard options and considered unconventional possibilities, using her individuality as her guide. Instead of passively picking, she made an active choice. She took a job as a receptionist at the University of Sound Arts.

By the lights of the Standardization Covenant, this was a foolish decision. After all, her job would consist of office work, not engineering work, without any guarantee that her temporary position would not become her permanent career. But her choice was rooted firmly in her knowledge of her micro-motives. A receptionist position was a service job, and Susan had a zeal for service. Thus, she knew her job would not be a grind and she would be able to perform her required duties at a high level. Susan hoped the position would allow her to get indirect access to the instructors and class materials and use this access to independently learn what she needed to become an engineer.

Susan also knew she enjoyed studying on her own, so she possessed justifiable confidence in her ability to be an effective self-directed learner—an essential quality if her plan was going to succeed. Though Susan's decision to work as a school receptionist in order to break into the music industry may have seemed dubious from the outside, it was a rational forecast based on her understanding of her micro-motives, the reality of her circumstances, and her assessment of fit.

She took the receptionist job and kept her ears open. After

just a few weeks, Susan "heard the sentence that would change my life." A teacher was talking to a student in Susan's office, when the student mentioned that he didn't want to be in the music business because he wanted job security. Since Susan's own priority was not fame or fortune but a way to procure a stable position in the industry, she tuned in to the conversation. The teacher told the student that the best way to get job security in the music business was to be a maintenance technician. "As soon as I heard that, I thought, *Okay, I will become a maintenance tech! But first, I gotta find out what that is!*"

It didn't take long for Susan to learn the difference between a maintenance tech and a recording engineer. A recording engineer is analogous to the cinematographer of a movie: they are in charge of all the sound on a studio recording. The maintenance tech is like the person who assembles and disassembles the camera. It was distinctly unglamorous work, far outside the spotlight. (Can you name a single maintenance tech? Have you even *seen* a maintenance tech?) That did not matter at all to Susan, since it would allow her to have a meaningful role in the industry and grant her what she wanted more than anything else: a front row seat to music-making.

Susan realized that to become a maintenance tech, she would need to learn about electronics. She heard from a friend that the best self-guided training program in electronics was a series of manuals published by the US Army. Susan called up the local army recruiting office and asked whether they might possibly be willing to send her their electronics manuals. They might. A week later, a huge set of paperback manuals covering everything from direct current principles to microwave technology arrived at her door.

"I devoured them. I spent every waking moment reading

them. I brought them to work, I brought them to the bathroom, everywhere." Even though she still did not have access to any studio equipment, she memorized everything she could and visualized how all the devices worked, the same way she used to visualize what was going on inside her toys.

Eight months after she took the receptionist job, Susan felt that she had enough basic knowledge about electrical engineering and studio equipment to try to apply for a job. She spotted an ad in the back of the *Los Angeles Times* for an audio trainee position at a company called Audio Industries Corporation in the heart of Hollywood. The company sold and serviced a very popular brand of tape machines and consoles, which meant it had access to all the major music studios and record labels. It was a competitive position with many applicants.

Susan got the job.

"I still remember the month—October 1978—because that was when my career began." When asked why she was hired, she told us, "I can't say for sure, but I know I was very enthusiastic. I really, really wanted that job. They probably never saw such enthusiasm for a trainee position. Also, I shared with them how much I was studying, how I was spending every day learning about electronics—and that I understood that it was a service role. 'Service' is the best word to describe the engineering and production arts."

She loved her new role as an engineering trainee. In short order, she was one of four maintenance technicians at the company, doing service calls to repair tape machines and consoles at recording studios throughout greater Los Angeles. She still wasn't seeing any music getting made, but at least she was finally in the industry. And it didn't take long for people to recognize her enthusiasm and talent. One of the studios where she did a lot of service calls, Rudy Records, owned by Graham Nash and David Crosby of the legendary folk rock group Crosby, Stills & Nash, began asking her to come work for the studio full time. Eventually Susan said yes, and she became a full-time maintenance tech at Rudy Records.

Not long after she started her new job, she got an opportunity to be an assistant recording engineer during live sessions. For the first time, she had a front-row seat to music-making, serving several major artists, including Crosby, Stills & Nash; Bonnie Raitt; and the Eagles. She was twenty-four years old.

"I sometimes hear people say that trying to make it in the music business is like standing by the side of the highway with your thumb out, just waiting to be picked up and hoping you get a lift," Susan asserts. "That was not the music business I was in. I never stood with my thumb out. I walked. And those of us who were successful, we all walked for a while. Eventually we got picked up, but we got help because someone saw us walking and everybody likes to see someone moving forward. But nobody likes to see someone standing around with their thumb out, waiting to get picked up."

6.

Luck is not a dark horse strategy.

Despite appearances, dark horses do not make riskier choices than those who hew to the straight and narrow. For one thing, dark horses are as apt to consider the worst-case scenario as anyone else. If they can't live with the worst plausible outcome of a choice they are considering making, they don't make it. Dark horses also take into account their economic realities. If they are raising two small children, and one plausible outcome of investing all their savings in starting their own business is that if it fails they won't have any reliable means of supporting their kids, they consider other opportunities. That's prudent advice whether you adopt the standardization mindset or the dark horse mindset.

And just like everyone else, dark horses minimize their exposure to unnecessary gambles by carefully evaluating the riskiness of a choice before they make it. What sets them apart, however, is *how* they evaluate risk.

Within the standardization mindset, risk has a very precise definition: the *odds* of success. It is a statistical concept describing the probability that the average person will succeed in a given situation. This is how most people evaluate the riskiness of a choice—especially when they evaluate *other* peoples' choices. Calculating the odds is ultimately an institutional, *top-down* perspective—not a personal, *bottom-up* perspective. Statistical risk is the perspective of an administrator who needs to select one applicant from a pool of many. For instance, if only one of every ten people who try to land a programming job at Google gets that job, then according to the standardization mindset the odds are very much against becoming a Google programmer. A risky career plan, that is to say. If you subscribe to this "risk as odds" philosophy, you would be justified in saying that anyone who pursues a programming job at Google is likely to fail, while anyone who gets a job is downright lucky.

But think about what is really going on here. We've so thoroughly embraced the individuality-erasing mindset of the Standardization Covenant that we think we can learn something useful about our own likelihood of success by asking how the average person fares. But no dark horse is average, and neither are you. An average is a linear concept, and the reason dark horses ignore the average is because their evaluation of risk rejects the one-dimensional reasoning of statistical averages in favor of a more sophisticated analysis.

In the standardization mindset, risk is determined by odds. But in the dark horse mindset, risk is determined by *fit*.

Dark horses evaluate how well their personal pattern of micromotives matches up with the features of an opportunity. Thus, fit is a multidimensional interaction between the individual *and* the opportunity. Both sides play an equally important role in determining fit, like a hand and a glove. The more of your micromotives that will be activated by a particular opportunity, the greater the passion you will engineer by choosing it—and the lower the riskiness of your choice.

If there is good fit, the opportunity is low risk. If there is poor fit, the opportunity is high risk.

As long as you Know Your Micro-Motives—and have a realistic appraisal of the demands of an opportunity—then you will be a better judge than anyone else of the riskiness of a choice, because you will be a better judge of fit. When others tell you that your choice seems perilous, they are usually adopting the standardization mindset and ignoring your individuality. They are playing the odds instead of playing the player.

When Susan Rogers took the receptionist job in hopes of becoming a musical engineer, she was not rolling the dice in a game of craps. She was a multidimensional individual considering a specific multifaceted opportunity. Though the *odds* of the (nonexistent) average person successfully ascending from a school receptionist job to a music engineering career are low, Susan concluded that there was a snug enough fit between her mosaic of motives and the features of the opportunity that she could count on the fierce passion engineered by the fit to thrust her past the inevitable challenges she would face. It was this engineered passion that enabled her to walk along the side of the road without putting her thumb out—and without worrying about whether someone would come along to pick her up.

By choosing the opportunity with the best fit, Susan harnessed her individuality in the pursuit of fulfillment, and thereby attained excellence.

7.

Luck is what we call the things that are not under our control. This is the problem with measuring risk in terms of odds—the moment you accept this institutional perspective, you become impotent. There's nothing you can do to alter the odds—the statistics are the statistics—and therefore there is nothing you can do to alter the risk. This is why luck plays a much greater role on the straight path, where our institutions of opportunity confiscate the power of choice.

Perhaps the greatest illusion perpetrated by the Standardization Covenant is the presumption that the straight path is the safest route to professional excellence. In reality, it's only safe if you are one of the lucky few who naturally fit the institutional mold. But for everyone else, when you must passively pick instead of actively choose, the gap between your individuality and the institutional mold represents pure, unadulterated risk.

The dark horse mindset, in contrast, grants you the power to influence risk. You can reduce the role of chance in your choices by increasing your knowledge of your micro-motives. The more you understand yourself, the greater your ability to judge fit and decrease the role of luck. By knowing yourself and having the confidence to act upon that knowledge, you take control of your destiny.

Within the Standardization Covenant, playing the odds makes perfect sense. It might even be wise. But it's fatal to personalized success.

8.

At the age of thirty-two, Alan Rouleau divested himself of the small-town business conglomerate that he built, brick by brick, out of a bartending job, and moved to Boston.

Considering that his hospitality enterprise was doing very well—his restaurant, bars, and club shared inventory and customers, feeding off each other in a tight-knit circle—his decision to sell them off because of a vague feeling of dissatisfaction with his life was viewed by others as highly risky, if not outright daft. But when he made his decision, Alan wasn't playing the odds.

He was playing the player.

Alan understood that the reason he had been such a successful entrepreneur in the first place was because of his particular set of micro-motives. He had a penchant for the numbers side of business, with a keen interest in the unglamorous calculation of profit margins and overhead. He relished situations where he was accountable only to himself, taking great satisfaction when a venture's success or failure depended solely on his own acumen. "I can't stand corporate environments, where you have meetings to discuss more meetings," Alan elaborates. "Working on my own, I can implement a change, have it fail, then solve the issue before a consensus would ever get reached in a corporation." Alan approached any task that involved marketing or selling with unfeigned enthusiasm, in large part because he is naturally sociable, deriving pleasure from getting to know customers, negotiating with vendors, and glad-handing clients. All in all, managing a hospitality enterprise was a pretty good fit for Alan, which is why he had prospered in central Massachusetts. And when he made the bold move to dispose of the pieces of that enterprise in order to pursue something new and unknown, Alan was confident he could rely on this same set of micro-motives to establish himself in Boston in whatever new enterprise attracted his interest.

But his confidence in his decision was based on something more. The reason Alan wanted to relaunch himself in the big city was because he possessed other micro-motives that were not getting satisfied in small-town America. For one thing, Alan loved culture. He had been devouring books since he was a child, sometimes at the rate of a book a day. He loved to learn about new places and people and the world beyond his hometown. He ran a jazz night at his bar every Thursday, even though the old mill town of Gardner, once known as "Chair City" for its furniture factories, did not supply a terribly robust audience for jazz. Alan enjoyed conversing with all manner of patrons at his bar, but he gravitated toward those with whom he could discuss books, the arts, and the pressing events of the day. Boston, "the Athens of America," held out the opportunity to make culture a more consequential feature of his life.

In addition, Alan longed to be in the heart of the action—he was stirred by the prospect of engaging with society's movers and shakers, rubbing elbows with the influencers, power brokers, and up-and-comers. "I was a big fish in a small pond," Alan explains, "but I was ready to swim in the ocean."

Alan's understanding of his individuality made him willing to bet that—even though he did not know *exactly* what he would end up doing in Boston—the fit between his micro-motives and the financial, cultural, and social opportunities of Boston would provide him with a better shot of achieving fulfillment.

It was a smart bet.

After arriving in Boston, Alan hung out his shingle as a consultant, evaluating commercial properties and crafting business plans for small-business start-ups. One young man hired Alan to assemble a business plan for a retail clothing store that would specialize in men's luxury accessories. Alan spent a week writing a detailed and thoroughly researched fifty-page document. He proudly presented it to his client, but once the young man realized how complicated it would be to actually get the store off the ground, he walked off without paying Alan for his efforts. Annoyed, Alan filed the plan away, hoping that one day another client might request a business plan for a similar project.

Five months later, Alan was strolling through Faneuil Hall, a shopping complex in downtown Boston, when he happened to notice a small vacant retail space for lease. Something made him stop and look the space over. The discarded business plan that he had spent so much effort crafting suddenly sprang to mind. "Until that moment, I had zero interest in retail, let alone clothing retail. But it occurred to me that this was a perfect spot for the store. It was right in the heart of the Financial District with plenty of foot traffic from professionals. And it seemed like it would be a lot of fun to do."

Alan made his next bold move. He rented the space and put all his money into opening his very first shop, executing a plan for a business that he never expected to become his own. "The original plan called for custom tailoring, so I added to the window lettering, 'Custom Suits and Shirtings.' I didn't know the first thing about tailoring, I just thought it would give the store a little panache. I honestly didn't think there was a market for it. Then a few months later a gentleman walks in and asks for a custom suit."

At that point, Alan had a decision to make. He could tell the customer that the store was no longer doing custom suits, the no-hassle choice. He could have hired a professional tailor to start handling custom orders, the Business 101 choice—stick to the things you're good at and outsource the rest. But something about the idea of making a suit appealed to a deep-rooted yet barely unacknowledged yearning inside him. Instead of ignoring the feeling, Alan made a decisive choice. "I told the guy we were fully booked at the moment and told him to come back in two weeks."

Sometimes bold moves are dramatic, like quitting a political career to become a professional organizer, or selling everything you own to fly to England to learn gardening, or dropping out of a graduate program at UC Berkeley without a clear backup plan. But sometimes a bold move can be as simple as saying yes to a client with an unusual request. "People ask me why I decided to become a tailor when I knew nothing about tailoring. I tell them, I didn't know anything about running bars or restaurants, either. But what I've learned over time is that when you do something you love, you tend to become really good at it."

As soon as the customer left the store, Alan sprang into action. He called up a prominent custom clothing company in Baltimore and asked what he needed to do to make a custom suit. They suggested that he attend their next tailoring class—in three months. Alan couldn't wait that long. Instead, he flew one of the company's employees up to Boston to give Alan a one-day crash course on measuring and fitting suits. "I brought him up the day before I met with the customer to make sure I wouldn't forget anything he taught me," Alan says. When the man returned, Alan carefully measured and fitted him and helped him select a suit. Six weeks later, it was ready. "It was a medium gray glen plaid two-piece. It came out *beautiful*. The customer was thrilled. And I thought, *This is pretty cool.*"

Up until that moment, Alan had never been involved in creative work. He had been an entrepreneur: selling, strategizing, managing, and a whole lot of hustling. He loved all those activities, but now, to his immense surprise, he discovered that the challenge of using his own abilities and judgment to contrive stylish attire resonated with him in a whole new way. Making custom suits appealed to his business sense, sure—Alan was quick to recognize that bespoke suits featured much less financial risk and far better profit margins than retail—but it also appealed to an artistic part of himself that had lain dormant within him, undernourished and ignored.

Of course, making custom apparel was a significant career pivot, to say the least. If Alan wanted to make money at it, he knew he couldn't approach it as a side hustle or a weekend gig. It was a towering professional mountain that would require enormous effort to climb. But Alan began scaling the slope, crag by crag, propelled by that boundless drive that arises when you're pursuing an opportunity that fits the entire spectrum of your micro-motives.

To learn the basics of fitting, tailoring, and custom design, Alan took classes at locations around the country that he believed offered the best match for his own way of learning. After that, he began "hounding" master tailors, following them around and watching them toil at their craft, doing grunt work for them in exchange for private lessons. He found he had a talent for the mathematics of tailoring, just as he had for the mathematics of business. But in a more surprising revelation, he discovered he possessed an unexpected instinct for fabrics—a native flair for identifying the right type of cloth for a particular sartorial end, the way a chef knows which spices will pair with a given ingredient. Soon, Alan was conducting deep dives into the study of fabrics. He investigated how cloths react to different temperatures, different levels of humidity, and different levels of wear. He even went so far as to study the history of fabric mills—then decided that if he really wanted to understand how mills produced fabrics, he should actually visit them.

Alan began voyaging to Italy and England, home to the world's finest luxury textile mills. Such pilgrimages were not common practice among aspiring tailors. Alan was almost always the first American to show up, which caused more than a few employees to suspect that Alan was some kind of industrial spy. But the effort paid off. "I got *really* good at fabrics. Now I can look at cloth and immediately tell you its quality, the length of its fiber, and usually the mill it came from, because each mill has their own proprietary way of finishing fabric that's passed down from generation to generation."

Since Alan was coming to tailoring rather late in life, we might excuse him if he decided to focus on some narrow niche of his new profession in order to reduce the burden of his formidable learning curve. But Alan had engineered maximum passion. He constantly pushed himself out of his comfort zone, embracing opportunities to design difficult or unusual outfits, including nineteenth-century Western wear, cruise wear, and leather biker outfits. Such projects offered little that was directly relevant for selling premium suits to professionals, but Alan was motivated to acquire any skills or techniques that might improve his overall competence. His unorthodox approach to learning would not work for everyone, but it was the right approach for him.

Barely two years after he made his first custom suit, Alan won his first National Fashion Award of Merit in Houston—precisely for making one of those unusual outfits: a vintage cowboy tailcoat, hand-pleated in the back to go over a horse's rump. "By that time, I had two retail stores, one in Boston and one in Nantucket, but my custom suit business was 72 percent of my gross. And it was way more fun!" He closed his retail stores and opened Alan Rouleau Couture, which has sustained itself as a fixture on Newbury Street for almost three decades.

Alan has never forgotten his roots—there is still plenty of Leominster in his speech and in his swagger, and he is a man who never puts on airs—but he became the person he hoped to become when he looked in the mirror many years ago, wishing for something more. It may never have happened if he had remained in central Massachusetts. But instead of hedging his bets or waiting for something better to come along, he boldly acted on the knowledge of what mattered most to him—and was rewarded with his very best life.

Alan achieved excellence and fulfillment not by taking thoughtless risks, but by embracing the power of fit.

9.

When you make your first choice based upon your genuine micro-motives, it's almost always going to be a good one. That's because a choice based upon a little self-knowledge is better than a choice based upon none at all. Not only that, in the early going, you have a lot to gain and not much to lose; the potential fallout from making a bad choice is relatively low.

As your understanding of your individuality increases, you will make choices that fit you better and better, your life will become more fulfilling, and you will steadily ascend toward excellence. Eventually, you will reach that happy moment when you've strung together a series of victories. You will look around and realize, with no small delight, that all the opportunities available for you to choose from are pretty good ones.

Paradoxically, that's when Know Your Choices becomes harder than ever.

Now you have something meaningful to lose. Once you become conscious of that fact, the vanquished influence of the Standardization Covenant will resurrect itself and begin to whisper in your ear. We've spent our lives in a standardized culture that forces us to operate without a safety net. We are taught to avoid bold moves that could threaten the stability and comfort of what we've already acquired. You worked so hard to get here—why risk your gains by pursuing a new and uncertain opportunity? Suddenly, playing the odds starts to look appealing again. You might even begin to experience grave doubts about the wisdom of fit.

Don't fall for it.

Nothing has changed. The same assumptions still hold, the same math is still in effect, and the same mindset that got you here has not come close to reaching its limit. Keep evaluating opportunities the same way you always have: if a new opportunity provides a better fit than your present one and you can live with the worst-case scenario, then no matter how seemingly stable and satisfactory your current opportunity appears, you should still choose the more fulfilling option. The reason is simple. Seemingly small differences in fit can lead to very large differences in fulfillment and excellence.

Fulfillment is a dynamic experience that must always be nurtured with growth, development, and self-improvement. The moment you stop trying to get better is the moment that fulfillment begins to wither on the vine. The winding path never ends. The moment you close yourself off to opportunities that will increase your sense of authenticity, you risk losing something worse than stable comfort.

You risk losing your sense of purpose.

10.

Megan Stanley was working as an information technology manager at a home automation company in Calgary, Alberta, when she was presented with two great options. One was a passive pick. The other was an active choice.

Megan had worked at her firm for five years. It was a comfortable position with decent pay and good benefits, and her boss and colleagues liked her. Megan excelled at her job, so much so that in 2002 she was offered a contract that would guarantee her job security if she committed to working for the company through the next ten years. Her family and friends were unanimous: sign the contract! The problem was, even though Megan genuinely liked her job, she knew something vital was missing from her life that her current job could never satisfy.

Dogs.

Megan had wanted to work with dogs ever since she was a young girl and watched the Tom Hanks movie *Turner and Hooch*, which starred a large French mastiff as Hooch. "There's a veterinarian character, Emily, who has a vet clinic in her home. I wanted to be her," explains Megan. "I had even picked out the house in Calgary where I imagined I would live and run my vet clinic." When she entered high school, Megan began to research what the work of veterinarians was actually like. This helped her clarify her exact micro-motives—and made her recognize that being a vet was not the right fit for her.

"Vets spend their time mostly *doing* things *to* animals—surgery, treating sick pets, putting animals to sleep, and dealing with upset owners," Megan explains. "I realized that's not the kind of relationship I wanted with dogs. I wanted to have more of a personal connection. Unfortunately, if you want to work with dogs, there really wasn't any other path available that I was aware of."

When Megan was offered the ten-year contract, she still had no idea how she might be able to work with dogs or how she might make a career of it. But she knew she wanted to try.

"There's something I refer to as my itchy feeling, and my itchy feeling just told me that signing was not right for me," Megan says.

Imagine Megan is your own child. You learn that she wants to forsake a decade's worth of stable income and benefits to chase her dream of improving canine welfare. What advice would you give her? Megan's parents insisted the odds were too risky, that she had too much to lose—and anyway, she could always volunteer to help dogs in her spare time. But Megan understood one thing better than anyone else: herself.

First and foremost, Megan possessed a deep and abiding love for dogs that she was sure would be an unquenchable source of motivation. And she had a heartfelt desire to improve the quality of care for animals. But just as important, she also knew she enjoyed performing many of the tasks necessary to run a business, and she suspected that if she wanted to work with dogs she would eventually need to start her own company. She liked accounting, financial planning, and web programming. Indeed, it was her excellence at these tasks that made her company offer her the contract in the first place. She liked being creative, and the idea of devising marketing strategies for her business appealed to her. She took great pleasure in working with people, and she knew she would enjoy building lasting relationships with dog owners and any employees she might need to hire.

To the total shock of her colleagues—not to mention her parents—Megan turned down the contract and resigned from the company.

Despite its lower pay, Megan took a job as a full-time dog trainer, which she hoped would give her more exposure to dogs and possibly allow her to learn about other opportunities. As she went through the process of training dogs, she discovered that the company was using punishment-based training methods. "One of the trainers pulled out a prong collar. I thought it looked like an ancient torture device. I was completely shocked and mortified that they were training dogs this way."

That experience, along with her growing awareness of what she calls the "dark side" of the pet industry, impelled Megan to become a voice for the animals. "I decided I needed to create my own facility to help dogs exist in our crazy human world and to fight for change across the entire industry."

Megan had a vision of creating a facility with two components. First, it would offer classes and programs to teach dog-training methods that were positive and oriented toward teaching dogs to thrive in urban environments. Second, it would offer humane and professional day care for dogs, since Megan had visited other day-care businesses and discovered that almost all of them mistreated the dogs in their care, out of either ignorance or apathy.

So in 2006, at the age of twenty-six, she opened her company, dogma training & pet services. The word spread fast about Megan's commitment to positive care and effective results. Her classes and day care filled up so quickly that in 2008 she was able to open a second facility. She won the Top Choice for Dog Train-ing in Calgary in 2016, 2017, and 2018 and was a finalist for the Calgary small business of the year in 2017. Megan currently serves as the chair of the Association of Professional Dog Trainers.

These days, Megan's parents no longer regret their daughter's bold move. Megan earns more than twice as much as she would have if she had stayed with her former company. She could be earning even more, but she puts as much money as she can back into her business and her employees' salaries. Over the past cou-ple of years, there's been a major drop in the Calgary economy, with massive layoffs in information technology. Megan says that if she had signed the contract, she would probably be unemployed right now. Instead, the past two years have been the best yet for dogma training & pet services.

Even when all your options are good ones—*especially* when your options are good ones—the dark horse mindset implores us to choose the one with the best fit, no matter how hazardous it may seem to others.

11.

Susan enjoyed working at Rudy Records. She was doing mean-ingful work for influential bands in a role that suited her. Even so, she admitted to herself that the studio's style of music was not precisely her "resonant frequency." As Susan explains, "If in the summer of 1983 you had asked me to write down on a piece of paper what my dream job would be, I would have immediately written 'to be a recording engineer for Prince.' "

She had felt a deep connection to Prince since 1978, when his music started playing on soul radio stations. She owned every-thing he had ever put out. But Prince moved in entirely different industry circles than Susan. She certainly never expected to have a professional relationship with him.

Then one day, a friend in the music industry called Susan. He had just heard about a new job opportunity, one that instantly made him think of her. Someone was looking for a maintenance technician. That someone was Prince.

There was just one catch.

"There was a reason the position was available," Susan remembers. "The engineer would have to move to Minneapolis. Nobody wanted to live in Minnesota. Nothing was happening there musically. It was a dead zone. In Los Angeles, if you needed equipment, if you needed help with equipment, if you needed a job, everything was right there. Moving to Minnesota was viewed as a career killer."

At this point in her life, Susan had something to lose. She had worked so hard to secure a career in the music industry, blazing her own winding path through a thicket of obstacles. Now all that labor would be in jeopardy if her career sputtered out in the Land of 10,000 Lakes. The standardization mindset told her that she had already beaten the odds, so why take another risk?—she should hold on to what she had already earned.

But Susan knew better. "I didn't even hesitate. It was Prince! I packed my bags and shipped off to Minneapolis."

The job site turned out to be Prince's basement. He was installing his own home recording studio and needed Susan to help him set it all up and then maintain the equipment. She spent her first week in Minneapolis working nonstop getting the studio up and running. During that time, she often heard Prince strolling around the house above her, but she never encountered him. On the afternoon she finished, he walked down the stairs and spoke to her for the first time.

"He asked me a few technical questions about what I had set up. I answered. Then he turned to go. No introductions, no small talk, nothing. He was about to vanish back into the house when a little voice went off inside my head. *Don't let things start this way.*"

She was thinking about what had happened with her marriage, when she had immediately accepted a deferential status without speaking up. "I've moved twenty-three hundred miles for the sole purpose of working with this man, please don't let the relationship start with me accepting this kind of role."

In that moment, Susan made a crucial decision that grew out of that first transformative decision to make her own choices. She stuck out her hand very formally and said, "I'm Susan and I'm here to be your engineer." A look of bemusement passed across Prince's face, but he came back down the stairs and shook her hand. "I'm Prince. Nice to meet you."

It was the start of a beautiful collaboration.

"I am very glad I did that," Susan emphasizes. "We are all equal as humans. We created this artificial construct on a professional level where I do this work for him in return for a paycheck. You can fire me, I can quit, but those are professional roles that we are agreeing to play for each other. There's another playing field on which we're equal and we'll always be equal. It was very important to me to establish that even though I was there to serve his musical needs, my role was important for the success of his music and that it needed to be respected. And he understood that and he treated me with respect for the entire duration of our working relationship."

Susan gradually earned Prince's trust by demonstrating her elite technical knowledge and, just as important, demonstrating that they shared the same musical tastes and sensibilities. That was the entire reason Susan moved to Minneapolis, after all—to be with the one musician whose musical style made her soul tingle. Though Susan had been hired as a maintenance tech, Prince apparently did not know or did not care that there was a difference between the person who maintains the equipment and the person who records and mixes the tracks. So Prince invited her to sit at the recording console as he began to record his next album.

Purple Rain.

It became one of the most influential and successful albums of all time, selling more than twenty-five million copies and earning Prince two Grammys and an Oscar. It stayed at number one on the *Billboard* 200 for twenty-four weeks, the fourth longest run in history. Susan had helped her favorite artist record and mix his greatest album. It was an amazingly fulfilling achievement.

But there was more to come.

When Prince went on his Purple Rain Tour, he asked Susan to accompany him as one of his sound engineers, to record his concerts at the bigger venues. And one of the venues was none other than the L.A. Forum.

"I still get shivers when I think about it. I returned to this place where my life was at its absolute low point, where I had made this impossible vow, and now it was coming true. I wasn't mixing live sound, but there I was, recording sound for my favorite artist in the world. It mattered to no one else in the world, but it mattered to me."

After the show, Susan went to Prince's dressing room and told him about her vow.

"We shared this incredible moment where we were like two kids together because he really got it. My dream had come true, but he was living his own dream at the same time. We had both been teenagers who had struggled with some really lonely times,

and now we were sharing this amazing moment where we recognized that we had each helped one another reach this magical
place. He gave me a smile that was like, YEAH!!"

12.

Dark horses don't follow their passion; they engineer it by understanding and activating their micro-motives. And dark horses
aren't given their purpose; they engineer it by making bold moves.

Each time you make a meaningful choice based on your
assessment of the fit between your micro-motives and an opportunity, you are forging your own purpose. You are dictating the
meaning and direction of your life.

When Susan took the receptionist job, her purpose became to
find a way to train herself for a technical job in the music industry. When Doug moved to England, his purpose became to train
himself in horticulture so that he could become a master plantsman and landscape architect. When Megan quit her IT job, her
purpose became to make a living—and make a difference—by
caring for dogs. In each case, their purpose was defined by the
consequential opportunity they chose to pursue.

If you follow the call of the Standardization Covenant and
passively pick a standardized option based on the perceived odds
of success instead of actively choosing the one that best fits your
individuality, you are robbing yourself of your rightful sense of
purpose. That's why dark horses fully invest themselves in their
choices. They do not equivocate, hedge, or treat their choice as
a trial balloon. They act decisively because they are committing
to a particular direction.

Whenever you make a bold move, you are announcing to the
world, "This is where I'm headed."

chapter 4

know your Strategies

In general, we're least aware of what our minds do best.

—Marvin Minsky

1.

The Rubik's Cube is one of the world's most beloved and enduring puzzles. Though its popularity peaked in the 1980s, there has recently been a resurgence of competitive "speed cubing." Experts can twist the candy-colored puzzle into its correct configuration in less than thirty seconds. Elite cubers can solve it in eight seconds flat.

You might guess that there is some prescribed strategy for solving the Rubik's Cube, an algorithm of moves guaranteed to get the job done. If you wanted to learn how to solve it yourself, you might instinctively go online and search for a YouTube tutorial demonstrating the proper sequence of steps to follow. Speed cubers, we presume, simply memorize this recipe and practice it over and over until they can execute it effortlessly.

Except there is no single recipe. Instead, there are at least twelve well-established strategies for solving the Rubik's Cube, including the Roux Method, Petrus Method, Human Thistlethwaite Algorithm, ZZ Method, and Shadowslice Snow Columns. There are also a half-dozen different techniques for solving a part of the cube (such as My World and Winter Variation) as well as additional techniques for increasing one's speed, including a variety of "fingertricks." Some strategies are indeed algorithm-based, specifying a sequence of twists to perform for any given pattern, though for any given pattern different strategies prescribe different maneuvers. Some "block-building" strategies don't strictly follow an algorithm but instead rely on the speed cuber's pattern-recognition capabilities. Most of the advanced strategies are hybrids that switch between algorithmic and block-building techniques and often rely upon the cuber's intuition as well.

Any newcomer is likely to ask the obvious question: Which strategy is *best*? By this point, you probably know the answer. There's no way to evaluate a strategy without taking into account the individuality of the person wielding it. For a given Rubik's Cube starting arrangement, eight different experts might follow eight different combinations of moves to reach the same outcome. Speed-cubing championships have been won using at least six different strategies.

For speed cubing or anything else, there is no best strategy for developing excellence. There's only a best strategy for *you*. That's why the third element of the dark horse mindset is *Know Your Strategies*.

2.

In the dark horse mindset, a strategy is a method for *getting better*. Thus, every strategy involves improving yourself over time. You need a strategy for learning how to hit curveballs, a strategy for increasing your sales, a strategy for becoming a more effective leader. Identifying the right strategy for you is the key to attaining excellence.

Know Your Strategies is about letting your strengths guide you to the right study method, training regime, or learning system, instead of passively following strategies handed down to you from on high. When you do, you might very well come up with ideas that appear strange to others, even though they seem entirely natural to you. What if you needed to solve the Rubik's Cube while blindfolded, for instance? What strategy might you adopt?

A dark horse by the name of T. V. Raman came up with a strategy that allows him to solve a cube in twenty-four seconds without ever looking at it once. How does he do it? Raman has a highly acute tactile sense, so his first step—which came very naturally to him, given his personal strengths—was to glue little bumps to the squares of his Rubik's Cube, with a different pattern of bumps corresponding to each color. Instead of seeing the cube with his eyes, he could now "see" the cube with his fingers. (Some might wonder whether that's cheating—but imagine if you were blindfolded and someone handed you a Rubik's Cube covered with complex patterns of bumps and asked you to solve it. Would you find the task any easier?)

A tactile strategy for solving the cube opens up new options, while impairing or eliminating others. Any visual strategy allows you to see a maximum of three sides of the cube at a time, though you can see *all* the squares on those three sides. But a tactile strategy affords a different perception. When you hold the cube with your fingers, you can "see" *portions* of all six sides of the cube—but you cannot "see" all the squares on any single side at once. To observe the squares on an entire side, you must move your fingers across the face of the cube.

T. V. Raman spent a few months developing his own unique "tactile" strategy for solving the cube—one that involved conceptualizing patterns of movements of the cube in a different way than any of the visual strategies. It wasn't a better or worse strategy than the others.

But it was the right one for Raman.

3.

Standardized institutions are not designed to help you discern the best strategy for you. On the contrary, they anoint a single strategy for everyone to follow—a One Best Way. Indeed, the biography of Frederick Taylor, father of standardization, is titled *The One Best Way* because the bulk of Taylor's efforts to standardize industry focused on determining the optimal method for performing a task, then arranging everything in the system (including people) to perform the ordained method as efficiently as possible.

By sanctifying specific strategies as "best practices" or "gold standards," the Standardization Covenant certainly makes the lives of administrators and managers easier. They don't need to spend the effort figuring out each person's individual strengths and tailoring institutional systems to accommodate them. Instead, it's the One Best Way or the highway.

Over time, the One Best Way has become so entrenched

within our standardized systems that we have difficulty imagining that there might be far better alternatives. Instead, we presume that institutions know more about our abilities than we do.

Today, we instinctively measure our worth by observing our performance on standardized methods of learning, training, and achieving. Of all the ways that the covenant can make you underestimate your own potential, perhaps the most deflating is when an institution insists that you adopt a strategy that does not suit you—and then reprimands you when you struggle, condescendingly attributing your failure to a lack of talent.

But just because you can't do it the One Best Way doesn't mean you can't do it.

4.

Astronomy is a field that depends heavily on mathematics. Kepler's equations describe the orbits of planets; Maxwell's equations describe the detection and interpretation of electromagnetic radiation from distant stars; and Einstein's equations of general relativity describe the behavior of galaxies, white dwarf stars, and black holes. Every graduate program in astronomy requires students to pass courses in calculus, linear algebra, and differential equations. Unfortunately for Jennie McCormick, she dropped out of high school before taking a class in basic trigonometry.

Perhaps if she had managed to stay in high school she might have developed more sophisticated mathematical skills—or perhaps not. "I always hated maths," Jennie says. "I could never get it right and often felt very frustrated—so much so, I must have switched it off." Thus, to develop astronomical excellence, Jennie needed to come up with a strategy that did not require much math.

Fortunately, Jennie possessed other strengths. For one, she is endlessly curious. She is comfortable asking for guidance and is not afraid of appearing uninformed. After her stellar epiphany in the wet grass, Jennie began attending free public lectures about the moon and planets at the Auckland observatory. After these lectures, she introduced herself to the professional astronomers who worked at the observatory. They responded to her enthusiasm and disarming congeniality, and one of the astronomers lent her a small telescope that she could take home. "I set it up in my backyard and said to my husband, come look, come look at Jupiter! He said, 'I don't want to look at that crap,'" Jennie recounts with an infectious laugh. "But that didn't deter me. I couldn't get enough of looking at the sky."

Jennie is also very comfortable with technology. She became proficient at wielding both the computer hardware and software used for contemporary astronomical observations, not by studying books or taking classes, but by jumping in and learning by doing. Jennie never shied away from asking someone for assistance with a new task, whether it was measuring the brightness of a variable star, calibrating a CCD camera, or performing differential photometry on microlensing fields. She gradually became adept at programming the kind of custom software necessary to automate telescopes during nightlong observations.

Jennie is also patient, detail focused, and methodical. She spent night after night, month after month, year after year, gazing up at interesting objects in the Southern Hemisphere sky, especially "planetary nebulae such as the hauntingly beautiful Ghost of Jupiter." She focused on developing her accuracy at aiming her telescopes at these targets, learning how various lenses, mirrors, cameras, and assorted electronics influenced the quality of her observations. Her methodical approach to observations gradually enabled her to make the kind of precise technical manipulations necessary to obtain a clear, stable image of a celestial object thousands of light-years away and produce a great-looking "light curve."

As she got better and better at observations, her newfound competence activated new yearnings—that is to say, new micromotives. "After a while, you start feeling like it's not enough to just *look* at things," Jennie explains. "I wanted to *contribute*. And to contribute to science in a meaningful way, I knew I needed a bigger telescope."

So she built the Farm Cove Observatory on her back patio.

Astronomy is a discipline where global collaboration is essential to success, since no single observatory can view all parts of the sky, or even one part of the sky, all the time. Thus, research projects frequently draw upon observational data harvested from many different telescopes.

In October 1999, Jennie began to work with professional astronomers at universities around the world. They supplied her with targets of interest, and in return she supplied them with observational data. Professionals quickly realized that they could count on her for high-quality light curves. Impressed that she had obtained such useful data with a homemade telescope, astronomers became increasingly eager to help Jennie obtain even better observations. International teams began to donate resources to Farm Cove Observatory. A team from Ohio State University supplied Jennie with a better telescope. An organization at Columbia University gave her a better camera. A Korean group shipped her a better dome. The astronomy department at Ohio State University even flew her to Columbus to give a lecture to its faculty, which she describes as one of the high points of her career: "Imagine me, this mom from Wanganui, dropped out of school at fifteen, speaking to all these professors about astronomy!"

To date, Jennie has contributed to the discovery of nearly two dozen new planets. But she also enjoys working on her own. In 2008, while conducting a routine observation of a distant comet, she noticed a tiny speck in the corner of the image. It obviously had nothing to do with the star she was monitoring, and many astronomers might have ignored it as a bit of uninteresting "noise." But Jennie, as usual, was curious and thorough. She liked to account for everything in her data, and so she investigated the origin of the speck to determine whether it was a computational artifact or an actual object. It turned out to be a previously unknown two-mile-long asteroid, which Jennie officially named "New Zealand."

Believe it or not, these days discovering a new asteroid is an even more impressive feat than discovering a new planet. Astronomers often know in advance which stars are worth targeting in their search for new planets, and when Jennie discovered her planet she was aiming her telescope at coordinates suggested by the lead scientist of the Microlensing Follow-Up Network. Other astronomers, both professional and amateur, who were part of the same project also made observations of the same planet, so Jennie shared codiscoverer status with other members of her globe-spanning team.

In contrast, she discovered the asteroid entirely on her own, unprompted and unguided. The reason this was so unlikely is because there are academic and government projects that do nothing but search the sky for new comets and asteroids, such as the Catalina Sky Survey, Siding Spring Survey, and Near-Earth

Object WISE. Virtually all new asteroids are now detected by these systematic surveys—not by amateurs in their backyards. She was awarded the New Zealand Order of Merit for her contributions to astronomy.

There is a term in academic circles for people like Jennie. That term is *successful*.

Know Your Strategies does not require that you come up with some kind of ingenious, game-changing tactic. Dark horses are no more or less creative than the rest of us. Nor does it require an uncanny instinct for zeroing in on strategies that suit you perfectly. Dark horses are no more or less intuitive at picking strategies than anyone else. But there is a way that the dark horse mindset's approach to strategies does differ markedly from the standardization mindset's.

Know Your Strategies demands a new way of thinking about the nature of strengths.

5.

A strength is a fundamentally different kettle of fish than a motive.

Your micro-motives comprise part of your core identity and are therefore potent and resistant to change. Our brains are designed to know—to *experience*—our motives very directly. Indeed, desires often elbow their way into our consciousness entirely unbidden. Even if we cannot quite put a label on a particular yearning, appetite, or aspiration, it is always possible to perceive the nuances of our micro-motives through introspection: when we want something, we *feel* it.

We know with confidence whether we want to go skydiving or eat a plate of eel sushi or watch the latest Marvel movie. But unlike the steady beacon of motives, strengths are *inaccessible*, *contextual*, and *dynamic*.

In other words, strengths are *fuzzy*.

Our brains are not designed to intuit our strengths. It's no mystery why. Almost everything we label as a personal strength is an artificial construct imposed on you from outside yourself rather than something that emerges naturally from within yourself. Composing limericks, programming web apps, and performing ballet pas de chat are culturally defined abilities that do not preexist within you; they are assembled—with sustained effort—through learning. Micro-motives, in contrast, are enduring psychic entities wired into your brain that consistently exert their presence in any environment. Unlike micro-motives, strengths are *inaccessible* to introspection because with a strength there is usually no real there there.

Just consider: How naturally gifted are you at riding a hippopotamus?

You probably feel very little ambiguity about whether you would even *want* to climb aboard a hippo, but until you mount the surly creature's back and feel its massive weight beneath you as you attempt to guide it forward, there's simply no way to know for sure what latent hippopotamus-riding ability you might possess.

Do you know whether you would be naturally adept at finding truffles in the woods? Singing with your mouth closed? Sorting different-sized thimbles? Handling a venomous snake? Speed eating gumdrops? Raising grasshoppers? Blowing bubbles out of your eyes? Balancing a paperclip on your nose? Knowing exactly when a minute has passed? Accurately estimating the temperature difference between your hands when they are plunged into two different liquids? Unless you've previously attempted these or similar tasks, it's extremely difficult to estimate your innate aptitude for them. The only way to know for sure is to go out into the world and try them.

You discern your strengths not through introspection, but through action.

Strengths are also *contextual*. Any personal quality can be either an aptitude or a handicap, depending on the situation. Let's say you have difficulty reading printed text. This might understandably seem like a shortcoming, especially if you want to be a literary critic, a profession heavily dependent on the parsing of texts. But if you want to be an astronomer, the same apparent shortcoming could turn into an unexpected strength. The brains of many people who have trouble reading are better at detecting black holes and other celestial anomalies in astronomical images than the brains of individuals without reading difficulties. A facility for empathy is an asset for a nurse, but a shortcoming for a military drone pilot. Being tall is an advantage for an NBA player, but a disadvantage for a coal miner.

Even if you exert a personal quality in a context where it's a strength today, it might not remain a strength tomorrow. That's because strengths are *dynamic*. They are highly malleable, improving with practice and deteriorating through neglect. Though your micro-motives can change over time, albeit usually quite slowly, they are rarely altered from the mere act of harnessing them. Making a bold move might reveal new micro-motives or clarify facets of existing ones but is unlikely to modify the motive that impelled you to make the choice. In contrast, the whole point of selecting a strategy is to improve your existing skills or knowledge—that is, to *alter* your strengths.

Since strengths are fundamentally different from motives,

you should take a fundamentally different approach when choosing a strategy than when choosing an opportunity.

6.

If you Know Your Micro-Motives, you can choose opportunities with assurance, because you can be confident about the fit between your motives and a given opportunity. But since your strengths are fuzzy, selecting a strategy is a far more uncertain proposition. Whenever you make a choice based upon your micro-motives, you are declaring, "This is who I am!" But whenever you choose a new strategy, you are making a more provisional claim: "This is what I'm trying next!"

This is very different from the Standardization Covenant's prescription for choosing strategies, which commands us to stick with the One Best Way—and if that isn't working for you, well, you just need to show some gumption and soldier on. Keep on grinding! Don't give up! And if you never master the One Best Way, then it's time to face facts—you just don't have what it takes.

In the standardization mindset, choosing strategies is a matter of *staying the course*. In the dark horse mindset, choosing strategies is a matter of *trial and error*.

The idea of flitting from strategy to strategy instead of staying the course might strike some as sloppy and undisciplined. Tell that to scientists. All of science, from metabolic biochemistry to sedimentary petrology, is a grand and never-ending game of trial and error. Scientists propose a hypothesis, put it to the test, and when it fails to prove out—as it usually does—they come up with a new hypothesis to test. That's because scientific truths, like personal strengths, are inaccessible, contextual, and dynamic. If a hypothesis does hold up, scientists never stop proposing new ones that might work even better.

Compared to life choices, which can be irrevocable and costly, strategies are trial balloons. The process of Know Your Strategies, in fact, will be the first time you should *expect* outright failure while wielding the dark horse mindset. Welcome it. Failure is an essential component—perhaps the *defining* component—of the process of developing excellence. Failure is the only way you can unearth the hidden contours of your fuzzy strengths. Every attempted strategy is a personal experiment. Does this approach suit me? Is it helping me make progress? If so, what might that say about my strengths? If not, what does this failure suggest about what I might try next?

Know Your Strategies is a highly iterative and dynamic process of discovery and refinement. Even if you find a strategy that works for you, that's rarely the end of the story. The strategy will help you get better, which means it will change your strengths, which might in turn suggest new strategies to try that make better use of your altered strengths, which can further change your dynamic matrix of strengths, and so on ad infinitum.

The Standardization Covenant does not leave much room for trial and error. If you are a college-bound straight-A science student and decide to try a poetry class and get a C, this most certainly does not give you a leg up on your fellow applicants. If your philosophy professor asks you to demonstrate your understanding of the readings through a multiple-choice test and you write an essay instead, you will not pass—even if that's the best way for you to effectively communicate your knowledge.

When institutions do grant us permission to try a strategy other than the One Best Way, they do so only grudgingly. In education, for example, they sometimes even use condescending language to describe such a request, calling it an "accommodation." They often go so far as to require official certification of a "disability" or "special need" before granting the request. Part of this reluctance to tolerate a diversity of strategies is the usual institutional aversion to inefficiency, of course. But there's often something darker at play: an implicit judgment that we are not capable or worthy, or at the very least, that we are obviously less talented than someone who does not need to make such a demand.

T. V. Raman demonstrates just how hollow such an attitude truly is.

7.

T. V.—short for Tiruvilwamalai Venkatraman—Raman was born with broken plumbing in his eyes. The optic fluid did not properly drain, creating excessive pressure inside his eyeballs, which led to the appearance of glaucoma shortly after his birth. The doctors in Bombay (now Mumbai), India, operated on his eyes when he was five months old in a valiant attempt to fix his plumbing, but the surgery left him blind in his left eye. They had limited success with his right eye, leaving it with less than 10 percent of its original vision—but still able to see. The doctors told Raman's family that he might retain partial vision for the rest of his days.

Some of Raman's fondest childhood memories consist of working on British crossword puzzles, math puzzles, Mystic Squares, the labyrinth marble game, and chess. This would prove to be one of his most prominent micro-motives: *solving puzzles*.

He also came to realize that he delighted in thinking about

the structure of things. As a teenager, he taught himself German and French for fun, because he enjoyed learning the grammatical structures of languages. He figured out how to calculate the day of the week that any given date in the past or future would fall on, because of the interesting mathematical structure of the Western calendar. Thus, another emphatic micro-motive was *exploring structure*.

Raman was also motivated by *competition*. He owned a chess set, and when his brother (older by fourteen years) brought his friends home, they sometimes wanted to play chess against each other. Whenever they asked to borrow Raman's chessboard, he told them that they had to beat him first. "Most of the time, I got to play chess all afternoon," Raman recounts with a smile.

In school, his interest in solving puzzles and exploring structure drew him to mathematics. The study of math is considered a highly respectable pursuit in India, with none of the connotations of nerdiness or eccentricity associated with mathematics in the United States. Most Indian parents are proud and relieved if their child wants to pursue a mathematical education. Though he could see out of only one eye, and not very well, it still looked like it might be possible for him to eventually pursue a mathematical career in the rigidly standardized Indian educational system with the aid of large-print textbooks and by sitting in the front row of school lectures.

Then, catastrophe.

When Raman was thirteen years old, elevated pressure in his right eyeball caused his retina to detach. On his way to the hospital, the retina ripped apart, rendering him totally and irrevocably blind. Raman entered a world of eternal darkness.

The standardized career track for mathematics now seemed closed to him. He would never again read another equation, parse another algebraic expression, or view another geometric figure. There is a standardized educational path in India for blind students, but it's not one you'd want for your own child. Its guiding assumption is that since everything in the educational system is designed for sighted students, the best approach is to give blind students the exact same education—just *much slower*.

"In tenth grade, they're usually teaching material that other kids have in sixth grade," Raman explains. "And everything is half-hearted. They believe that blind kids are all going to end up as telephone operators, so there's no point in giving them a full education. I remember a friend telling me, don't worry, I wouldn't need to be an operator, he just met a blind guy who worked at a bank—maybe I could work at a bank, too. I asked him what the blind man did at the bank. My friend said he didn't know, he'd go find out. Turned out the guy was the bank's telephone operator."

Raman realized that he had better start coming up with his own strategies for learning—or what Raman calls "hacks." To get an idea of how he devises hacks, consider his trial-and-error approach to solving the Rubik's Cube. He first heard about the cube in the 1980s when he noticed that everyone around him was trying to solve a fun new puzzle—and failing. The fact that most people could not solve the cube activated his competition micro-motive. The cube also activated his puzzle-solving and structure-exploring micro-motives, so he purchased one.

He didn't start out by adding bumps to the cube. That came later. Instead, he started out by manipulating its smooth surfaces with his hands. "Since I couldn't see the colored patterns on the cube, it gave me the impression that it wasn't going to be very dif-

ficult. This was a very lucky misconception, because it prevented
me from getting discouraged."

As he explored patterns of movement, he learned to hold the
cube in a fixed orientation so that he could track his manipulations. He mentally assigned a number to each of the six faces
and began to think about manipulations of the cube as strings of
digits. Still working with a smooth cube, he realized he needed to
solve the cube one horizontal layer at a time and *not* one face at
a time. Eventually, he realized that he needed to *feel* the distinct
squares on the cube to make further progress. His brother pasted
five different kinds of Braille stickers to five colors of the cube,
leaving the white face smooth. "Now I learned why everyone had
so much trouble solving the cube. It was much more difficult
than I had initially anticipated. Fortunately, I had already built
up an intuitive feel for how the cube worked. I fixed up my original notational system for common patterns, adding new nota-
tions for direction."

He began to develop mini-algorithms for solving particular
patterns by mentally proceeding through strings of digits corresponding to the patterns he felt with his fingers. Though remembering all these different patterns and their relationships without
the benefit of visualization techniques would be prohibitively
difficult for most people, Raman's facility with complex structures, his ability to hold numerical patterns in mind, and his
well-developed tactile sense endowed him with a set of strengths
quite well suited for his "tactile" cube-solving strategy.

After a few more weeks of trial-and-error experimentation,
he figured out a system of moves that would solve any possible
arrangement of the cube. It was an exhilarating moment, but
Raman's competitiveness didn't let him stop there. "After that, I
worked on getting faster. I derived shortcuts that allowed me to

move multiple pieces into position in parallel. Now I was really taking advantage of the fact that I could see all sides of the cube at once, which I consider a leg up. Eventually I could solve it in twenty-four seconds, which was faster than anybody else I knew could solve it."

Of course, solving a children's game is one thing. Getting an education that can lead to a fulfilling career is quite another.

8.

Most of the early challenges that Raman needed to tackle involved attending classes with sighted kids without falling behind. For example, one of the first hacks he needed to figure out was how to take notes quickly during lectures. It was the early 1980s, a time before laptop computers and mobile devices, when the only way to record real-time notes was by writing them down by hand. Though Raman quickly taught himself Braille, writing in a language of raised dots involves an awkward and time-consuming process of poking out holes, one by one, in a sheet of paper. There was simply no way he could keep up with a lecture by taking notes in Braille. So he invented his own form of shorthand.

"It was a problem of structure," Raman explains. "What is the minimal information you actually need to record a letter or a word using dots? I created a highly compressed form of notation that minimized the number of dots I needed to punch to communicate a single idea."

In his math classes, he faced another communication problem. He needed a system of mathematical notation that would enable him to effectively express and read complex equations filled with subscripts, superscripts, mathematical symbols, and

Greek letters. "There was only one system of mathematical notation for the blind, the Nemeth Braille system, except it was
only available in the US, and nobody there ever responded to my
requests for the Nemeth code. There was no way I could take
notes in class using the traditional Braille system, and it didn't
work for the math I was doing. So I expanded upon the ideas I
came up with for my Braille shorthand and devised a new system
of mathematical notation for the blind."

Using his hacks, Raman graduated from high school with hon-
ors. "When I was young I managed to slip through the cracks in
the Indian educational system, but in a good way. I really should
have been compelled to go to a school for the blind, but because
my parents never officially filled out any paperwork saying I was
blind, and since I always managed to excel in school, nobody ever
intervened."

So far, so good. But getting into college was a whole new challenge. The Indian educational system is modeled after the highly
standardized British system, including rigid entrance exams that
determine where you can go to college. Raman wanted to attend
the best science and engineering school in the nation, the Indian
Institute of Technology (IIT), the subcontinent's equivalent of
MIT or Caltech. The entrance exam for IIT consisted of two
parts. The first part was a multiple-choice test, which Raman expected he could do well using his existing strategies. The second
part was the real challenge: a written test that would require him
to solve full-length problems.

"On American tests, it's usually enough just to calculate the
right answer to get the points. But in India, you have to show
your work for every step of your calculations, and all your intermediate work has to be correct, too, to get the points. The big
problem for me was that the second part was timed, so if I took

too much time writing out my intermediate work, I wouldn't be able to finish before the clock ran out."

Raman took the multiple-choice part of the exam and passed without trouble. Now came the hard part.

"The written test required learning a new kind of self-discipline. My mind naturally likes to jump right to the solution, and I could usually figure out the final answer pretty swiftly, but I had to make sure that I systematically completed each step and wrote it out before moving to the next one. It was a different way of working, but I was very motivated because I knew if I could crack it I would stand a very good chance of going to IIT."

Crack it he did. Raman was admitted, excelled in all his classes, and became the first blind person to graduate from the Indian Institute of Technology. He went on to get a PhD in computer science from Cornell University, writing his dissertation about natural language-processing algorithms. When he graduated, he went to work for Digital Corporation and then for Adobe and IBM. Today, Raman is a senior research scientist for Google.

Many people hear the story of T. V. Raman and think, *What an amazing genius he must be to have succeeded against such odds!* Though Raman is assuredly amazing, this is the wrong lesson to take from his journey. He is no more or less a genius than Jennie McCormick, or Alan Rouleau, or Susan Rogers, or any of the other dark horses in this book. He did not succeed because his mathematical gifts were so extraordinary they transcended his circumstances. He succeeded because he chose opportunities that fit his micro-motives, and selected strategies suited for his strengths.

In other words, just like every dark horse, he figured out how to get better at the things he cared about most.

9.

In a standardized profession, you have little choice but to adopt the institutionally sanctioned strategies for learning. If you want to become a doctor, for instance, you must first go to medical school and earn passing grades in each required course. But in professions without a standardized training path, we have a rare opportunity to examine the organic development of personal strategies "in the wild" as aspiring professionals figure things out on their own, freed from institutional interference. And when we do, we discover something remarkable. When a profession stops imposing a One Best Way for developing excellence, every member becomes a dark horse.

Sommeliers are a perfect example. The most esteemed position in the entire hospitality industry is the coveted title of master sommelier, a credential awarded by the Court of Master Sommeliers. There are only 157 master sommeliers in the Western Hemisphere. That's fewer than the number of winners of the Nobel Prize in physics. That's fewer than the number of American neurosurgeons who graduate in a single year. That's fewer than the number of people who have visited outer space.

A sommelier is a wine steward. The profession first arose in restaurants in France after the French Revolution, though it blossomed into its modern form when wineries began bottling their own wine in the 1930s and 1940s. Today, sommeliers assemble wine lists for fine-dining establishments and help guests figure out the perfect pairing for a meal based upon the tastes of the diners. A master sommelier can famously describe the distinct taste and scent components of a wine, pronouncing, for instance, that a California chardonnay is "oaky and sharp, with hints of raisins and burnt caramel" or proclaiming that an Australian shiraz tastes of "superb pepper, red fruits, and violet aromas with ultra-fine texture and a mouth-filling palate."

To outsiders, the abilities of an expert sommelier can seem otherworldly. A more cynical soul might be inclined to posit that a sommelier's poetic interpretations of fermented grape juice are rife with pretension and outright fakery. But getting certified as a master sommelier is no joke. It's easier to become a NASA rocket scientist than a master sommelier. But unlike developing excellence as a rocket scientist, if you want to develop excellence as a sommelier, there is no One Best Way.

Though there is a specific thing you must do to become a master sommelier—namely, pass the Master Sommelier Diploma exam—the path to take to develop enough skill to pass is entirely up to you.

The MS exam is what is known as a "competency exam," meaning that it is designed to evaluate the specific skills that a sommelier must perform on the job, in the same functional context that the sommelier will be performing them. The MS exam has three parts: *Service*, consisting of serving highly demanding customers in a fine-dining setting under stressful conditions; *Theory*, consisting of wide-ranging factual questions about wine, viticulture geography, science, and history; and its most famous component, *Tasting*, consisting of blindly tasting six different wines and correctly identifying each one and accurately assessing their components. All three parts of the MS exam are oral, reflecting the actual conditions under which a sommelier operates: a working sommelier needs to answer a customer's questions at the table, rather than writing down responses in a booklet or checking off answers on a computer screen. Only about 5 percent of those who take the MS exam pass.

As you might guess, the hardest part of the exam for most

people is Tasting, the core ability that distinguishes sommeliers from any other vocation. To become a master sommelier, you need an effective strategy for developing a highly esoteric skill: identifying variations of yeast-metabolized grapes by their taste and smell. If we asked you to predict what kind of person would be most likely to pass the MS exam, you might speculate someone with a natural-born gift for identifying scents. And in fact, one of the master sommeliers we interviewed possessed exactly such native skill.

Brahm Callahan oversees a list of more than nineteen hundred wine selections at Boston's Grill 23 restaurant, winner of *Wine Spectator*'s Grand Award. Brahm is blessed with a heightened sensitivity to smell. When he was a boy, scents took on the same personalities as the characters in a play; he recalls, for instance, doing everything he could to avoid the "overwhelming odor" of dogwood trees, even though most people take little notice of their subtle fragrance. Adding to this powerful natural advantage, Brahm grew up in an agricultural region where he was exposed to a wide variety of odors relevant to the classification of wine. He can vividly recall the fruity redolence of pears on the tree as well as the juicy burst of pears sliced open on a kitchen cutting board and the fetid aroma of pears rotting in the compost.

Thus, when Brahm first began to evaluate wines professionally, he was usually able to instinctively sort out their constituent components with the same natural ease that most people might name the colors in a painting. Just as a freshman art history major has little difficulty distinguishing a Van Gogh from a Picasso, Brahm had little difficulty distinguishing different wines even before he began studying for the MS exam.

As such, his training strategy for the Tasting portion of the

MS exam was straightforward: integrate his instinctive olfactory prowess with the formal deductive tasting method demanded by the MS exam, which requires candidates to precisely identify a grid of specific wine qualities such as dryness and acidity. He just barely failed Tasting the first time, but the following year Brahm passed Tasting handily.

You might expect that most master sommeliers also possess superior olfactory and gustatory gifts. But Brahm is the exception, not the rule.

10.

Most aspiring sommeliers are not born with a special talent for remembering tastes or scents, and thus Brahm's "olfactory library" strategy is not feasible for them. If that's the case, what strategies *do* they use to pass the Tasting portion of the MS exam?

Aspiring sommeliers usually start with the "brute force" strategy: taste as many wines as you can, as often as you can, until through simple repetition your brain learns to pair the taste of a wine with its identity. This is the strategy Emily Pickral adopted while preparing for the MS exam. It helped that she had tasted more than two thousand wines over seven years of working at Gramercy Tavern in New York City, Kysela Pere et Fils in Virginia, and the Farmhouse Inn in California. Unlike Brahm, Emily doesn't focus as much on the individual constituents of a varietal as on its holistic identity. "You get so used to smelling something and the smell becomes so familiar to you that you don't break it down anymore. You're just like, *Oh that's what that is*," Emily explains. "I put my nose in the glass and I smell California pinot noir. I don't think, *Oh, it smells like ripe bing cherries and licorice and oak*—I think, *Wow, that's California pinot noir.* Or, *Oh, yeah, that's a Syrah from the Northern Rhone region, and it can't be anything else.*" When she took the MS exam, Emily drew upon what she calls her "muscle memory" strategy for wine and passed Tasting on her first try.

Pascaline Lepeltier, in contrast, used a somewhat idiosyncratic strategy to prepare for the MS exam. She had a lifelong love of philosophy, which she studied in a doctoral program in France, specializing in the metaphysics of Plato and Henri Bergson. "Wine fulfills my inquisitive mind, because I enjoy figuring out the 'why,' " Pascaline says. "There is always a reason *why* a wine tastes as it does, and I use philosophical deduction to figure out what it is. It requires knowledge of chemistry and biology and physics and sociology and geology and geography and even linguistics and metaphysics—my specialties. Wine tasting is the physical equivalent of philosophy, so it came very naturally to me. I could connect all the dots." Using her "philosophical" strategy, Pascaline passed Tasting on her first try.

Other sommeliers use a more conventional approach but augment it with their own personal tactics. Elyse Lambert seeks out the subtle markers of color, taste, and scent that guide her to the identity of a wine, such as a cloudy maroon hue, the taste of peach, or the scent of wild blackberries. She pays special attention to the acidity of wine, and before any blind tasting she takes small sips of "calibration wines" to help her tune her response to acidity. Despite her diligent efforts, she failed the Tasting potion of the MS exam five times in a row.

She credits an unconventional strategy for putting her over the top on her sixth attempt. "I watched a video by Amy Cuddy, where she talks about the importance of body positioning and mental attitude. It helped me realize that you don't walk into the MS exam hoping to become a master sommelier. You walk in with the mindset that you *are* a master sommelier. I put my arms into the victory position before I went to the test, and ever since then I try to control the positioning of my body, especially when I'm on the floor dealing with demanding or skeptical customers." Elyse became the highest ranking female sommelier on the planet when she came in fifth in the Best Sommelier in the World competition, after becoming the first woman to win the Best Sommelier of the Americas competition.

Another aspiring master sommelier was Michael Meagher. He started out using the "brute force" strategy to prepare for Tasting. For an entire year he spent between twenty and thirty hours a week tasting wines. But he failed the Tasting portion, badly. Unfazed, Michael increased his study time to around forty hours a week, still following the principle that more tasting equals more success. He failed Tasting again, and then the following year failed it a third time.

Undeterred, Michael added a "visualization" strategy to his arsenal. This is another popular strategy among sommeliers where you attempt to associate the identity of a wine with a visual scene that you instinctively conjure up in response to a taste, imagining, for instance, a stormy sky in response to a Malbec or a desert of pale sand dunes in response to a muscadet. Armed with this popular strategy, Michael took Tasting a fourth time. And for a fourth time, he failed.

At this point, even his closest friends were gently suggesting that perhaps he didn't really need to be a master sommelier. Michael ignored them. But he couldn't ignore the fact that something needed to change.

"I realized that using other people's methods wasn't going to work for me. Aggregating other sommeliers' strategies didn't make me any better—it just made me understand how other people pass the test," Michael says. "We all taste differently and we all have a different way we perceive wine and a different memory of flavor. The descriptors of wine are really objective, but the way we get to those descriptors is totally unique."

For the first time, Michael began to take his own individuality seriously. He began letting go of many of his adopted strategies. He failed the test a fifth time, but he felt that his mind was in the right place and that he was becoming more in tune with himself. That's when he finally came upon a strategy perfectly suited for him—what we might call a "physiological" strategy.

"I started to realize that I was very sensitive to the physiological aspect of tasting and I decided to use that. I focused on how the wine affected my body, like the burn of the alcohol going down my chest or the acid on my jawline or the grain of the minerality that I could perceive on the roof of my mouth or that twinge in my eyes from sulfur dioxide."

Even though he was learning a completely new strategy, he drastically cut back the time he spent preparing for the test from forty hours to between five and ten hours a week. He understood that, with his new personalized approach, he no longer needed to cram nonstop. "I felt like I was seeing the wines with my entire body and not just my palate. You might call it nirvana or bliss or whatever, but it was finally that sense of hearing the wine talking to me now. I'm not telling you what you are. I'm just listening to you."

On May 20, 2015, on his sixth attempt, Michael Meagher became a master sommelier.

11.

Even though Michael was not born with the same olfactory gifts as Brahm, he does possess exceptional native talent in another domain tested by the MS exam: Service. Michael is world class at making other people feel comfortable and important. He adroitly responds to complex and demanding requests with elegance and little apparent effort. His mind attends to the most minute details of the mechanical and social requirements of practical restaurant service and salesmanship. One might reasonably wonder whether his natural instinct to accommodate others might have even hindered him from prioritizing his own individuality over others' recommended strategies. Yet, even though Michael struggled to find the right strategy to develop his wine-tasting skills, he passed the Service portion of the MS exam on his first try with flying colors.

On the other hand, even though Brahm possesses a preternatural tasting ability, he failed the Theory portion of the exam the first time, and badly. This came as a total shock to him. Before he entered the hospitality industry, Brahm had earned a master's degree in classics from Boston College, a field that demanded he learn and recall a wide range of knowledge about ancient history and Greek and Latin. Brahm's confidence in his academic prowess created an obstacle opposite to the one that may have hindered Michael. "I admit I didn't take Theory seriously enough, and that goes back to my arrogance. I had written it off because I thought, *I'm a pretty smart dude*, and I had an irrational confidence about it."

Thinking his failure was a fluke, he did not bother altering his studying strategy before taking Theory a second time—and failed again. "This time it bothered me *enormously*," Brahm says. "It *insulted* me. My memory is able to hold on to random facts very well. But I realized memorization is just raw data, and raw data in a vacuum doesn't do anybody any good." Now he had a moment of insight into himself similar to the one that prompted Michael to change approaches. "I was studying the way that everybody else was doing. Hammering flash cards, maps, that kind of stuff. That's when I asked myself, what was my strength? My strength was writing papers. So I decided I would write a thesis for everything that I need to have an understanding of."

Brahm's new "thesis" strategy consisted of writing an academic-style paper for every subject that gave him trouble. He forced himself to locate and cite three different sources for each paper and write out everything as a scholarly document that he might submit to a professor. This approach allowed him to create context and meaning around the knowledge that he was studying.

"When I took Theory the next time, I crushed it."

The strategies that master sommeliers used to learn Theory were just as diverse as the ones they used to learn Tasting. Some sommeliers found it easier to study for Theory in a group, taking turns quizzing one another; others preferred studying alone. One sommelier recorded himself talking about wine theory and listened to his personal audio whenever he studied. Another adopted a "visual navigation" strategy, writing out all the information he needed to study on blank pieces of paper, but instead of using these "cheat sheets" as large flashcards, he memorized *where* on each piece of paper the facts were recorded. If he needed to remember the names of vineyards in Argentina, for example, he visualized the "Argentina" sheet of paper and then could "see" the vineyards listed in the bottom right corner.

Take a step back and think about what all this means. To master the art of tasting and serving wine, you must first master yourself. At some point, every aspiring sommelier must confront their own inadequacies and face the daunting reality that the standard strategies that carried them this far—the One Best Ways—are not enough to get them to the supreme level of excellence.

Every would-be master sommelier first needs to accurately

assess the fit between their micro-motives and the sommelier profession. Those who misjudge their motivational profile simply won't have the necessary fuel to keep going when they realize they must step into the unknown without anyone holding their hand. They must have successfully engineered enough passion and purpose to propel them through the formidable and intensely personal process of trial and error as they seek the right strategies for their own unique mosaic of fuzzy strengths.

There is no straight path for becoming a master sommelier. You must *always* harness your individuality in the pursuit of fulfillment.

12.

When you learn to Know Your Micro-Motives, you can engineer your own passion, which endows you with energy and authenticity. When you learn to Know Your Choices, you can engineer your own purpose, which provides you with meaning and direction. And when you learn to Know Your Strategies, you can engineer your own achievement. When you do, you will experience a deep sense of pride and self-worth because you will have accomplished meaningful feats while remaining true to your authentic self.

But if you want to attain the supreme realm of personalized success—if you hope to achieve the highest levels of excellence and fulfillment of which you are capable—then there is one familiar lesson you must first *unlearn*.

chapter 5

ignore the Destination

The truth is, most of us discover where we are headed when we arrive.

—Bill Watterson

1.

If you don't play much chess, you might presume that grand-masters possess an exceptional ability to see many moves into the future. That when lost in contemplation at a chessboard, elite players are computing long sequences of "if I do this, and she does that, and I do this, and she does that . . . *checkmate.*" You might even think that what partly distinguishes champions from amateurs is the number of moves ahead they can readily calculate.

Except that's not how most great chess players operate. Instead, they focus on one move. Their next bold move.

They evaluate which choice, right now, will put them in the strongest possible position to win. This evaluation considers the specific arrangement of the pieces in front of them and their assessment of what the opponent is trying to do. Crucially, it also takes into account their understanding of who they are as a player. Are they aggressive and chaotic, like Garry Kasparov? Unorthodox and inventive, like Magnus Carlsen? Or patient and cautious, like Tigran Petrosian?

"I am convinced, the way one plays chess always reflects the player's personality. If something defines his character, then it will also define his way of playing," asserts former World Chess Champion Vladimir Kramnik.

Confronted with the same board, three different grandmasters may make three different moves. What they do *not* do is assemble a plan for the next ten moves and stubbornly stick to it—though from the outside, it may look as if everything was premeditated when they finally land their winning blow. "I'm good at sensing the nature of the position and where I should put my pieces," current world champion Carlsen told one interviewer. "You have to choose the move that feels right sometimes."

There's good reason that top players prioritize situational decision-making over long-term objectives. Even in a game as tightly constrained as chess, where one can exhaustively list every possible outcome for every possible choice, the future holds vastly too many possibilities for any human to calculate—or any computer, for that matter. When the IBM supercomputer Deep Blue played reigning world champion Garry Kasparov in the first match between man and machine, Kasparov defeated Deep Blue even though the computer could "see" between one hundred million and two hundred million positions every second, thus enabling it to consider up to twelve moves into the future.

But in the rematch between supercomputer and grandmaster, Deep Blue prevailed. It became the first artificial intelligence to defeat a human champion because its programmers altered its code so that it stopped relying solely on brute force calculations of future possibilities and instead adopted humanlike insight into the situational value of immediate moves.

It turns out that supercomputers can teach us a thing or two about personalized success. Perhaps the most impactful difference between conventional recipes for success and the dark horses prescription concerns goal-setting. The Standard Formula commands you to know your destination. In contrast, the fourth and final element of the dark horse mindset advises you to *Ignore the Destination.*

Destinations are great for institutions. They're catastrophic for fulfillment.

2.

Every standardized system produces standardized outputs. That's why standardization exists in the first place. And the entire point of adopting the Standardization Covenant was to convert excellence into a reproducible product no different from bottles, bolts, and blue jeans. Thus, under the covenant our institutions of opportunity are devoted to the standardization of excellence.

It made complete sense to obsess about your career destination during the Age of Standardization, because early in life you needed to select the educational ladder that would lead you there. Should you aim for an MBA? A nursing degree? The New York bar exam? Under the covenant, your chosen form of standardized excellence became your destination.

Dark horses take a different perspective. When they consider excellence, they presume that individuality matters. You've already gotten a taste of the unbridled variety of human individuality in this book. The individuality of micro-motives. The individuality of choice. The individuality of fuzzy strengths giving rise to a lavish variety of personal strategies. Put all these together, and you get infinite winding paths leading to an infinite variety of excellence.

What does it take to be a great novelist? Many pundits suggest it requires proficiency at a set of essential skills: the ability to create compelling characters, write compelling dialogue, devise compelling plots, and deliver unobtrusive exposition. If we were to standardize novelists in the same way we standardize radiologists or civil engineers, we might require every potential novelist to demonstrate excellence in all four of these aptitudes. If we did, many great novelists would undoubtedly fall short.

Elmore Leonard was world class at writing dialogue, dramatic scenes, and characters, but his plots are rather meandering and pedestrian. Stephen King is a master plotter, but his characters are often wooden and thinly drawn. Leo Tolstoy created some of the most unforgettable characters in literature, with engaging plots that steadily build toward momentous climaxes, but he sometimes delivers exposition in a professorial manner that brings his novel to a grinding halt. Perhaps we can agree that, at a minimum, a great fiction writer must be able to create *either* compelling characters *or* a compelling plot? Except Jorge Luis Borges crafted beguiling works of essay-like fiction that feature neither characters nor plot. All these authors attained literary excellence, but no two versions of literary excellence are very much alike.

The single most important finding of the Dark Horse Project might be the spectacular variety of individual expertise. In every field in which we interviewed multiple experts, we discovered meaningful differences in the way they approached their craft that were traceable to the individuality of the person. Ingrid Carozzi turned her back on the standard templates of floristry and forged her own form of reality-bending brilliance: she likes very large designs (sometimes twenty feet tall or forty feet wide; she once built an indoor jungle with a lily pad pond you could walk upon) and unexpected arrangements (such as hanging flowers upside down, taped to walls, dusted with glitter, or encased in blocks of ice). In contrast, another top florist, Laura Jean Pecci of LauraJean Floral & Design, pays special attention to understanding the life cycle of flowers. She learned about the growth, blooming, and death processes of plants from her grandfather, who grew peonies, roses, pansies, fuchsia, hibiscus, and many perennials and vegetables in his backyard garden as a memorial to Laura Jean's grandmother. "The biology and life cycle of plants always influences my approach to design," Laura Jean explains. "I create arrangements that mimic how flowers grow in nature. To me, 'keeping it real' is the most beautiful design."

It is not very surprising to find a variety of excellence in a profession fundamentally predicated upon creativity. But what about jobs where the work is more prosaic? Surely it's possible to standardize excellence in something as mundane as dog training? Recall Megan Stanley, who developed her own method for training dogs in Calgary, Alberta. She employs clickers and treats and other methods of positive reinforcement that are humane and extremely effective. Abraham Mashal also uses positive reinforcement methods, but ones that employ an alternate set of training tools that he acquired while serving in the US Marine Corps.

Abraham was tasked with training dogs for combat environments. His job took him to places where clickers and treats were sometimes unavailable. "When you're in Iraq and need a dog to sniff out IEDs, you need to find some way to handle it even if you've got nothing to work with but you and your dog." Based on those experiences, Abraham developed what he calls a "leadership approach" to dog training, where the human patiently demonstrates through calm and respectful authority what the dog should do. After leaving the marines, Abraham opened Always Faithful Dog Training in St. Charles, Illinois, about thirty miles outside of Chicago, and personally trained more than four thousand dogs. His approach to training, though humane and effective, isn't for everyone. Even so, his business was so successful that he decided to turn it into a national franchise. Today, there are twelve Always Faithful franchises around the country training dogs using Abraham's leadership approach.

If you believe in fuzzy strengths and the variety of excellence, then you can see that there is simply no way of knowing ahead of time what kind of virtuosity you might be able to reach. And if you don't know where you might end up, then it doesn't make much sense to unwaveringly march toward a constant destination. If you commit yourself prematurely to a straight path, you may close off numerous winding paths leading to far more satisfying versions of success.

But there is a more subtle way that the covenant's mandate to know your destination impairs your chances for fulfillment and excellence. It seduces you into submitting to a toxic conception of time.

3.

When building a standardized system of production, the first thing its managers must settle upon is what the final product will look like. Once the output is firmly settled upon, the managers must next establish a standardized process for converting inputs into outputs—the systems' One Best Way. And to ensure the One Best Way is uniform, consistent, and reliable, the managers must tightly regulate the flow of time.

It should come as no surprise, then, that every system for producing standardized excellence—including almost every modern school, university, and employee-training program—establishes and enforces *standardized time.* They administer fixed-pace periods of training with predetermined start and end dates, such as semesters, trimesters, quarters, seasons, academic years, and fiscal years. In the United States, most undergraduate programs require exactly four years (or 120 credit hours) to get a bachelor's degree, whether you are majoring in marketing or marine biology or Mandarin, whether you are attending a large public land-grant university or a small private liberal arts college, whether you are taught by Nobel Prize–winning professors or distracted teaching assistants—whether you learn fast or slow. To become a senior consultant at most management consulting firms requires a graduate degree, no matter how skillful or experienced you might be. Even landing a job as a manager at many retail stores requires a bachelor's degree, regardless of how many teams you might have previously managed or what results you've produced so far.

It's true that our institutions of opportunity must standardize time in order to produce standardized excellence. But let's be perfectly clear. Standardized time is solely for the benefit of the institutions, not for you.

Compelling everyone to conform to the same timeline makes it easier for administrators to manage educational processes by setting fixed dates for admissions, enrollment, course times, final exams, and graduations. By compelling all candidates to march along the same tracks at the same pace to reach the same way stations at the same intervals—or, more bluntly, by compelling you to conform your personal educational experience to the administration's workaday routines—institutions can more conveniently manage budgets, allocate personnel, and process tuition.

One consequence of this is that in a system explicitly designed to streamline the standardization of excellence, everything one needs to know about your progress can be concisely captured in a single number: *how much time has passed.* If you are starting your junior year in an American college, then you are exactly halfway to a bachelor's degree. If you are a Canadian high school senior who wants to become a lawyer, you can calculate the month eight years hence when you will start earning money as a licensed attorney. If you are a thirteen-year-old in Germany who wants to be a physicist, you can determine the month eleven years hence when you can expect to be hired as a professor.

All of this invites us to believe that getting better is simply a matter of time.

Not surprisingly, scientists are also susceptible to this seductive conviction, since they themselves passed through the same fixed-pace educational system to attain the necessary standardized credentials to conduct research in the first place. On top of that, most human subjects they study also trained or work in institutions enforcing standardized time. As a result, most researchers investigating excellence treat time as an independent variable rather than a dependent variable—which is to say, they view time as a cause of expertise. This leads scientists to pose the innocent-seeming question "How much time is necessary to develop excellence?"

When researchers then come up with tidy answers like "It takes an average of eight thousand hours of practice to develop mastery" or "The median time of schooling necessary to become an expert is twelve years," we internalize such assertions without protest, since these conclusions match our institutionalized understanding of the causal relationship between excellence and time.

But dark horses reject such conclusions out of hand.

In the dark horse mindset, time does not matter.

4.

How many hours of study and practice does it take to pass the Master Sommelier Diploma exam? The correct answer is *it depends*. It depends on the individuality of the sommelier—on his unique matrix of micro-motives and fuzzy strengths. But most of all, it depends on the specific choices he makes in the pursuit of excellence.

For Brahm Callahan, it took somewhere around four thousand hours of study and practice to pass the MS exam. For Michael Meagher, it took closer to eight thousand hours. But these numbers alone tell us almost nothing about the actual process of developing excellence. It would be misguided to use these durations as a rule of thumb for predicting how long it would take *you* to pass the MS exam, because they ignore the relationship between the individual and his search for strategies. If Brahm had continued doggedly employing the same "flashcard" strategy for studying Theory instead of switching to his personalized "thesis" strategy he might have ended up taking twice as long as Michael to pass. If Michael had applied his personalized "physiology" strategy from the start to prepare for Tasting, he might have passed in half the time that Brahm did. In each case, the most important temporal factor was not the inherent difficulty of the task they were trying to master or their general capacity for learning, but rather each man's ability to find the right strategy for his own pattern of strengths. Crucially, each aspiring master sommelier had to surmount a private mental hurdle that prevented him from recognizing that he needed a strategy (or suite of strategies) customized for his own individuality, and the time it required to come to that realization and find a strategy suited for his fuzzy strengths was far more impactful than the time necessary to develop competence once the right strategies were chosen.

Under the dark horse mindset, time is relative. Your pace of improvement is determined by the specific opportunities you decide to pursue and the specific strategies you decide to try. That means the time that passes on your journey of self-improvement will always be relative to the decisions you make. Time does not inexorably drive you toward excellence. It is your choices, not the ticking of some metronome, that propel you toward excellence. You should be skeptical of any "standard developmental timeline," and certainly any institutional timeline, since they were developed with respect to static, one-dimensional averages without any reference to your own dynamic and multidimensional micro-motives and fuzzy strengths.

Instead of asking pointless questions like "How long does it take, on average, to master tennis?" or "Why am I taking so much longer than my peers to understand organic chemistry?," the only question you should ever ask yourself is "Is this the right strategy for me?"

The Standardization Covenant will steer you away from this all-important question. It demands that we trade away the relative time of situational decision-making for the standardized time of knowing your destination and staying the course. That is the bargain we strike when we choose to embark upon the straight path, and most of the time it's a pretty raw deal. But when you embrace relative time by making your own choices at your own pace, time does not matter because you are maximizing your fulfillment every step of the way, which in turn will maximize the rate at which you will develop excellence.

When viewed through the dark horse mindset, it becomes apparent that standardized time actually *impairs* your ability to attain excellence, by making you lose hope when you fall behind the institutional pace car. If you see others graduate on time while you take a few semesters off, you may experience a gnawing sense of insecurity. If others get promotions while you stagnate on a lower rung of the corporate ladder, you may start to feel a lingering sense that life is passing you by. Every time you read about the average age of a Silicon Valley entrepreneur, professional athlete, or med school graduate, you might worry that you've missed your big chance. Even the institutional notion of retirement inhibits our sense of possibility as we endure the creeping sensation that the world is pushing us toward an exit date. In short, standardized time makes us focus on all the wrong things.

But there is a remedy. Ignore the Destination instructs us to focus on the opportunity at hand rather than the prospects at the end of the road.

5.

Every young person knows what it is like to be pestered with the question "What do you want to be when you grow up?" Compelled to declare a preference, many adolescents dutifully announce, "I want to be an engineer" or "I want to be a journalist." At first, such a declaration might be put forward reluctantly, but with perpetual pressure from family members, counselors, and teachers to *know your destination*, this tentative proposal often turns into a resolute plan. But an early commitment to a career is often doomed to failure because it disregards a fundamental feature of reality: the inevitability of change.

Attaining excellence requires that you engineer purpose. Engineering purpose requires that you maximize the fit between your micro-motives and the opportunity you choose to pursue. Thus, there are two obvious problems with pursuing a professional opportunity that lies somewhere in the far-off future. Number one, by the time you finally get there, your understanding of your micro-motives may have changed. And number two, the opportunity itself may have changed.

We've already seen how the covenant tends to stifle your understanding of your micro-motives, so coming to an awareness of your true identity is always an uphill climb when you are in a standardized institution. Blindly rushing into the rigid hierarchy of higher education may be more likely to suppress your self-understanding than elucidate it. But even in a world with a highly personalized educational system, it would still require plenty of bold moves and useful failures to gain insight into all the dimensions of your motivation. You simply have no way of knowing in advance whether your mosaic of authentic micro-motives will be a good match for the destination you are aiming for.

And even if you are fortunate enough to arrive at a fair understanding of your motives, there's no way of knowing how they might change over time. The very process of pursuing success will cause you to grow and develop in unpredictable ways, leading to a different set of micro-motives that will no longer be a good fit for the standardized notion of excellence you decided to chase so long ago. Needless to say, the farther off the destination, the more likely your understanding of your individuality will evolve before you arrive.

But it's not only you that can change. It's an iron-clad guarantee that the world will have changed by the time you reach your destination. New opportunities will appear that weren't there when you first embarked upon the straight path. Ten years ago, there were no social media community coordinators, smart car engineers, brand-experience designers, or 3-D printer entrepreneurs. Who knows what exciting opportunities will arise in another ten years?

Like chess grandmasters, dark horses teach us that you can achieve success without ever knowing your destination. You just can't reach it without knowing who you are.

6.

From an early age, Jenny Dorsey knew exactly where she wanted to go: the very top of the ladder. Her parents drilled into her the idea that success consisted of climbing higher and faster than anyone else. "I had Tiger parents," Jenny says, "and for them life was about perfect grades and outcompeting all the other kids to get a high-status job. Since I loved competing, I never really questioned any of this."

To say that Jenny excelled in school would be a gross understatement. She left high school at age fifteen and then finished the finance program at the University of Washington at the age of nineteen. "I did so well in my classes that I destroyed the curve, so the teachers simply took me off the curve so the other students could pass. I was usually the smartest person in the room. My ego was completely unchecked." Within months after she graduated, she was hired by Accenture as a management consultant. It was a job with a nice salary, decent benefits, and the opportunity to travel—an impressive career start by most standards, especially for a teenager. But Jenny was so obsessed with muscling her way to the top that she was already plotting how she could land one of the premier roles at the firm.

"I wanted to be a consultant for the luxury brands in the fashion industry," Jenny says. "That was the brass ring. The ultimate status." Unfortunately for Jenny, the company put her on the account for a discount department store instead, which was perceived as one of the dullest jobs at Accenture, with the least opportunity for advancement. "At first, I was like, *Okay, at least I'll get to be in New York and I can make a move from there.* But then they told me I had to work in Arkansas, and I was like, *Uh, no way.* I decided I would do whatever it takes to move up."

She proceeded to maneuver her way up the ladder by cajoling her superiors, twisting arms and throwing elbows, not hesitating to step over her colleagues, until she finally secured a position consulting for Theory, a Manhattan-based high-end global fashion retailer. At the age of twenty-one, she had already reached her destination.

Jenny's career trajectory is the perfect embodiment of the maxim "It's not personal, it's just business." If you feel a sense of disapproval, wasn't she simply doing exactly what the Standardization Covenant demands? Wasn't she simply ascending the ladder by being the same as everyone else, only much better? Wasn't Jenny exactly the kind of success story the system was designed to cultivate?

Jenny certainly thought so. She celebrated her arrival by proudly updating her social media accounts to showcase her glamorous life to the entire world. "I had everything I thought I wanted," Jenny says before drawing a long sigh. "And I hated my life."

Even though she had reached the destination she had longed for throughout her short life, she was anything but fulfilled. "I was obsessed with my Facebook and LinkedIn accounts. I updated them constantly. But in reality, I didn't have any friends. I thought they would slow me down, that in the corporate world it was kill or be killed," Jenny explains. She developed an unhealthy relationship with food. It got so bad that she would binge in the middle of the night and then go days without eating. "I was completely out of control, I wasn't sleeping, I wasn't even doing my work."

She finally reached her turning point.

"I looked in the mirror and realized—*I have no idea who I am.*"

She had been on the fast track for standardized success for so long that she had never stopped to think about what she actually wanted. "It suddenly became clear that I needed to start over. I was still living for my parents, for their expectations, for their idea of what it meant to be successful. I needed to find some way to figure out who I was, what I really wanted to do with the rest of my life."

So she quit her job and embarked on a lengthy period of soul-searching. She worked as a barista at a café. She peddled blended juice. She worked in the kitchen at several restaurants. Jenny's parents were angry and baffled by the abandonment of her career, and her relationship with them collapsed. She was unhappy about that, but she also understood what was at stake. After all, living her life according to someone else's notion of success is what got her here in the first place.

Over time, she began to form healthier relationships. She started making real friends. Then she married a man who liked her for herself, for the Jenny who was discovering her own way. He supported her choices without putting any expectations on her about what success looked like. She finally restored a healthy balance to her eating. She discovered that she thoroughly enjoyed cooking and began to dabble in cooking classes, then enrolled in the Institute of Culinary Education. To test drive her new skills,

Jenny and her husband decided that they would throw a five-course dinner party for friends.

Jenny cooked the food, and her husband mixed the drinks. "The food was a mess and the drinks were worse, but the dinner was kind of a revelation for me. For the first time, it was, something that was completely my own. I picked the menu, I cooked it, I organized the event, I was creative, I could just be myself and help my guests have a good time."

Jenny had so much fun that she and her husband made it a weekly event. More people came each time. "Then one day a stranger showed up who we didn't even know. We realized, wow, people are legitimately enjoying what we're doing, and we're having such a good time, maybe we should see if we can take it to the next level."

The next level required Jenny to make her first bold move based on her true micro-motives. She and her husband rented a huge space in New York City and sold one hundred tickets for their dinner event. "We spent a great deal of money, expecting to make it all back, but ended up losing half! That hurt, but I didn't care. It was amazing."

Jenny and her husband continued refining their "pop-up supper club" in New York, naming it "I Forgot It's Wednesday" since they always held it on Wednesday. "I was so proud of it. I never cared about anything the way I cared about the supper club, because it was something that was finally my own thing. For instance, one of our courses was named 'You Make Asian Food Right?' and the dish was a very non-Asian dish with lots of Asian influences, an ode to the fact that as an Asian American woman I am not a unidimensional thing. Another dish was named 'Fancy 'Cause It's French'—a mooncake with very traditional mooncake flavors (red bean, salted duck egg), but the ingredients were reimagined using the French technique for a small entremets so it presents as a patisserie item, mocking the fact that we assign status without true consideration for quality."

Jenny's bold move paid off. She and her husband moved to San Francisco and continued I Forgot It's Wednesday there. Within a year, they were named the number one underground supper club in San Francisco. Eventually they moved back to New York and were named the top secret dining club in the city by Guest of a Guest and one of the best tasting menus in the city by CBS New York. Their pop-up dinner series, now renamed "Wednesdays," is still going strong today.

After living the first two-thirds of her life chasing someone else's idea of success, Jenny has finally arrived at a place where her individuality matters. "We built our brand around authenticity, because everything about it is true to who we are."

7.

Dark horses may ignore destinations, but they don't ignore goals. In the dark horse mindset, there is a clear distinction between the two.

A goal always emerges out of your individuality. More pointedly, a goal is born out of an active choice you have made. In contrast, a destination is someone else's idea of an objective that you have acceded to. More often than not, a destination is defined by a standardized institution of opportunity.

A goal is actionable in an immediate, concrete way. You can try out different strategies, right now, that will enable you to reach a goal. Finishing your novel before the publisher's deadline, increasing your sales over the coming year, and winning your next soccer game are all legitimate goals within the dark horse mindset.

Reaching a destination, in contrast, is always *contingent*—contingent upon the intermediate, the unknown, or the unpredictable. Destinations require multiple future strategies that depend on the outcome of intervening strategies. The more contingent a destination is upon future events, the more it impairs your attainment of fulfillment because the more it requires you to ignore the reality of change. Winning the Nobel Prize for literature, becoming the number one sales associate at your company, and winning the World Cup are all destinations.

If you are in high school, then getting into Harvard Law School is a destination. There are too many unknowns and intermediate events between you and the destination, and the destination itself is entirely defined by the Standardization Covenant, anyway. But there are many purpose-driven goals you can work toward right now, such as reading philosophy books, winning your next debate club match, and trying to get an internship at a local law firm. Sure, it's certainly possible that you will end up at Harvard Law. But it's far more likely that the self-knowledge you obtain from your experiences pursuing these immediate goals will open up a whole new range of choices better suited for your authentic individuality.

The difference between a goal and a destination may seem like a game of semantics. It is nothing of the sort. They are divergent conceptions of what an objective ought to be that emerge from two distinct systems of reasoning. When you Ignore the Destination, you don't need to take a leap of faith.

You just need to trust the math.

Designed by Bruno Gazzoni

The Landscape of Excellence

8.

Imagine a landscape of peaks and valleys stretching as far as the eye can see, like the one pictured here. Your mission: climb to the top of the highest peak. The challenge: you don't possess a map of this unexplored terrain, so you don't know the locations or the elevations of the summits in this vast mountain range. Since you are starting your journey down near sea level, you can only see the rugged slopes immediately around you. How would you go about finding a promising route to climb?

This is not merely a thought experiment. It's an example of what mathematicians call a "global optimization problem."

Your pursuit of excellence is your own personal global optimization problem. The pinnacles and depressions all represent different levels of excellence that you could attain, given your unique set of micro-motives and fuzzy strengths. You can think of each mountain and valley as representing a different endeavor. As you can see from the many dips and chasms in this "landscape of excellence," you do not have the potential to be great at every-thing. But at the same time, the number of things at which you *could* be great is almost boundless. The question is, how do you reach one of your attainable peaks of excellence if you don't have a map telling you where to climb?

The dark horse mindset is perfectly designed for this challenge. From the outside, the winding paths that dark horses like Alan Rouleau, Susan Rogers, and Doug Hoerr followed to attain pro-fessional mastery can often seem the result of luck rather than a rational process. But mathematicians have a term for the unappar-ent though purposeful process that dark horses employ to attain excellence:

Gradient ascent.

Over the years, applied mathematicians have come up with a variety of gradient ascent algorithms to use in global optimiza-tion problems to locate the highest possible peak in the shortest amount of time. Many industries routinely use gradient ascent algorithms in the design of products, including lenses, vehicle suspension systems, wireless sensor networks, and information retrieval systems.

When applied together, the four elements of the dark horse mindset function as a gradient ascent algorithm.

Here's how gradient ascent works. First, you look around at all the slopes near your starting point and determine which slope is steepest. You climb in that direction for a while, then pause and look around from your new vantage point to see whether there might now be a more favorable direction to climb—specifically, a steeper slope. By repeating this process over and over again, you steadily climb higher and higher until you reach a summit. While this process may not find the fastest possible route to the top, it will reliably get you there.

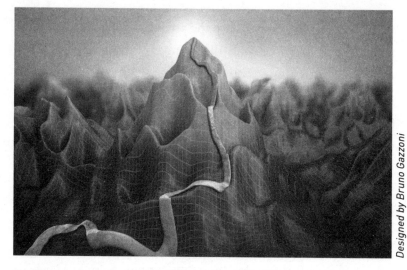

Designed by Bruno Gazzoni

Gradient Ascent: The Winding Path to Excellence

This process captures the mathematics underlying the trial and error method of Know Your Strategies: your search for strategies that fit your fuzzy strengths is a search for the steepest slope up the mountainside of the endeavor you are trying to master. If you choose a strategy that fits your individuality, you'll quickly ascend a steep slope. If you choose a poor-fitting strategy, you may ascend slowly or not at all.

You pursue one strategy for a period of time, then pause and look around to see whether there might now be a better strategy to try—a more promising slope to scale. Know Your Micro-Motives and Know Your Choices play a role in the dark horse mindset's gradient ascent process, too. Whenever you make a bold move and choose a new opportunity, you jump to an entirely new mountain with its own unique crags and ridges—and which might present an even higher summit than the last.

There is one crucial property of this excellence landscape that helps us understand why the dark horse mindset is much more likely to lead you to success than the Standard Formula of knowing your destination, working hard, and staying the course. Every person's landscape of excellence features its own one-of-a-kind topography, because each person bears their own unique pattern of micro-motives and fuzzy strengths. The peaks and valleys available to you are different from those available to your neighbor. But if no two people share the same landscape, this means that there can be no universal path to excellence. The idea of there being a One Best Way to develop expertise that holds true for everyone is, mathematically speaking, nonsense.

Gradient ascent also illuminates the distinction between goals and destinations. When you make the choice to advance in a new direction, you are setting a goal for yourself: to reach a specific point somewhat higher up the mountain, a point that you can see from here. You aren't aiming directly for the peak because unless you're already near it, you simply won't know where it is or the best route to get there. But if you rely upon situational decision-making—if you pursue near-term goals while maintaining the flexibility of changing course if a better strategy or opportunity presents itself—you will always be climbing higher.

Choosing a destination, in contrast, is ignoring the landscape entirely and declaring, "I am going to head to point X no matter what!"—even though point X might very well be hanging somewhere in empty space, inaccessible, impossible, a denial of your personal reality.

If you believe in the variety of excellence and the individuality of micro-motives and fuzzy strengths, then the mathematics of gradient ascent explains how you can reach your destination without ever knowing your destination. If you stay focused on engineering your passion, purpose, and achievement, then you can be confident that you will attain a personal peak of mastery.

9.

The process of gradient ascent explains how the dark horse mind-set can lead you to your own unique variety of excellence. But what about attaining the other half of personalized success—fulfillment?

The *Oxford English Dictionary* defines "fulfillment" as *Satisfaction or happiness as a result of fully developing one's potential.* That's not a bad definition. Of course, what's missing is *how.*

How do you fully develop your potential to achieve satisfaction and happiness?

The standardization mindset can't help you. Any system based on the assumption that individuality is a problem will never create the conditions necessary to support personal fulfillment. The Standardization Covenant's assurance that the *pursuit of excellence leads to fulfillment* was always a false promise. That's why fulfillment has been in such short supply during the Age of Standardization.

The dark horse mindset, in contrast, shines at its brightest when it comes to the how. It offers straightforward instructions for developing your potential to its fullest:

Get better at the things you care about most.

This is the dark horse prescription for personalized success. It elegantly summarizes all four elements of the dark horse mindset and converts gradient ascent into a simple set of directives: *Get better* consists of climbing toward a personal peak of excellence. It is the process of engineering achievement by Knowing Your Strategies and Ignoring the Destination. *The things you care about most* consists of choosing which mountain to climb. It is the processes of engineering passion by Knowing Your Micro-Motives and engineering purpose by Knowing Your Choices.

This prescription also shows how tightly coupled together are fulfillment and excellence. Only by prioritizing your own fulfillment can you advance toward your peak excellence, and only by advancing toward your peak excellence can you experience fulfillment. You need the energy of self-engineered passion and the direction of self-engineered purpose to scale the mountain of excellence, and you need the pride, self-worth, and sense of meaningful accomplishment from self-engineered achievement to experience the full flush of fulfillment.

When you apply the four elements of the dark horse mindset in your own life, fulfillment and excellence come under your conscious control. You are no longer a puppet of fate, but the master of your destiny. When you focus on getting better at the things you care about most, you are not wandering. You are blazing a trail up the mountainside guided by the glowing beacon of your authentic self.

The winding path is anything but aimless. It just won't ever be straight.

10.

Even though Susan Rogers experienced one of the most transcendent moments of her life working as Prince's engineer at the L.A. Forum, it didn't mean her winding path was done. She collaborated with him for three more years, but eventually realized that it was time to find a new mountain to climb. She parted on friendly terms and moved back to Los Angeles where she engineered a new sense of purpose.

At first, record labels hired Susan as a recording engineer, laying down and mixing tracks according to the sensibilities of a band or the executives at the label. But as she developed a reputation for her reliability, impeccable technical chops, ability to get along with cantankerous rock stars, and facility for adapting her musical sensibility to whatever artists she was working with, she was elevated to the powerful role of producer.

Through the 1990s, she produced albums by the Violent Femmes, David Byrne, Rusted Root, Robben Ford, Geggy Tah, and Selena. By 2000, she had become a true rarity in the music industry: a *successful* music producer.

Susan was very fulfilled. She had ascended another peak in her landscape of excellence. But her micro-motives continued to evolve. In her late thirties, she recognized that the time had come to make another bold move.

"I started becoming interested in the human brain," Susan says. "It's not that I lost interest in music, but I began wondering what might have happened if I had gone to college. Maybe I would have studied science. I always liked figuring out how things worked, and I was especially curious about consciousness. One of the questions that had interested me my whole life was—is there something in the brain that causes a particular style of music to become your 'resonant frequency'?"

Susan decided that she wanted to go to college and study cognitive science, with the hope of becoming a university researcher. Up until that point, Susan had spent virtually her entire adult life in the music business, one of the least standardized industries around, a vocation in which diplomas, credentials, and GPAs matter not at all. But now, Susan was considering stomping into the lion's den of standardization: American higher education.

She concluded that the only way for her to have the opportunity to become a cognitive scientist was by acquiring a PhD. And to do that, the Standardization Covenant required her to go to college and get an undergraduate degree.

As with her youthful pledge to return to the L.A. Forum,

Susan's new vow to leave behind a flourishing musical career—as a middle-aged woman—and become a cognitive scientist also seemed rather implausible, especially given that she had never graduated from high school.

Susan had no idea what to expect from her attempt at enrolling in college. Other than serving as a receptionist at the University of Sound Arts, a tiny postage stamp of a facility that only offered associate degrees in musical production and engineering, she had never been part of academia. Almost everything she knew about university life was from movies and friends. The first challenge, at least as she saw it, was coming up with the necessary tuition to attend a university with a decent cognitive science department.

Susan knew that if she could produce a hit album, she could use the windfall cash to pay for the tuition. Easier said than done, of course. Every producer wants to make hit records, but few succeed. But Susan accomplished it with her very next opportunity. She was hired by the Barenaked Ladies to produce their album *Stunt*. It went platinum. Its song "One Week" reached No. 1 on the *Billboard* Hot 100. And just like that, Susan had the cash for college.

Susan decided to leave California and apply to school in Minnesota, "the place where I received the golden ticket to achieve something. Minnesota to me was like Oz was to Dorothy—a place where I wasn't bound to notions of who I was." She naïvely presumed that attending college was a straightforward business transaction—you choose the college you want to attend, you fork over your money, and the school lets you take its classes. That's how they did things at the University of Sound Arts, at any rate. "The idea that there was an admissions process never occurred to me," says Susan.

So one summer day she walked into the admissions office at

the University of Minnesota with her checkbook in hand and announced that she wanted to register for the fall semester. The puzzled receptionist informed her that she needed to fill out an application. No problem, Susan replied, do you have one handy? The receptionist hesitantly handed over the form. Susan hurriedly filled it out and handed it back. The receptionist paused . . . then explained that there were other things that she needed to submit as part of the application. A personal essay, for instance. No problem, Susan replied, do you have any paper? The receptionist shook her head. Susan spotted a pad of sticky notes and said, no problem, I can just use those. She hurriedly scribbled an "essay" on several sticky notes, pressed them on her application, and handed it back to the receptionist.

The woman eyed Susan a long while before replying, "Please wait here."

The receptionist headed to the back of the office, carrying the application as if it had been dipped in radioactive waste. She returned a few minutes later with the director of undergraduate admissions. He looked Susan over.

"Well, Susan, you probably don't realize that the deadline for applying was several months ago." Susan was crestfallen. The man's eyes returned to the sticky notes and skimmed over her career working for hometown hero Prince and producing hit albums. He drummed his fingers on the desk. "But I tell you what, Susan. . . . You sure are one hard charger. Congratulations, you're admitted. Welcome to the University of Minnesota!"

Susan was forty-one. Though she was highly motivated to learn about the science of the brain, she was nervous that her ability to learn new technical material might have diminished with age. Instead, when classes began she discovered that she devoured knowledge with seemingly boundless energy. And even though she had already made her way through the male-dominated world of music, she was worried about being a middle-aged adult in a freshman class of teenagers. Instead, she discovered that the other students liked her and eagerly invited her to be in their study groups. "Attending U of M was four of the most self-indulgent years of my life," Susan says. "All I did was learn and study. And because I knew exactly what was at stake—why I had chosen to be there, what I wanted to do—it was a fabulous time."

After graduating, Susan was accepted to the doctoral program in musical cognition at McGill University in Montreal, studying under Daniel Levitin, one of the most renowned authorities in the field. After Susan got her PhD, she swiftly secured a job as a professor at Berklee College of Music in Boston, where she works today. The job suits her well. It's true that she wishes she had more time to devote to her research—but she is a respected scientist, she teaches courses she likes, she loves her students, and she can maintain the lifestyle she wants. It was a long way from being a high school dropout in an abusive marriage.

"I am very happy," Susan says, "but I will admit that I had to make some painful sacrifices to get here that maybe not every person needs to make. But I am at peace with my choices, because they were my own. I just hope that young people in the future will have the freedom to make the choices they want to make without needing to make the same sacrifices. We've got to try to make things easier for those coming down the road behind us."

the battle for the Soul of human potential

Managers . . . scientifically select and then train, teach, and develop the workman, whereas in the past he chose his own work and trained himself as best he could.
—Frederick Taylor, *The Principles of Scientific Management*

To find out what one is fitted to do, and to secure an opportunity to do it, is the key to happiness.
—John Dewey, *Democracy and Education*

In the introduction, we told you that this book was first and foremost a user manual for the dark horse mindset. That manual is now complete.

You know how the Standardization Covenant influences how you see yourself. You know there is a different way of thinking about what is possible in your life. But the standardization mindset and the dark horse mindset do not merely represent opposing ways of seeing yourself. They are opposing ways of seeing other people, too, and therefore they entail two opposing prescriptions for how we can best help every human being live up to their full potential.

At heart, they entail two opposing visions of what we *owe* each other.

To appreciate just how antithetical these mindsets truly are, let's lay them out side by side:

STANDARDIZATION MINDSET	DARK HORSE MINDSET
Ignore Your Micro-Motives	Know Your Micro-Motives
Ignore Your Choices	Know Your Choices
Ignore Your Strategies	Know Your Strategies
Know Your Destination	Ignore Your Destination
The pursuit of excellence leads to fulfillment	The pursuit of fulfillment leads to excellence
Know your destination, work hard, and stay the course	Harness your individuality in the pursuit of fulfillment to achieve excellence
Be the same as everyone else, only better	Be the best version of yourself
Institution-centered	Person-centered
Straight path	Winding path
The standardization of excellence	The variety of excellence
Universal motives	Micro-motives
Follow your passion	Engineer your passion
Picking	Choosing
Odds	Fit
Stay the course	Trial and error
Destinations	Goals
Standardized time	Relative time
Climb the ladder	Gradient ascent
Individuality is a problem	Individuality matters

When laid out so starkly, it becomes clear that the chasm between these two mindsets is not hyperbole. Their prescriptions for success are fundamentally incompatible. There is no way to meet halfway or split the difference. There is no neutral ground or middle course. Their contradictory sets of assumptions about the development of individual excellence prescribe mutually exclusive mandates for how society should organize its system of opportunity.

The conflict between these two mindsets represents nothing less than a battle for the soul of human potential.

You have to choose a side.

chapter 6

tricking the Eye, cheating the Soul

Somebody once observed to the eminent philosopher Wittgenstein how stupid medieval Europeans living before the time of Copernicus must have been that they could have looked at the sky and thought that the sun was circling the earth. . . . Wittgenstein is said to have replied: "I agree. But I wonder what it would have looked like if the sun *had* been circling the earth."

—James Burke

1.

In 1632, Galileo published *Dialogue Concerning the Two Chief World Systems*, a book that marked a turning point in our understanding of the cosmos. In it, Galileo weighs in on the ongoing battle between the heliocentric mindset and the geocentric mindset. The book contributed to the dawning awareness that all the bitter differences between the two opposing theories of our place in the universe were ultimately rooted in each side's reckoning of one fundamental phenomenon.

Gravity.

For those who believed that the Sun orbited the Earth, the Earth was the only entity that exhibited gravity. That was the reason it lay at the center of everything. All the other objects floating through the heavens were attracted by Earth's gravitational pull without exerting their own.

Those who believed that the Earth orbited the Sun held a contrary view. They came to argue that *all* celestial entities exhibited gravity, including the Sun, planets, comets, even the moon.

The publication of Galileo's book ignited a contentious period of struggle during which many temperate scholars hoped there might be a way to reconcile the two frameworks. Some searched for a "conversion formula" that would transform the math of the geocentric mindset into the math of the heliocentric mindset, the same way you might convert Fahrenheit to Celsius. But gravity forced the issue, making it plain that a reconciliation between the two chief world systems was impossible.

The old mindset declared, "Only one special celestial body has gravity"; the new mindset declared, "Every celestial body has gravity." Both assertions could not be true.

In the battle for the soul of human potential there is no possibility of compromise, either. All the bitter differences between the standardization mindset and the dark horse mindset ultimately stem from their divergent views of *human potential.* The old mindset declares, "Only special people have talent"; the new mindset declares, "Every person has talent." Both assertions cannot be true.

You have to choose a side.

Just as the two opposing theories of gravity led to profoundly different conceptions of the physical universe—one in which the Earth is the center of the universe, the other in which the universe has no center and the Earth is one of countless planets—the two opposing theories of human potential lead to profoundly different conceptions of the relative roles of individuals and institutions in our social universe. According to the standardization mindset, only a small minority of people are capable of attaining excellence (and therefore only a minority are capable of attaining fulfillment) and our institutions should possess the exclusive power to identify and reward these talented individuals. According to the dark horse mindset, everyone is capable of achieving excellence and fulfillment, and our institutions should help every individual develop his or her potential to its fullest.

The single greatest obstacle to making the leap from the old mindset to the new one is no different now than it was four hundred years ago: overcoming the obvious. It sure *seemed* like only the Earth possessed gravity, just as it sure *seems* like only special people possess talent.

But as Galileo demonstrated with his telescope, this is merely a trick of perception.

2.

From the end of World War II until the collapse of its government in 1991, the Soviet Union was the planet's most reliable manufacturer of elite talent. During the years the USA and USSR both competed in the Olympics, the USSR won more medals, including more gold medals. In fact, the USSR won more Olympic medals on average per Olympiad than any country in history.

Soviet musicians, composers, opera singers, and ballet dancers dominated international competitions in the performing arts. They ruled chess, too. Out of seventeen world chess champions between 1945 and 1991, sixteen were Soviet. They crushed the USA in math, with Soviet-bloc nations winning the International Mathematical Olympiad twenty-six times; the Americans won twice. During those rare incidents when the Cold War adversaries faced off in air-to-air combat, Soviet pilots shot down five times as many planes as American pilots. While the Americans eventually took home the greatest prize in the space race—the first *manned* lunar landing—throughout the 1950s and most of the 1960s the communist nation beat the wealthier West to virtually every space "first," including the first satellite, first animal in space, first man in space, first woman in space, first lunar landing, first interplanetary probe, first spacewalk, first space station.

Even though its economic system was a disaster and its totalitarian government rejected the very notion of individual freedom, throughout its postwar existence the USSR confidently maintained talent parity with the USA. Indeed, Americans justifiably viewed themselves as the underdog in most head-to-head contests with Soviet prowess. We celebrate the "Miracle on Ice" at the 1980 Winter Olympics when the US hockey team beat the Soviet team not because the victory was the culmination of a longstanding rivalry, but because the Soviets had relentlessly crushed American teams for decades. Chess grandmaster Bobby Fischer became a national hero because it was downright unfathomable that American brains could compete with Soviet genius.

But we shouldn't be surprised that Soviet talent managed to keep pace with the free world. After all, the Soviets were using the same talent development system as everyone else, only better.

3.

From the start, the Soviets threw their arms around the Standardization Covenant in a bear hug. There was one and only one path to excellence in Union of Soviet Socialist Republics, and it was a straight one. In every field of endeavor—academic, athletic, artistic—Soviet-bloc nations established a talent ladder that any aspiring student, athlete, or performer attempted to climb, rung by rung, until they reached the very top. The criteria for ascending to each successive level was perfectly transparent: you needed to demonstrate more talent than your peers.

The first rung of the ladder typically consisted of local school "clubs"—such as swimming clubs, physics clubs, or ballet clubs—that were set up at grade schools or high schools and open to any student who wanted to join. There were also specialist schools, such as music schools and engineering schools, that children as young as seven could attend if they passed an entrance exam. From there, all candidates were relentlessly pitted against one another to determine who deserved to rise to the next echelon.

At fixed milestones, aspirants were ranked by comparing their performance on a standardized set of tasks specific to their field, such as their speed running the one-hundred-meter dash, their score on a physics exam, or their performance during a cello recital. Superior candidates were promoted to the next rung, while the rest were booted off the ladder without sympathy. At each successive rung, the surviving candidates received more resources. They studied and practiced even harder. And the competition grew fiercer.

As one example, an athletic-looking ten-year-old girl named Heidi Krieger was encouraged by her teachers to join a track and field club in East Berlin, East Germany, a Soviet-bloc nation.

Her trainers saw something special in her and four years later promoted her into an elite sports-focused school in the city. After each round of competition within the school, students who did not make the cut had to leave within two weeks. Heidi was never asked to leave. She excelled in the shot put, and after only two years at the school she came in second in shot-putting at the Spartakiad, a national sports competition for youth in East Germany. From there, she was promoted to the SC Dynamo, a state-sponsored organization for the nation's top professional athletes, where she received the best training the Iron Curtain nation could offer. In 1986, after seven years of steadily ascending the athletic talent ladder by consistently demonstrating her superior ability, Heidi won the gold medal in the women's shot put at the European Championships.

This is exactly how the Soviet system was supposed to work, and if it sounds familiar, it's because it replicates the system of talent development in every democratic nation. In the USA, you need to beat everyone else in high school to get into the best colleges, beat everyone else in college to get into the best graduate programs, beat everyone else in graduate school to get the best jobs, and beat everyone else at your job to get the best promotions.

In structure, operation, and output, the Soviet and American systems of education are identical. To attain excellence, you must climb a rigidly standardized talent ladder. To ascend to a higher rung, you must exhibit more talent than your peers. Only the most talented individuals will reach the top.

The design of the system of talent development is the same in every nation that abides by the Standardization Covenant because they all share the same assumption about human potential:

Talent is rare.

4.

We seldom question the notion that talent is rare. It seems perfectly obvious that talent is something uncommon and special because very few people ascend to the top of the ladder. Very few people make the national track and field team or the national Mathematical Olympiad team. Very few people manage to win academic scholarships or athletic scholarships. Very few people get to play for the Boston Symphony Orchestra or write a book that makes the *New York Times* bestseller list or become a NASA astronaut.

Nowhere does the rarity of talent seem more apparent than in higher education, where very few students get admitted into elite universities. Princeton accepts around thirteen hundred students each year. So does Yale. MIT and Columbia accept about fourteen hundred students. Harvard and Brown accept approximately sixteen hundred, and Stanford accepts just over two thousand. These are tiny numbers for a nation with a population of 330 million.

We instinctively presume that the small number of admittees at prestigious institutions corresponds in some meaningful way to the available talent in the population. But here's the thing.

None of these universities wait to evaluate the pool of available talent before deciding how many candidates to accept. Without looking at a single application, every eminent academic institution goes into its admissions process with a specific number in mind, a number that does not grow or shrink based upon the quality of the applicants. More to the point, they do not accept *all* qualified candidates. They accept a predetermined number.

Said another way, our foremost institutions of opportunity enforce a *talent quota*.

Schools originally adopted quotas for sensible reasons. During the Age of Standardization, there were severe limits on how many students a brick-and-mortar institution could physically accommodate. There were only so many seats in the available classrooms. There were only so many beds in the available dormitories. There were only so many faculty, students, and staff who could fit on campus. Thus, as the number of students applying to college began to rapidly increase in the early twentieth century, both private colleges and public universities placed quotas on the number of students they could admit because of the practical constraints of their physical infrastructure. (Today, schools restrict admissions for other reasons, too, most notably to maintain their image as a luxury brand.)

But this means our institutions cap the number of individuals who may attain excellence before they know the actual number of students with the potential for excellence. It doesn't matter how many applicants possess talent, because universities are chained to their self-imposed quotas.

The national track and field team, Mathematical Olympiad team, athletic scholarships, academic scholarships, Boston Symphony Orchestra, *New York Times* bestseller list, and NASA also enforce their own quotas. The Boston Symphony Orchestra doesn't add an additional row of violins just because there is an unexpected abundance of talented violinists; the *New York Times* doesn't triple the length of its bestseller list just because a large number of books are selling especially well; NASA doesn't train thirty extra astronauts just because a surplus of qualified candidates apply.

We infer that it's an immutable fact of human nature that very few have the *potential* for excellence because we see very few *attaining* excellence. It sure appears that only special people have talent—but that's just a trick of the eye.

Under the Standardization Covenant, talent is not rare by empirical fact. Talent is rare by institutional decree.

5.

Of course, once you establish a quota you need a way to decide who to let in and who to keep out. If human beings were identical, then filling a quota would be straightforward. If you needed to produce one thousand graduates, you could simply choose one thousand applicants at random. That would represent a genuine system of talent *development*: cultivating the potential of *any* person who seeks to achieve excellence.

But even the most devoted advocate of standardization recognizes that people vary. No two applicants are ever exactly alike. Thus, every standardized system of talent development needs a set of selection criteria it can use to decide who merits a slot in its precious quota. The most obvious selection criteria to use are ones that distinguish between candidates who already exhibit talent from those who don't. That certainly makes sense—but it also means you are not *developing* talent. You are *selecting* talent.

Thus, *a standardized system of talent development is always a system of talent selection.*

Consider Gifted and Talented programs. In most American school systems, the selection criterion for getting admitted into a Gifted and Talented program is to score in the upper percentiles on a standardized test like an IQ test. These programs are not actually set up to *develop* the gifts of any student who may want to join. They are set up to *select* those students who match predefined criteria for "giftedness." We can imagine a Gifted and Talented program that accepts all students who want to join and helps them understand their individual motives and strengths, but that's not how it works. Instead, to decide who gets in, Gifted and Talented programs do the same thing that every standardized educational program does: pick someone who *looks* like a winner.

Indeed, our educational system is the only system of production that we evaluate primarily based upon its raw materials, rather than its final product. When *U.S. News & World Report* ranks American universities, it relies upon a set of "indicators of academic excellence" to determine which school to rank higher than another. The grades and SAT scores of admitted students are two major indicators. So is the percentage of applicants that a school admits. Which indicator is given the greatest weight of all? The opinions of institutional administrators. How much weight is given to the opinions of the students who actually attend these institutions? Zero.

In fact, zero is the weight granted to all the things that most families care about: the starting salary of graduates, how long graduates take to find a job, and job satisfaction among graduates. None of these are useful "indicators of academic excellence," according to *U.S. News & World Report.* The only indicator that involves the student experience at all is the institution-reported alumni giving rate.

Just think about that for a moment. *Nothing* in these rankings reflects the actual process of developing talent that occurs in our institutions of talent development. When our schools impose quotas on educational opportunity, we end up caring more about what administrators think than what students, parents, or employers think. We end up caring more about who gets in then who comes out.

The fact that we continue to accept this state of affairs without protest shows just how far down the rabbit hole we've gone. Every day, families of every background and socioeconomic level rely upon such rankings to make life-altering decisions about where to apply and how much money to spend. But strip these rankings bare, and we find they have nothing to do with developing our potential and everything to do with securing a spot in a quota.

Nevertheless, even if we agree that our system does not furnish every talented individual with the same opportunity to succeed, we might still presume that our system ensures that the individuals it does bestow opportunity upon deserve it. The reason we don't protest our quota-based system is because we take it as an article of faith that, whatever their limitations, our institutions award opportunity according to objective standards of merit.

6.

Every set of standards for evaluating talent has one essential feature: a fixed and predetermined threshold. If you exceed this bar, you qualify as talented. If you fall short, you do not. That's the dictionary definition of a standard: *a fixed metric of merit*. Nothing could be simpler.

This integrity is precisely what makes a standard objective and legitimate. The Master Sommelier Diploma exam is a perfect example. To get recognized as a master sommelier, you must score higher than its fixed cutoff score. The driver's license exam is another. In most states, you must pass both a knowledge test and a road test to obtain a license; the passing score for each part is transparent and unvarying. If you fail to score enough points on either part, you won't be driving.

By definition, a standard does not change depending on the person being evaluated or what other people taking the test look like. If the guy ahead of you crashes into a mailbox during his road test, it doesn't affect what you need to do to pass. If the gal next to you gets a perfect score on her MS exam, it doesn't influence the score you need to attain to become a master sommelier. Nor does the threshold get raised or lowered according to the whims of the evaluator. If a road test evaluator personally believes that obeying the speed limit is a more important skill than parallel parking, he doesn't get to increase the points assigned to obeying the speed limit and reduce the points assigned to parallel parking.

By evaluating candidates against a consistent and incorruptible benchmark, our institutions of opportunity earn the public's confidence and trust. One big reason we bought into the idea that talent is rare is because we presume that our institutions are using scrupulous if stringent criteria when making judgments about who deserves a spot in their quotas. We take it for granted that "highly selective" means the same thing as "high standards."

But all standards have one very important limitation, a limitation that leads to profound consequences for our institutions of opportunity. Whenever you employ a fixed threshold for evaluating talent, you can never know in advance how many candidates will make the cut.

If just one person exceeds the passing score on the MS exam, then just one person will become a master sommelier. If one hundred people exceed the passing score on the MS exam, then one hundred people will become master sommeliers. Over the past decade, somewhere around three million Americans passed their state's driver's exam each year, but the exact number varies widely: sometimes a few hundred thousand more pass, sometimes a few hundred thousand less.

Why is this unpredictability so important? Because it poses

an unavoidable dilemma for our institutions of opportunity, a dilemma so intractable that it prevents *any* standardized system of talent development from ever being fair or equitable.

If an institution employs standards, it must accept all applicants who exceed a fixed and predetermined set of criteria. There's no way of knowing in advance what this number will be.

But if an institution employs a quota, it must accept a fixed and predetermined number of applicants, no matter how many talented candidates apply.

These two numbers will almost never match up.

The simplest solution for resolving the contradictory demands of quotas and standards is to keep one and drop the other. Maintain a quota and acknowledge that you will not be using objective standards. Or maintain a set of standards and abandon your quota.

But our institutions want to have their cake and eat it, too. They want the public trust that is earned from appearing to have standards while preserving the efficiency (and exclusive brand image) generated by using quotas. Rather than make a choice, they decided to resolve their contradiction the same way an astronomer named Ptolemy once resolved another unresolvable contradiction.

By fudging it.

7.

For more than a thousand years, scholars and astronomers who believed that the Earth was the center of the universe were able to accurately predict the appearance of planets, comets, and eclipses. How were they able to accomplish this feat when they were completely and utterly wrong about the operation of the cosmos? By employing a devilishly tangled set of equations. This mathematical system was laid out in a treatise published in the second century by the ancient Greek astronomer-mathematician Ptolemy, a work entitled the *Almagest*.

The equations in the *Almagest* were based upon an even older set of geocentric formulas assembled by the Greek stargazer Hipparchus. But Ptolemy came to realize that Hipparchus's original equations were incomplete. They failed to account for a contradiction.

Most ancient astronomers believed that the planets must be moving at a uniform rate around the Earth. But even though Hipparchus's equations accurately predicted the location of the planets in the sky, these calculations also produced results where the planets sped up, slowed down, and even moved backward. According to Hipparchus's math, if the planets were circling the Earth, then they must be moving at ever-changing speeds, but if the planets were moving at uniform speeds, then they must not be circling the Earth.

One solution to this contradiction would have been to reject the geocentric mindset entirely and replace it with the heliocentric mindset, as Galileo and Newton would eventually do. But Ptolemy decided to cheat instead. He introduced a fudge factor, a kludge that made the math work out the way everybody wanted, with geocentric orbits and uniform speeds. Ptolemy's fudge factor is known as an "equant."

An equant is the location in space where you should start your calculations so that the solutions will show the orbits moving the way you want. Thus, an equant is what mathematicians politely call "self-defining"—it is assigned whatever value will give you the answer you are looking for.

For more than fourteen hundred years, nobody questioned the validity of the equant. After all, if you used it, the Earth remained at the center of everything and everything moved the way you thought it should move. Sure, there were some inconvenient errors when using equants for predictions, errors that grew steadily worse and worse over the centuries, but since the results remained intuitively satisfying—and since there was no practical alternative—the *Almagest* endured as the One Best Way in astronomy throughout the Middle Ages.

Throughout the Age of Standardization, our system of talent development has employed its own kludge to produce the results it's looking for. Our educational institutions use a deceptively simple ploy to preserve quotas while maintaining the public illusion of employing objective standards.

We call this intuitively satisfying fudge factor a *talent equant.*

8.

What are the criteria for getting into Johns Hopkins? What are the criteria for getting into MIT? What are the criteria for getting into any of the hundred top-ranked schools on *U.S. News and World Report*'s list?

In each case, the answer is the same: *it depends.*

It depends on the other applicants who are trying to get in. It depends on the immediate needs of the school. And it depends on the subjective opinions of the institutional evaluators. What it does *not* depend on is an impartial evaluation of your merits. Which is to say, it does not depend on objective standards.

Every quota-driven institution of higher education requires that applicants submit specific metrics of ability to gain entry. In the United States, these metrics almost always include grades and test scores. Institutions explicitly advise applicants that to gain admission they need superior grades and test scores, which certainly seem like objective benchmarks of talent. So why don't

such criteria constitute a standard? Because the institutional definition of "superior" is self-defining.

There is no test score cutoff you must attain, no grade point
average threshold you must exceed. There is no *fixed* benchmark
at all. Instead, the bar you must exceed for gaining admission
into any quota-enforcing educational program is raised or lowered on the fly in order to provide institutions with the flexibility
they need to precisely fill their quota.

An institution might decide that an applicant from Florida
has a high enough GPA for admission, but an applicant from
Texas with an identical GPA does not. It might decide that an
applicant who wrote a witty essay has a high enough SAT score
for admission, but an applicant with an identical SAT score who
wrote a somber essay does not. A violinist who spent her summers
building houses in Guatemala might be considered worthy of
admission, while a trombonist who spent her summers teaching
English in Uganda might not. Such endlessly mutable criteria for
evaluating candidates constitute a talent equant.

When you lack objective standards for evaluating merit,
then the appraisal of talent is placed squarely in the eye of the
beholder. It does not matter *what* criteria an institution relies
upon for evaluating talent, or for that matter, *how many* criteria.
Whether a school considers solely a candidate's grade point average or employs a hundred different metrics as part of a "holistic
admissions process," unless each candidate is measured against
the same fixed and pre-established benchmarks, then the assessment of applicants will remain a subjective fudge that enables
institutions to obtain the results they are looking for. Though
holistic admissions are often a marked improvement over non-
holistic admissions, they don't solve the underlying dilemma.
They still leave most talented students on the sidelines while

inserting even more fudge into the equant by granting evaluators even more freedom to select candidates according to their
own private conceptions of merit.

If an institution truly wanted to objectively evaluate candidates *and* preserve its quota, there is a rational and practical
solution that is indisputably fairer than an equant: a lottery. The
institution could publish its standards in advance—then randomly select the exact number of candidates it needs to fill its
quota out of the pool of applicants who meet those standards.
Obviously, a lottery would not be nearly as fair as eliminating quotas entirely, but it would be a marked improvement in
both transparency and impartiality compared to self-defining
equants—and would eliminate the wholly unjustified perception that only people who get admitted into selective academic
institutions are special and talented. In fact, elite institutions
could even make public the list of applicants who met their standards; those applicants who qualified for the lottery but lost out
on the random drawing would then be able to demonstrate to
potential employers or other educational institutions that they
were indisputably "good enough to get into Harvard."

The reliance on talent equants is not merely an academic
problem. Equants insinuate themselves into any institution of
opportunity that relies upon quotas, even in domains that on
the face of it might not seem particularly conducive to self-
defining criteria for evaluating talent, such as athletics. Most
high school sports programs have quotas, since some kids make
the team or training program and some do not. But whenever
you impose a quota on talent, no matter what the reason, then
the assessment of individual potential is moved into the eye of
the beholder.

For example, the USSR employed an arbitrary and subjective

mold for appraising female shot-putters. Coaches evaluated aspiring athletes by how far they could hurl a shot, of course. But they also judged how closely a woman's physique resembled their notion of what shot-putting talent *looked* like. And in their eyes, it looked like male shot-putting talent. Consequently, Soviet-bloc nations tended to seek out and encourage female shot-putters whose bodies had a masculine physique. As an adolescent, Heidi Krieger was broad-shouldered and flat-chested, with narrow hips and strong arms. Heidi exhibited objective talent at throwing the shot, and she worked exceedingly hard. But she received early opportunities to develop her talent because she fit the subjective Soviet mold for athletic talent. A young shot-putting hopeful with weak upper body strength and accentuated feminine curves would never have been selected for advancement in the Soviet system of talent development.

Think about what talent equants mean for the legitimacy of the Standardization Covenant. The covenant commands you to know your destination, work hard, and stay the course in order to climb the ladder to standardized excellence—but also requires you to submit to an opaque and capricious evaluation process to determine whether you are worthy of ascending to the next rung. Our system of talent development seems fair and meritocratic. But the reality is that our standardized institutions force each of us into the role of a contestant in a beauty pageant, pleading, "Pick me! Pick me! Pick me!"

All the power lies with the judges, who use their own personal template of merit to select the winner.

9.

It took all of society to maintain the false assumptions of the geocentric mindset. Ordinary folks looked out their windows and saw with their own eyes that the Sun was revolving around the Earth. At the same time, respected academic institutions declared that they possessed special formulas that justified the public's beliefs.

Of course, you know how the story ends with the geocentric mindset. At some point, the jig was up. Equants were exposed for what they are. But merely divulging the truth about equants, as Copernicus did, was not enough to get rid of them. Two equally necessary things needed to happen before society was able to make the momentous shift from the geocentric to the heliocentric mindset. First, we needed concrete *proof* that the geocentric mindset was wrong. We needed indisputable evidence that Earth was not the only celestial body in the universe that possessed gravity. Second, we needed a *practical replacement* for the equant. We needed a new logical formalism that could make actionable predictions about the operation of the universe if every celestial body did indeed possess gravity.

The first irrefutable evidence that Earth was not the only entity with gravity came when Galileo looked through his telescope at Jupiter and discovered, to his utter surprise, that the planet was orbited by four moons of its own. The moment Galileo saw them, it was clear the proposition that the Earth was special was *false*. Other planets had gravity, too. The moment people began seeing Jupiter's moons with their own eyes (without saying their heads hurt), they knew the foundational assumption of the geocentric mindset was irretrievably *wrong*.

To disprove the standardization mindset's view that talent is special, all we need to do is aim our telescope at the social universe and see whether anybody has talent other than those individuals who manage to climb to the top of society's talent ladder. We need hard evidence, in other words, that there is a greater variety of talent than what is found in our standardized institutions.

Fortunately, the evidence is all around us.

The dark horses.

10.

Heidi Krieger vs. Michelle Carter

Shot-putter Michelle Carter would have been cut from the very first rung of the Soviet shot-putting ladder, and not just because she is African American. Michelle's body is much different from Heidi's. For one thing, Michelle is far curvier. Some might even call Michelle voluptuous, though when she was younger she was more apt to get teased—or shamed—for the size of her body. Michelle weighs 256 pounds, compared with Heidi's 165. Michelle doesn't possess the superior upper-body strength that Heidi did; in high school and college, she could barely do a single pushup. Put it all together and Michelle's physique doesn't resemble anyone's stereotype for an athlete.

"Sometimes looks are deceiving," says Michelle. "I'm faster than I may look. I'm also very flexible for what I do compared to most throwers. There are a lot of positions I can hit that others struggle with. I'm able to get a lot of torque. And I learned how to use my legs early and that's my strongest asset. I have big, muscular thighs. I learned how strength comes from your legs and not your arms."

Michelle competed in the Olympics in Rio de Janeiro in 2016. Using her own personal style, she threw the shot 20.63 meters, setting a new American record and taking home the gold. "It just goes to show that you can't judge a book by its cover," Michelle asserts. "You can't go looking for a certain body type because sometimes a person may have exactly what you need, it just may be packaged differently."

Michelle's mold-breaking talent is not an isolated case. Throughout the Dark Horse Project, we found new moons wherever we looked: expert after expert who was excellent in a way that did not conform to any institutional template.

But demonstrating that the standardization mindset is wrong is the easy part. It's not much of a revelation to point out that a multitude of women and men attained excellence even though our system told them they didn't have what it takes. What we really require if we hope to build a better and fairer system of opportunity is a logical formulation that explains how everybody can have talent—and how we might design a new system around such a conception.

11.

The scientific upgrade that eventually supplanted Ptolemy's equants was Isaac Newton's law of universal gravitation. Newton's law was far more concise and elegant than the labyrinthine equations and self-defining fudge factors of the *Almagest*, and it also explained *how* the heliocentric mindset actually worked: every object with mass attracted every other object with mass with a strength that was inversely proportional to the square of the distance between them. Newton's formulation paved the way for Einstein's theory of general relativity and our modern conception of a vast, expanding, and finite universe.

This book is not the first to suggest that everyone has talent. This conviction can be traced all the way back to a handful of philosophers in ancient times, though it did not enter mainstream thought until the Enlightenment, the first epoch to fully embrace individuality. But what was always missing from previous proposals was a law of universal gravitation for human potential, a logical formalism that explained how everyone can be talented, not just special people. Fortunately, the science of individuality offers such a formalism as one of its basic concepts.

The jagged profile.

12.

Are you smart? This is a question frequently asked by the gatekeepers to our standardized institutions of opportunity. To determine the answer, they employ a variety of standardized benchmarks for measuring intelligence. The most familiar is the IQ score.

An IQ score is a one-dimensional measure of mental talent that varies on a continuum ranging from high to low. It reduces everything about a person's mental ability to a single number. According to those who create and use IQ tests, someone who scores 100 is average, someone who scores 130 is a genius, and someone who scores 70 is what the test-makers originally called a "moron," though later this appellation was softened to "mildly retarded" and today is rendered as "cognitively impaired."

These labels are a not particularly subtle clue regarding the attitudes and intentions of those who wield IQ tests.

The IQ score would appear to be the perfect metric for evaluating intelligence, which is why it is used as a criterion for admission to many educational programs. Deciding which of two students is smarter involves a simple comparison that even the least mathematically inclined administrator can make: Whose IQ score is higher?

The IQ score is the average of several distinct dimensions of mental ability that are evaluated by an IQ test, each with its own subscore. For example, the Wechsler Preschool and Primary Scale of Intelligence, Fourth Edition—usually known by its acronym WPPSI-IV—is the most common IQ test given to young children. It measures ten dimensions of mental ability (such as a child's ability to search for symbols, build objects out of blocks, and comprehend vocabulary) and assigns a subscore to each dimension.

The standardization mindset has little use for these subscores. After all, it views individuality as a problem, and the complex details of each individual's performance on an intelligence evaluation are far less useful than boiling their mental ability down to a single number that can be used to conveniently rank students from smartest to dumbest.

But in the dark horse mindset, individuality matters—which means the details matter. To assess mental ability, the dark horse mindset replaces one-dimensional talent *scores* with multidimensional talent *patterns*.

To understand the power of patterns, look at the following figure, which shows the actual subscores obtained by two Massachusetts boys who took the WPPSI-IV. Which boy is smarter?

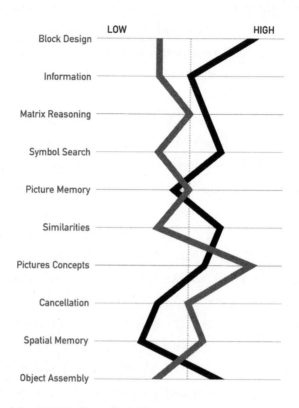

Two Boys' Jagged Profiles of Intelligence

It's not very easy to figure out which boy is smarter merely by comparing the patterns of their subscores. Given the difficulty of interpreting these zigzagging lines, the natural temptation is to retreat behind the simplicity of a single number. But the dark horse mindset views these multidimensional patterns as providing a far better account of each boy's mental strengths than a unitary score.

This zigzag pattern is known as a "jagged profile."

A jagged profile has a technical definition within the science of individuality. A jagged profile is any human quality composed of multiple dimensions, with low correlations between the dimensions. A low correlation simply means that it is not easy to predict the value of one dimension from the value of another dimension. The US stock market has a high correlation with the British stock market, because when the US stock market goes up, it's a safe prediction that the British stock market will probably go up. The US stock market has a low correlation with the rainfall in Britain, because when the US stock market goes up, you can't make a good prediction about whether or not it's raining in Britain.

More than a century of research has demonstrated that the correlation between most proposed dimensions of human intelligence are low. Just because you have a large vocabulary doesn't mean you will be good at writing. Just because you are good at trigonometry doesn't mean you will be good at calculus. Just because you are good at remembering names does not mean you will be good at remembering melodies.

So which boy is smarter? Look at their jagged profiles once again. One boy is much better than the other on *four* dimensions of mental ability: block design, symbol search, similarities, and object assembly. The other boy is much better than his classmate on *three* dimensions: picture concepts, cancellation (a type of image processing), and picture memory. This might lead you to guess that we've asked a trick question—that the two boys share similar IQ scores.

But you would be wrong.

One boy's IQ score is 117, corresponding to the eighty-fifth percentile. The other boy's IQ score is 98, corresponding to the forty-fifth percentile, or roughly half of the other boy's percentile rank. Thus, according to the standardization mindset, one boy is smart while the other boy is below average. This difference in IQ scores means they will likely be afforded different educational resources and opportunities under the Standardization Covenant, starting with the fact that one boy could be eligible for many Gifted and Talented programs, while the other most certainly would not. Over time, these divergent opportunities will lead to cumulative differences in their success as adults, since one of them will receive more support developing his talent than the other.

The dark horse mindset looks at things quite differently. It interprets the distinctiveness of each jagged profile as indicating that each boy has his own unique potential for excellence. Though the differences in their jagged profiles suggest different types of strategies that might be suited for each boy's strengths (one boy might consider focusing on object-based strategies, the other might consider focusing on image-based strategies), their potential for excellence ultimately depends on the full pattern of their mental abilities, including innumerable dimensions not evaluated by the WPPSI-IV. But bear in mind that according to the dark horse mindset, the most important factor influencing the variety of excellence that each boy might be able to attain is their pattern of micro-motives—which are not captured by any IQ test.

Everything important about your individuality and your potential for excellence is erased by an IQ score—and will be ignored by any talent equant (or any talent standards, for that matter) that relies upon an IQ score as a criterion for opportunity. With a one-dimensional score, you can pretend that someone possesses more talent than someone else. With a jagged profile, you cannot.

This is crucial, because everything important about you is jagged.

13.

Your body is jagged. Just because your neck is thick does not mean your wrists will be thick. Just because you have long arms doesn't mean you will have long legs. There is a reason department stores have dressing rooms: just because a shirt is labeled "medium" doesn't mean it will fit you, even if other medium shirts fit you fine. In his book *The Sports Gene*, journalist David Epstein talks about the "Big Bang of Body Types"—the growing awareness that the physiognomy and musculature of human anatomy is so infinitely variable that for any given sport, jagged bodies exist that are naturally tailored for particular athletic demands. The jaggedness of the human body is the basis for personal training and bespoke wardrobes.

Your physiology is jagged. The immune system, endocrine system, digestive system, pulmonary system, and metabolism all vary widely from person to person. The cancer treatment that works for you might not work for someone else; you may be vulnerable to a strain of flu that does not affect your neighbor; your body might be able to harness more oxygen during physical exertion than your brother's. Even your microbiome, the bacterial ecology of your body, is jagged. The jaggedness of human physiology is the basis for personalized medicine and personalized nutrition. Your genome is jagged, too, which serves as the basis for personalized genetics. Surprisingly, even identical twins have divergent sets of DNA.

Your emotions are jagged as well. The patterns, causes, and expressions of human emotion are not universal, as was believed by mainstream psychology for most of the past half century, but instead vary dramatically from person to person. As psychologist Lisa Feldman Barrett details in her 2017 book *How Emotions Are Made*, "Even after a century of effort, scientific research has not revealed a consistent, physical fingerprint for even a single emotion. When scientists attach electrodes to a person's face and measure how facial muscles actually move during the experience of an emotion, they find tremendous variety, not uniformity. You can experience anger with or without a spike in blood pressure. You can experience fear with or without an amygdala."

You have a jagged mind, a jagged body, and a jagged heart. Put these together, and you end up with a uniquely jagged profile of talent.

14.

The jagged profile is the conceptual basis for the variety of human excellence. It is a logical formalism that explains how everyone can have talent.

It's not wishful thinking to say, "Everybody is good at something." Whenever the human sciences break down the physical, mental, and emotional profiles of individuals into increasing numbers of distinct dimensions, at some level of granularity they eventually find that every person possesses some dimensions that are above average (and some that are below average). Everybody is highly motivated by something (and every person is highly *unmotivated* by something). Everybody has a part of their body that is larger than average (and a part that is smaller than average). Everybody is naturally proficient at some tasks (and everybody is naturally limited at some tasks). Finding them is just a matter of expanding your dimensions.

The contextual nature of our strengths also helps us understand how everyone can have talent, by suggesting that it is not only individuals who possess jagged profiles, but environments. Sometimes a dimension of ability that appears to be a weakness becomes a strength in the right context. Fortunately, in the emerging Age of Personalization, society offers an unprecedented variety of contexts for meaningful human achievement.

We have sampled a few in this book, such as professional organizing for working moms, managing underground urban supper clubs, and developing legislative strategies for midwives. Today, it is possible to make a living selling handmade iPhone cases, programming apps to find parking spaces, providing therapy to cats, organizing wine and painting parties, and doing math for professional basketball teams. With an infinite variety of jagged profiles of talent and a rapidly expanding variety of professional opportunities, there is all but guaranteed to be a great fit for your own individuality.

If the idea of searching through all of life's possibilities for one of those great-fitting opportunities seems daunting, remember the power of gradient ascent—the power of getting better at the things you care about most. The math tells us that's all you need to do to ascend to a personal peak of excellence.

By declaring that talent is limited to those individuals who fit self-serving institutional equants, the Standardization Covenant cheats you out of the opportunity to develop your potential to its fullest.

Let's sum up. We have hard evidence that the standardization mindset's assumptions about talent are erroneous: the ubiquity of dark horses. We have a logical formalism that explains how everyone can possess the potential for excellence: the jagged profile. This same logical formalism explains how to convert your potential into proficiency: by harnessing your jagged profile of micro-motives and using trial and error to find strategies that fit your jagged profile of fuzzy strengths.

And when you have one mindset that is coherent and backed by evidence, and another mindset that is self-contradicting and negated by evidence, the jig is up.

They didn't call it the Dark Ages for nothing.

15.

Anybody who believes in the individual freedoms and egalitarian principles that democratic societies are founded upon should be asking themselves, *How did we get so far from our roots? Why are we using a system of opportunity that is equally at home in the Soviet Union as in the United States? How has such a defiantly undemocratic social covenant endured for so long?*

There is no bogeyman here. No villain hiding behind the curtain. The culpable party is perfectly plain. In the Soviet Union, the Standardization Covenant was imposed upon its population by a tyrant's edict and enforced by a totalitarian government. Here in the West, we did it to ourselves.

We chose to embrace a system of opportunity demanding that we fit the mold to climb the ladder. We chose to affirm a view of human potential holding that only a small number of special people deserve access to society's best opportunities. We chose to reckon success through simple numbers: How high did you climb? How long did you study? How high did you score?

Fortunately, the mold-shattering success of so many dark horses gives us all hope. The true value of the dark horse mindset does not lie in flouting our misguided, cynical, and profoundly unfair system of opportunity. It lies in empowering us to build a better one.

All we need to do—all *you* need to do—is make a choice.

chapter 7

the Dark Horse Covenant

It is also possible that the explosion of top incomes can be explained as a form of "meritocratic extremism," by which I mean the apparent need of modern societies, and especially U.S. society, to designate certain individuals as "winners" and to reward them all the more generously if they seem to have been selected on the basis of their intrinsic merits rather than birth or background.

—Thomas Piketty

1.

Our quota-based system of talent selection is usually called a meritocracy. The word has tremendous rhetorical power. It implies a system of opportunity based on merit, where anyone who works hard and possesses talent can climb to the top. At this point, you know that's not true. You can work as hard as you want, but if your jagged profile doesn't fit a fickle institutional mold, it might not matter. The presence of talent quotas ensures that many people with merit will remain stuck at the bottom.

If we had called our system of opportunity a talent aristocracy rather than a meritocracy, perhaps we would have been more wary about what we were getting ourselves into. Ironically, that was the exact intention of the man who coined the term "meritocracy." In 1958, the British sociologist Michael Young wrote the book *The Rise of the Meritocracy*. This satirical work of fiction was no celebration of the test-based system of standardized talent selection sweeping through Britain. Instead, Young contrived the word "meritocracy" as a mocking rebuke, drawing a contemptuous parallel with "aristocracy." As Young wrote, "We have our modern society: by imperceptible degrees an aristocracy of birth has turned into an aristocracy of talent."

Yet, to Young's chagrin, his derisive label was co-opted by the very people he intended to condemn. Educators, professional organizations, and government officials began to proudly tout the "meritocracies" they were fostering and overseeing. They hijacked Young's term for good reason. Though Young intended merit-*ocracy* to be suggestive of arist-*ocracy*, all most people heard was *merit*. Young's term seemed to denote fairness and egalitarianism, enabling the authorities to convincingly argue that they were replacing a system of opportunity based on privilege with a system based on talent. They declared they would find merit even among society's most underprivileged and provide them with a ladder to achievement and status.

By insisting the new system of opportunity would identify,

select, and nurture talent wherever it lay hidden, advocates of the
"meritocracy" confidently assured us that it would even *maximize*
excellence in society. But a system that only makes opportunity
available to an arbitrary quota is not a true meritocracy. It is a
quotacracy.

And in a quotacracy, excellence is always a negative-sum game.

2.

Tennis, backgammon, and sumo wrestling are all examples of a
"zero-sum game." The term comes from the science of game theory and refers to situations where one person's gain results in an
equal loss for someone else. If I win, you lose; if you win, I lose:
that is a zero-sum game.

If a quotacracy consisted of 50 percent winners and 50 percent losers (such as 50 percent of college applicants getting admitted and 50 percent getting rejected), it would be a zero-sum
game of excellence. Half of those aspiring to climb the ladder would realize their potential for excellence, the other half
would not. It wouldn't matter *who* the winners or losers are,
because for each person who develops excellence, someone else
would not.

But that's not how a real-world quotacracy works.

Instead, it consists of a small minority of winners and a large
majority of losers. For every applicant who gets into Yale, fifteen others will not. For every applicant who gets into Stanford
Medical School, forty-two others will not. For every student who
wins a Rhodes Scholarship, hundreds of other candidates will
not. As long as quota-enforcing institutions are the gatekeepers
to opportunity, then my chance to attain excellence comes at the

expense of yours—and at the expense of your siblings, friends, and neighbors, too.

In a quotacracy, the opportunities of the many are sacrificed for the opportunities of the few. This is worse than a zero-sum game. This is a *negative-sum game.*

As long as we have a system that disproportionately rewards educational opportunity to an arbitrary minority, we will always be stuck with a negative-sum game of excellence. Make no mistake about what this means for any society that abides by the Standardization Covenant:

Far more than half the population will never even get the chance to realize their full potential.

Each year close to fifteen thousand new freshmen will attend Ivy League schools, one of the de facto gatekeepers to society's most advantageous opportunities. But that means that 2.2 million other first-year college students, or 99 percent, will not. Incredibly, a smaller percentage of the US population attends name-brand universities than the percentage of the population who were nobles during the peak periods of aristocracy in Britain, Spain, Italy, and Russia. Most of us must be content with our mediocre lives (as judged by the quotacracy) so that a tiny number of special folks can attend Princeton, Yale, or Harvard and enjoy the lion's share of American opportunity. The rest of us must fight for the scraps. Sure, a quotacracy guarantees that society will always produce a reliable number of superstars—they just won't be you.

Jennie McCormick, high school dropout, was consigned to a paycheck-to-paycheck career in fast food. Ingrid Carozzi, mediocre college student, was shunted into low-wage hospitality jobs. Susan Rogers, high school dropout, found work on a medical-device assembly line. But we shouldn't be concerned by their plight, our quotacracy assures us—also-rans like Jennie, Ingrid, and Susan earned their fate. They were simply outperformed by those with superior ability and gumption. According to our quotacracy, if they truly had the right stuff, they would have climbed to the top of the institutional ladder.

We could imagine tolerating a negative-sum game of excellence if those who received the best opportunities were objectively deserving of their rewards. But whenever a system relies upon equants to evaluate talent, that system will not only abolish objective standards, it will inevitably become corrupt.

3.

In the United States, one of the most obvious and pernicious ways our purported meritocracy is corrupted is through "legacy" admissions to universities. All the most desirable American universities admit large numbers of applicants based upon their bloodlines. Many Ivy League schools admit 30 to 40 percent of the legacy applicants who apply compared with 11 to 17 percent of other applicants. At Harvard, legacy applicants are six times as likely to be admitted as merely "talented" applicants.

This is not an "-ocracy" of merit. This is an "-ocracy" of privilege.

But that's not the only way our purported system of merit is undermined. Universities are in constant competition with each other for the same pool of "talented" students, since they all employ similar talent molds to fill their quotas. The prime way they compete for applicants is by offering more impressive physical facilities. They build sports stadiums, food courts, dorms with concierge service, and many other projects that have little to do with developing excellence and everything to do with recruiting students. Such projects are expensive, so universities are perpetually seeking money.

One way they boost their revenue is by admitting students
who are willing to pay more tuition, rather than students who exhibit more talent. These days, state colleges and universities give
an edge to out-of-state applicants because they pay more than instate applicants. A state audit of the University of California system in 2016 found that its universities "gave favorable admissions
treatment to thousands of higher-paying out-of-state and foreign
students, to the detriment of Californians." In their never-ending
quest for cash, many of these state taxpayer-funded universities
ignore the local communities they were built to serve in favor of
those who can pay the most.

In a quotacracy, the well-endowed schools that don't need
money inevitably get co-opted by bloodlines, while the schools
that do need money sell themselves to the highest bidder. And
as long as we maintain a system with arbitrary quotas and self-
serving institutional criteria for accessing educational opportunity, the wealthy and the privileged will always have an advantage
over the rest of us.

In a very real sense, the talent equant implements the famous
farmyard dictum in George Orwell's *Animal Farm*: "All animals
are equal, but some animals are more equal than others."

4.

A quotacracy is at best a half-meritocracy, sharing as much in
common with an aristocracy as with a true meritocracy. Talent
and hard work are a genuine advantage, sure—provided your jagged profile of talent happens to fit the institutional mold. But you

certainly don't need talent or hard work to climb the ladder. You just need the right family or a fat wallet. For generations, a majority of the population has been pressured to accept their place at the middle of the ladder while others no less deserving seem to enjoy an express elevator to the upper rungs. Sometimes one group or another seems to get the advantage at the top, leading to resentment and bitterness among everyone else. In a quotacracy, we are doomed to a perpetual Hunger Games of social opportunity with no way to break the cycle, since there will always be fewer slots in the quota than the demand.

Though we think of our form of meritocracy as the only one of its kind, in truth it was always a fledgling system of merit, a rudimentary first draft. It was a system of talent development based upon the values, beliefs, and mathematics of the late nineteenth century. But we can imagine other systems of opportunity based upon a twenty-first-century conception of talent. Until recently, the quotacracy was the best we could realistically hope for.

No longer.

The time has arrived when we can finally do better.

5.

Over the past century, many people have recognized and lamented the deficiencies of our standardized system of talent development. American psychologist and educator John Dewey, British mathematician and philosopher Bertrand Russell, Italian physician and educator Maria Montessori, US labor leader Samuel Gompers, and American educational psychologist Benjamin Bloom all delivered savage indictments of the standardization of work and learning. Many artists, too, have taken sharp aim at the Age of

Standardization, including novelists George Orwell (*1984*), Lois Lowry (*The Giver*), and Thomas Pynchon (*Gravity's Rainbow*) and in movies such as *Brazil* and the *Matrix* trilogy. These critics identified and assailed many of the soul-crushing hallmarks of a society predicated upon the notion that individuality is a problem.

But what none of them could offer was an alternative.

Since the dawn of the Age of Standardization, anti-standardization critics were in much the same position as anti-war critics: condemning the obvious evils of the phenomenon and demanding its swift termination, without specifying any practical means for doing so. Throughout the twentieth century, you could say the same thing about standardization as a form of social organization that Winston Churchill famously said about democracy as a form of political organization: *It's the worst— except for all the others.* There simply wasn't any feasible hope of reforming our quotacracy because we lacked the necessary economy, science, and technology to get the job done.

But the Age of Personalization offers the first real chance to change everything.

So far, we usually think of personalization as iPhones, Facebook, and video-on-demand, as gadgets that make it easier for us to express ourselves, find things we like, and customize our environment to suit our tastes. But the real promise of personalization is something so much larger. It is how we move from a negative-sum game of excellence to a positive-sum game of excellence. It is how we move from a universe where the Sun revolves around the Earth to a universe where the Earth revolves around the Sun.

The Age of Personalization empowers us to create a system of opportunity that institutes a radically expanded form of fairness. A system where you still have to earn your success, but where opportunity is available to anyone *and* everyone, instead of those who fit an institutional mold. A system that delivers on the promise of personal fulfillment. For the first time, we finally have everything we need to build a meritocracy that is worthy of the name.

A democratic meritocracy.

6.

We have the right economy for a democratic meritocracy. When the United States first embraced the Standardization Covenant, an abundance of standardized industrial and managerial jobs were available to anyone who completed a standardized education, and you could expect to work for the same employer for life. No longer. Economic standardization has been overtaken by a massive increase in economic diversity, with far more kinds of jobs than ever before and a burgeoning ecosystem of entrepreneurs and small businesses with few or no barriers to entry. Manufacturers can alter their products weekly, or in many cases, daily. We have a gig economy populated by contractors, freelancers, and other free agents. We have a long-tail economy, where it's possible to target small consumer niches on a global scale. We need a diverse, flexible, and personalized economy in order to provide opportunities for the expansive variety of excellence generated by a democratic meritocracy.

We have the right technology for a democratic meritocracy. More than a century ago, the father of standardization, Frederick Taylor, argued that standardization was necessary because people were cheaper and easier to rearrange than machines. But a century later, machines are cheaper and easier to rearrange than people. Smartphones, smart watches, smart homes, social media apps, and digital assistants like Alexa, Siri, and Cortana have become part of the daily fabric of our lives. A century ago, the largest corporations were the undisputed masters of standardization. Today, the largest corporations are increasingly driven by personalization. Even Bristol-Myers Squibb, once a pioneer of standardized medicine, has made the shift, joining the Personalized Medicine Coalition and formally rejecting "one-size-fits-all" medicine. Most important, we now possess a nearly universally available internet—the ultimate personalization technology. We need robust, low-cost, and ubiquitous personalization technologies to provide the kind of personalized learning and individual choice necessary for a democratic meritocracy.

We have the right science for a democratic meritocracy. A science of individuality has emerged that provides new methods and mathematics for understanding, evaluating, and nurturing individuals, drawing upon the twenty-first-century mathematics of dynamical systems instead of the nineteenth-century mathematics of statistics. The blooming fields of personalized medicine, personalized nutrition, personalized genomics, personalized training, personalized learning, and personalized manufacturing draw upon the principles of the science of individuality and are advancing every day. A passionate and growing platoon of scientists is developing new research programs and departments solely devoted to the study and empowerment of individuals. We need a healthy science of individuality to constantly improve and refine the inherently flexible design of a democratic meritocracy.

We have almost everything we need to make a seismic switch from our antiquated quotacracy to a genuinely democratic meritocracy. There is only one thing missing—one thing that each of us must actively *choose* instead of passively accept.

We must ratify a new covenant.

7.

The truths animating a society's social contract are inextricably linked with a society's perception of merit and its system of opportunity. In recent history, first came what we might call the Aristocratic Covenant, predicated upon the belief that *only special bloodlines possess merit* and endorsing a core value of *tradition*, leading to a system of opportunity where *neither anyone nor everyone* could succeed. This system was enforced by the nobility, without the consent of anyone else.

Then came the Standardization Covenant, predicated upon the belief that *only special individuals possess merit* and endorsing a core value of *efficiency*, leading to a system of opportunity where *anyone but not everyone* could succeed. This quotacracy was enforced by institutions, with the consent of individuals.

Now we have the chance to ratify a Dark Horse Covenant, predicated upon the belief that *everyone possesses the potential for their own variety of merit* and endorsing a core value of *fulfillment*, leading to a system of opportunity where *anyone and everyone* can succeed. This democratic meritocracy will be enforced by individuals, with the consent of individuals.

8.

We might presume that a social contract should be a lengthy legal document with many provisions and clauses. But the real authority of a social contract does not derive from a piece of parchment, but from a few simple truths that we all abide by, truths that implicitly structure the relationship between individuals and the institutions we create to serve us. At its heart, a social contract defines what we owe one another.

Recall the terms of the Standardization Covenant:

Society is obligated to reward you with opportunity if and only if you abandon the pursuit of personal fulfillment for the pursuit of standardized excellence.

If we want a democratic meritocracy for ourselves and our children, then we must each choose to ratify a new social contract:

Society is obligated to provide you with the opportunity to pursue fulfillment, and you are accountable for your own fulfillment.

The supreme institutional obligation under the Dark Horse Covenant is to provide *Equal Fit*. The supreme individual obligation under the Dark Horse Covenant is *Personal Accountability*. These two obligations—when conjoined together—are necessary and sufficient to inaugurate a democratic meritocracy.

9.

As the Age of Standardization picked up steam, the free world elevated and enforced a core value of *Equal Opportunity*. In principle, Equal Opportunity holds that every person, no matter their bloodline, gender, or creed, should be granted a fair shot at society's opportunities. In practice, Equal Opportunity has manifested largely as an attempt to remedy the inevitable corruption of quotacracies.

As we've seen, access to the quota can be gamed by the wealthy and the privileged. Access to the quota is also deeply vulnerable to sexism, racism, and other systemic prejudices, since the talent equant places merit in the eye of the beholder. Consequently, throughout the Age of Standardization, the bulk of our talent quota has been occupied predominantly by a narrow and homogenous segment of the population. To combat this, Equal Opportunity sought to provide everyone, no matter what their background, with an equal chance at being admitted into the quota. Equal Opportunity attempted to ensure that the demographics of the quota resembled the demographics of the population. In short, Equal Opportunity has always been defined as Equal Access.

Equal Access is certainly a noble and necessary effort. But Equal Opportunity as Equal Access leaves the fundamental unfairness of a quota-based system of opportunity unaltered and intact. First, the elites still retain the seats that have always been reserved for them at the top of the ladder. Equal Access policies did not prompt universities to reduce the number of spots in their quotas available to the wealthy and privileged. Equal Access only influenced the spots available to the rest of us.

More to the point, Equal Opportunity as Equal Access fails to change the underlying dynamics of an inherently negative-sum game. Since the quota is fixed, providing access to one person, no matter how underprivileged, always ensures that many others with merit who worked equally hard will be left out. If you think Latino Americans are underrepresented in the quota, then Equal Access can help increase the number of Latino Americans who are admitted into the quota. But this thereby decreases the number of spots available to African Americans, Native Americans, and Asian Americans—and will also decrease the number of spots available to other equally talented Latino Americans.

Equal Opportunity as Equal Access isn't increasing opportunity. It's an attempt to reserve seats in a game of musical chairs with fifty times more players than chairs. It marginally increases the fairness of an inherently unfair system by helping mitigate systemic disparities based upon race, gender, and socioeconomic status under a social contract in which everyone is doomed to battle for the same artificially limited opportunities. It changes the identity of the players in our Hunger Games of merit, but not the outcome. The number of winners remains staunchly fixed.

Equal Opportunity as Equal Access is the best we could hope for in a quotacracy. But the fact that it was necessary and decent doesn't eliminate the reality that Equal Access is a standardized solution to a standardized problem. It's using one equant to fix another equant. Its ultimate aim, and ultimate achievement, was to help ensure that anyone—but not everyone—had a chance to attain excellence and fulfillment.

Today, we can do better.

We can adopt a new covenant whose obligations entail a very different notion of fairness. If we want to provide genuine equality of opportunity for anyone *and* everyone, then we must redefine Equal Opportunity as Equal Fit.

Under Equal Fit, every person is given their best opportunity to succeed, according to their individuality. It's not concerned with adjusting the talent equant, because there is no equant—no mold you must fit, no judge you must please. Instead, Equal Fit adjusts to accommodate your unique jagged profile. In a system with Equal Fit, we are not competing with each other to ascend to the next narrowing rung of the ladder; we are each performing our own gradient ascent. With Equal Fit, your win is not my loss. Your goal under the Dark Horse Covenant is not to become the best in the nation (a massively negative-sum game), but to become the best version of yourself, through a process that does not limit the ability of others to become their own best self.

Unlike Equal Access, which focuses on providing access to standardized excellence for a more diverse segment of the population, Equal Fit is focused on guaranteeing the pursuit of fulfillment as a universal right, thereby maximizing the variety and volume of individual excellence.

You can ratify a Dark Horse Covenant by adopting Equal Fit as your personal notion of fairness. But to implement a working democratic meritocracy, our institutions must fully commit themselves to *delivering* Equal Fit.

10.

Practically speaking, how can institutions provide Equal Fit? This is where the Age of Personalization comes in, because Equal Fit is a guarantee of authentic personalization for everyone.

Under the principle of Equal Fit, institutions become obligated to personalize all human-facing systems that support how we learn, work, and live. More pointedly, institutional systems and services should accommodate the jagged profile of any individual, of any background, of any age. The design mandate for institutions under the Dark Horse Covenant is flexibility rather than efficiency. In a democratic meritocracy, personalization is not some kind of perk, upscale add-on, or after-market frivolity. It is the only possible way to ensure Equal Fit and the universal right to fulfillment.

Fortunately, we don't need to invent this stuff. Some of the most successful businesses in the world already harness sophisticated and well-developed personalization technologies to cater to every customer's individual needs and wants. We merely need to move these personalization technologies from the periphery of our experience to the center—from consumer products into education and the workplace.

The true promise of personalization is not some fancy digital gizmo or all-encompassing commercial ecosystem. It is creating the systems and services necessary to provide Equal Fit to all. If we do, then anyone and everyone will be empowered to achieve success on their own terms.

Delivering personalization to everyone might seem like the most difficult hurdle for building a democratic meritocracy. It used to be. Not anymore. Khan Academy, for instance, is the story of one man—not even an educator or technologist, but a financial analyst—who in the brief span of a decade created a nonprofit system of personalized online learning that has already delivered a billion self-paced, self-determined lessons to more than sixty million students and two million teachers—entirely for free.

No, the real challenge for providing Equal Fit is not delivering personalized technology to everyone. Practically speaking, that task is about as hard as it is for Netflix to figure out how to deliver movie recommendations to all of its customers.

The hard part of providing Equal Fit—the part that requires a new social truth vested in a new covenant—is guaranteeing individual choice.

11.

Choice is utterly essential for fulfillment. Genuine choice is necessary to find, compare, and select different opportunities that fit your micro-motives. Genuine choice is necessary to freely explore different strategies that might suit your fuzzy strengths. Choice is the navigation system for gradient ascent.

We can evaluate whether any institution's system or service is providing Equal Fit by asking a simple question: *Does it provide both personalization and individual choice?*

Choice without personalization is mere picking. This is what we have now. Our institutions curate their menus and compel you to select one of their self-serving options. Only by providing processes and pathways flexible enough to adapt to the individuality can institutions provide meaningful choice. Personalization technology is necessary but not sufficient to accomplish this.

Providing true choice means that an institution must be willing to relinquish some perceived control. Though there are tremendous benefits from doing so—including expansive growth potential and increased employee engagement and productivity—it does require a major perceptual shift in an institution's leadership. It's a shift the rest of us must do our best to encourage, or we will end up with something far worse than a quotacracy.

Though the Age of Personalization is an epoch of unprecedented promise, it is also an epoch of monstrous peril. There is something far more oppressive than choice without personalization, and that is personalization without choice.

Systems that adapt themselves to your individuality without offering you genuine choice are systems with unlimited power to control you. This is not alarmist scaremongering. There is a growing list of countries where all the democratizing potential of the internet has been subverted by totalitarian governments as an unprecedented means of monitoring, manipulating, and repressing their populations. And make no mistake, without intervention, this is where things are headed right now in the West.

Large corporations already possess enormous troves of personal data about you that they use to deliver personalized advertising to sell you the products they want you to buy, personalized search results that guide where you go on the internet, and personalized news that influences what you think and whom you vote for. We are creating a world where governments and corporations—and their ever-smarter artificial intelligence systems—make increasingly important choices for you without your knowledge or consent.

These institutions most definitely want to provide you with more and more personalization. They just want to give it to you on their terms and for their own ends. More to the point, they want to give you personalization without the corresponding power of choice.

12.

Why would an institution ever want to hand over the power of choice to the individuals it serves? Because institutions that provide Equal Fit will flourish in the Age of Personalization. This is not merely a theoretical assertion. Right now, this moment, it's possible to live your whole life inside a democratic meritocracy by engaging with healthy institutions that offer a fledgling version of Equal Fit.

One example is Summit Public Schools. Summit is a network of eleven public charter schools in California and Washington state serving grades six through twelve. They were built upon a personalized approach to learning and teaching called Summit Learning. The popularity of these schools and the success of their graduates demonstrate the real-world effectiveness of Summit's mission: "to equip every student to lead a fulfilled life."

The Summit educational program is explicitly designed to help every student engineer their own passion, purpose, and achievement through three main components. Every Summit student has a dedicated mentor who meets with them one-on-one every week to support them in understanding and harnessing their individuality. In class, students apply the knowledge, skills, and habits they've learned to projects that prepare them for the scenarios they'll encounter after they graduate. Lastly, all students are guided through a learning cycle that teaches them how to set achievable goals, make effective plans, demonstrate their abilities, and reflect on themselves and their progress.

Under the Standardization Covenant, we're taught that we must make a trade-off between the pursuit of professional competency and the pursuit of fulfillment. This conviction is reflected in most people's first question about Summit: it sure sounds nice, *but do Summit graduates get into college?* Under the Dark Horse Covenant, of course, getting into college is not a valid metric of fulfillment nor excellence. But to answer the question, yes—99 percent of Summit Public School students are accepted into four-year colleges, compared to a national average of 66 percent. Even more impressively, Summit students graduate from college at double the national average. In fact, on any standardized measure of academic excellence, Summit students consistently rank near the top.

The physical infrastructure of the schools, designed to be small communities of learning, limits the number of students who can enroll. As you might imagine, there is tremendous demand to get into the Summit schools, and far more applicants than there are slots. To solve the quota problem, Summit uses a lottery, randomly selecting students out of the pool of those who wish to enroll. Thus, acceptance is not a reflection of academic merit or financial need: any child who wishes to develop their talent at Summit will receive an equal opportunity to do so.

Why should you care about eleven schools in the northwest? Because Summit can deliver genuine choice to your own children, no matter where you reside in the US. The real potential of Summit's unique approach is its Summit Learning Program, a complete package of curriculum, in-person and on-demand professional development, a dedicated mentor for schools, and Summit's technological platform. What began as an effort by Summit to share its practices, tools, and knowledge with other educators who visited the Summit schools has grown into a robust nationwide program to support schools across the country in adapting Summit Learning for their community—*entirely for free*. This is how Summit is attempting to get around the limitations of a quota to provide personalized education to anyone and everyone.

Across the United States, over 330 schools are already participating in the Summit Learning program. Crucially, Summit encourages each school to tailor the Summit experience to suit its community's needs and values, recognizing that delivering Equal Fit requires institutions to maximize the flexibility of their particular implementation. You could go to your child's school right now and ask them to partner with Summit, and your child would get their first taste of a democratic meritocracy.

Let's move beyond K–12 to higher education. On the face of it, higher education has the most to lose from a Dark Horse Covenant demanding they provide Equal Fit to its students.

These institutions have maintained a near-monopoly on social opportunity for more than a century by remaining committed to standardization and quotas and by hoarding the power of choice for themselves. But we are finally seeing farsighted institutions like Western Governors University, Arizona State University, and Southern New Hampshire University take the plunge into personalization.

Consider Southern New Hampshire University (SNHU). Originally founded in 1932 as a standardized school of accounting and secretarial science, over the past decade SNHU has transformed itself into one of the nation's leading institutions of personalized learning by launching the College for America in 2008. College for America (CfA) became the first accredited undergraduate program in the United States that completely eliminated grades and credit hours, replacing them with competency-based evaluations. Every CfA student is provided with a personal mentor who helps the student make the best educational choices for their individuality, helping them decide which competencies to master and in what order—and helping them manage the expansive control they now have over their learning. There are no formal instructors—only academic coaches and reviewers who evaluate whether students have mastered the material yet. This means that students can control how fast or slow they progress, instead of getting imprisoned within standardized time.

To gain admission to CfA, there are no talent quotas to fight your way into and no capricious institutional molds to which you must conform. Anyone who wants to take classes in the College for America can do so. The average tuition for a bachelor's degree from a private four-year college in 2017 was around $155,000.

The total tuition to obtain a bachelor's degree from the College for America? Ten thousand dollars. And for students who progress more quickly, the cost can go down to five thousand. For many students, tuition subsidies from employers bring the price down still further. The great majority of CfA students graduate with no debt whatsoever. In 2017, enrollment in CfA was seven thousand students. However, Paul LeBlanc, the exuberantly student-empowering president of SNHU, expects enrollment to rise to twenty thousand by 2021.

The college partners with more than one hundred companies, including hospitals, nonprofits, hotels, insurance companies, food service companies, fashion companies, and media companies, since the College for America focuses heavily on preparing graduates for actual jobs. The CfA especially caters to those who are usually underserved in standardized universities, such as members of the armed services, stay-at-home moms, full-time workers, and older students.

"Much of the attention paid to our College for America program has had to do with its low cost and high quality, but we have come to more fully recognize how powerful a tool it is for letting people access education on their own terms, in ways that fit their life circumstances," emphasizes LeBlanc. "A CfA education is flexible and accommodates the needs of individual students in a way that a one-size-fits-all educational model just can't. And the best part? They excel. They read Kant. They master tough math. They become good writers and thinkers. The more we see the program in action, the more convinced we are that it represents a paradigm shift in how we think about education."

Let's move out of education into the workplace. In a democratic meritocracy, you have control over your professional destiny because you have control over your winding path. You can pursue your own version of excellence on your own terms. However, this freedom might lead you to wonder: *If I follow my own path, might I end up on a lonely career road? Will I be doomed to be a profession of one?*

Choosing personalization over standardization might seem like you are choosing between the chance to be part of a professional community, however flawed, and going it alone. In fact, just the opposite is true: by opening society up to the full variety of human excellence, a democratic meritocracy makes it much easier for individuals with common professional interests to find one another and spontaneously form their own passionate collectives. The Court of Master Sommeliers is one shining example of what is possible when we free ourselves from the Standardization Covenant. Another is NAPO.

The National Association of Productivity and Organizing Professionals is the organization that Korinne Belock joined after leaving her political career to become a professional organizer. What makes NAPO so interesting is that there is no institutional talent ladder to climb to become a professional organizer, no college diploma to obtain, no quotas or equants to squeeze through. Instead, NAPO members are purpose-driven individuals who followed their own winding path to excellence—before discovering, often to their complete surprise, that there were other people who shared the same two burning motives as themselves: the desire to help people and the desire to organize.

The origins of NAPO date to 1983, when five women began meeting together in living rooms in Southern California. They had responded to a small classified ad placed by Karen Shortridge in a local community newspaper that said, "If you like to organize, call me." Some of the women had earned money from cleaning or organizing clients' homes or offices, while others had simply been organizing for friends and family. One of the women, Stephanie Culp, had been running errands for Hollywood folks under the business name "The Grinning Idiot." One day Stephanie went into a client's home and discovered a chaos of boxes and hoarding and realized that she might be able to make a living by decluttering for people who could not do it for themselves.

Though the five women initially had no designs on anything larger than functioning as a club for sharing organizing tips and socializing, Stephanie believed they could be something more. "I saw that what we were doing needed to be recognized and respected as a legitimate profession," Stephanie says. "At the time, people thought we were maids. They didn't take us seriously. That's why I came up with the name 'professional organizers.'"

Under Stephanie's direction, the quintet of professional organizers formed their own nonprofit organization. "I wanted to create a nonprofit rather than a business entity because I strongly believed in women helping women," Stephanie explains. "Other professions have books and classes and college majors, but all we had was each other. I viewed it as a kind of network of mutual support."

In 1986, after their nonprofit opened a chapter in New York, they rebranded themselves as the National Organization of Professional Organizers. Stephanie admits things grew slowly at first. "There still wasn't a lot of equal opportunity for women. Communication was mostly by phone. It was hard to explain to the public what we were doing." But as the Age of Personalization began picking up steam, with new technologies, new economics, and new social values, things began to change. "The year 2000 was a turning point. The internet made it easier to connect with one another and form a genuine national community. And women were becoming more empowered, taking big steps forward in what society perceived they could do. It's astonishing to see what's happened since then."

Today, NAPO has more than four thousand members in forty-nine states and twenty-six countries. The leadership of NAPO is intensely engaged, highly effective, and fiercely ambitious. That's what you get when you have an organization composed of dark horses. In a democratic meritocracy, vibrant and flexible professional communities like NAPO that self-organize out of the identification of shared professional micro-motives will become the norm, rather than the exception.

Let's be perfectly clear: three examples do not make a new system of opportunity. We're not saying that Summit, SNHU, and NAPO solve all the problems of creating a democratic meritocracy. We are not presenting them as ideal models to emulate, but as bold proofs of concept. They are pioneers, like dark horses themselves, bravely blazing their own trails through the wilderness. There will never be One Best Way when it comes to implementing Equal Fit. Every institution will need to figure out its own solutions for providing personalization and individual choice. But Summit, SNHU, and NAPO demonstrate that when you liberate people through personalization and individual choice, you don't get chaos.

You get personal fulfillment *and* professional excellence.

If we want to bring about the world foreshadowed by these pioneers, it's not only institutions that must change. We each owe something to one another, too. Under the Dark Horse Covenant, each of us bears a personal obligation that is no less important to building a democratic meritocracy than the one borne by our institutions.

13.

Fulfillment is not something that can be given to you. It can only be earned. That's why the supreme individual obligation under the Dark Horse Covenant is *Personal Accountability*. But just as the Dark Horse Covenant views equal opportunity in an unconventional light, it takes an unaccustomed view of personal accountability.

In the past, we indulged in systemic hypocrisy as a society when it came to accountability. We insisted you needed to own your choices, then took away your freedom to choose. We insisted you needed an education to access professional opportunity, then enforced a talent quota. We declared that everyone had an equal opportunity to climb the ladder, then imposed a talent equant.

This is passive picking masquerading as choice, and sometimes not even that. In far too many instances, meaningful choice was reserved for the wealthy and privileged. We created a corrupt system of opportunity with a strictly limited number of winners, then told the losers to take accountability for losing.

Things are different in a democratic meritocracy that implements Equal Fit. You are no longer a cog in the machine. You are no longer a contestant in a beauty pageant. When you are offered genuine choice, you have genuine control over your life. But this increased power demands increased responsibility. When you are empowered to Know Your Choices you become fully accountable for the decisions you make in the pursuit of fulfillment.

Under the Dark Horse Covenant, the calculus is simple: with greater freedom of choice comes greater personal accountability.

You are accountable for Knowing Your Micro-Motives. You

are accountable for Knowing Your Choices. You are accountable for Knowing Your Strategies. And when you are accountable for all of these, then you are responsible for your own fulfillment.

Thus, a democratic meritocracy can *only* function properly if you are willing to view your pursuit of fulfillment as a duty you owe society. This is how you can personally drive institutions to provide Equal Fit. Places like Summit and the College for America will grow and improve only if we choose to support their nascent democratic meritocracies instead of pursuing standardized excellence and surrendering our right to choose.

14.

At heart, the Dark Horse Covenant is a simple declaration that fulfillment is both an individual right and a civic duty.

When presented in such a forthright manner, the Dark Horse Covenant can sound fatuous and quixotic. It might even strike some as un-American. At a time when society appears to be coming apart at the seams, the Dark Horse Covenant can easily be misconstrued as dignifying a sense of personal entitlement as a bedrock value.

Fulfillment hardly seems like a stalwart and dependable tenet upon which to build a social contract. Critics ensconced within the standardization mindset may scoff, "So you're telling me it's my *obligation* to focus on those things that matter most to me? It's my *civic duty* to pursue my own personal version of happiness? I mean, has there ever been a nation whose founding document declared that fulfillment was both a human right and a civic duty?"

As a matter of fact, there was.

The nation was the United States. The document was the Declaration of Independence.

the pursuit of Happiness

He who receives an idea from me, receives instruction himself without lessening mine; as he who lights his taper at mine, receives light without darkening me.

—Thomas Jefferson

1.

The most influential sentence in Western political history must surely be the first sentence of the Preamble to the American Declaration of Independence: "We hold these truths to be self-evident, that all men are created equal, that they are endowed by their Creator with certain unalienable Rights, that among these are Life, Liberty and the pursuit of Happiness." The most celebrated phrase in this hallowed sentence is its trio of unalienable rights. Yet, curiously, one of them does not sound like the others. It's easy to forget, but when the extraordinary minds who fashioned the world's oldest enduring democracy set down the most important rights due every human being, they afforded the rather eccentric "pursuit of Happiness" the same supreme status as Life and Liberty.

Two and a half centuries later, Life and Liberty remain steadfast fixtures in the public arena. We still furiously debate the right to life and the right to die. Every electoral season, American politicians of all stripes denounce perceived violations of liberty as a surefire means of garnering votes. But the pursuit of happiness rarely appears in public discourse. On the rare occasion when Americans happen to ponder the presence of this phrase in the Declaration at all, they usually suspect its inclusion was a mere literary flourish, a bit of aspirational embroidery intended to stir the hearts of a people yearning to be free. Indeed, on its first appearance upon the world stage, "the pursuit of Happiness" was promptly mocked throughout King George's Britain. Barely a month after the publication of the Declaration of Independence, this salvo by "An Englishman" appeared in an Edinburgh magazine:

> Their next self-evident truth and ground of rebellion is, that they have an unalienable right to the pursuit of happiness. The pursuit of happiness an unalienable right! . . . Did ever any mortal alive hear of taking a pursuit of happiness from a man? What they possibly can mean by these words, I own is beyond my comprehension. A man may take from me a horse or a cow, or I may alienate either of them from myself, as I may likewise anything that I have;

but how that can be taken from me, or alienated, which
I have not, must be left for the solution of some unborn
Oedipus.

In fact, the enigmatic phrase held profound currents of
meaning for the founders. It reflected a moment in history when
the greatest thinkers in the American colonies were pondering
the ideal form of social organization for a free people, united
by the shared conviction that reason, philosophy, and civil debate could offer more effective solutions for government than
tradition, religion, or bloodshed. And no American was more
deeply engaged in the reasoning, philosophizing, and debating
of the age than the author of the Declaration of Independence,
Thomas Jefferson.

Jefferson considered the Declaration the crowning achievement of his storied life. The epitaph on his gravestone, written
by Jefferson himself, lists his authorship of the Declaration of Independence as the foremost achievement by which "I wish most
to be remembered." And no phrase from the Declaration more
succinctly expresses Jefferson's vision of a society predicated upon
universal fulfillment than "the pursuit of Happiness."

2.

Each of Jefferson's known drafts of the Declaration from first
to last contained the four-word phrase, including the preferred
version that he published for friends and posterity, a kind of "director's cut." The all-star drafting committee for the Declaration
of Independence, which included two other towering writer-
philosophers in John Adams and Benjamin Franklin, made several edits to Jefferson's "rough draught" but left "the pursuit of

Happiness" untouched. Though the content of the Declaration was intensely debated by Congress, who eventually decided to cut about a fourth of Jefferson's original material, there is no record of anyone asking for the removal or modification of the phrase. Its inclusion, then, was neither an accident nor a compromise, but the deliberate annunciation of one of history's most gifted political thinkers as he was crafting what he believed was a transcendent document for all humankind.

Twelve-score and two years later, the notion of the pursuit of happiness as a basic human right remains a distinctly American concept. Consider the core rights delineated in the founding documents of other democratic nations. Canada touts "Life, Liberty, and Security." (The Canucks also endorse "peace, order, and good government.") Germany upholds "Unity, Justice, and Liberty." France advocates "Liberty, Equality, and Fraternity." These are all important principles, to be sure, and they each have a role as a basic right in a civil society. But these principles are primarily *collective* ideals. What is distinctly absent from each of these other nations' social contracts is the notion of *individuality*.

A government can institute the protection of Life and Liberty across society as a whole without accounting for individual variations. The death penalty can be declared illegal, for instance, which would guarantee that the government cannot take anyone's life, regardless of the details of your particular crimes. The pursuit of happiness, in contrast, manifests differently within each person. Protecting the right to *pursue* happiness, therefore, demands recognition of the individuality of the pursuer.

There was nothing particularly original about including Life and Liberty in the Declaration. Both values were publicly safeguarded as far back as the Magna Carta of 1215. What made the

United States exceptional among the nations of Earth is that, astonishingly, its creators believed that the ideal society was one where individuality matters.

A society where, above all, *fulfillment* matters.

3.

Jefferson's political ideas were most heavily shaped by the same source of influence that shaped the minds of the other founders: the Scottish Enlightenment. And the Scottish Enlightenment was very, very concerned with fulfillment.

Today, we associate Scotland with bagpipes, *Braveheart*, and Sean Connery's brogue. But that cold and rugged nation was also the undisputed leader of Enlightenment thought; the man often cited as the first Enlightenment philosopher was a Scotsman, Glasgow professor Francis Hutcheson. Jefferson was exposed to Scottish ideas from his earliest youth. Two out of three of Jefferson's most influential mentors were Scots: Reverend William Douglas and Professor William Small, the latter of whom Jefferson viewed "as a father, to his enlightened & affectionate guidance of my studies while at college I am indebted for everything."

Jefferson's library, during his formative years and when he was penning the Declaration, was filled with volumes by Scottish philosophers, which he copied and annotated extensively. These volumes spent far more ink contemplating "happiness" than life, liberty, or property.

Nowadays we think of happiness as meaning merriment or pleasure. But that's not what it meant during the Age of Enlightenment. The word "happy" is the adjectival form of the noun "hap," which meant an event or a situation. This definition provided the basis for an assortment of "hap" words: mishap (a bad event), hapless (without any favorable events), and haphazard and happenstance (chance events).

Thus, in its original form, the adjective "happy" referred to something that fit a particular event. A "happy thought" was one that was perfectly suited for the conversation; a "happy garment" was one that was appropriate for a social event. Scottish Enlightenment philosopher David Hume spoke of a "happy theory" because it kept fitting new data; Hume also penned a line that could serve as the dark horse motto: "He is happy whose circumstances suit his temper."

Though the meaning of "happiness" was originally neutral, meaning "the state of fitting one's circumstances," by Jefferson's time it had become a synonym for "goodhap," meaning "the *favorable* state of fitting one's circumstances," just as the word "lucky" evolved from meaning "random" to "favorable luck," and "fortunate" evolved from "random" to "favorable fortune."

The first reference to happiness in an American political document was in the Virginia Declaration of Rights published by Jefferson's friend George Mason just a few months before Jefferson wrote the Declaration of Independence. Mason wrote, "All men are by nature equally free and independent, and have certain inherent rights . . . [that include] *pursuing and obtaining happiness*" (italics added). Analyzing Mason's use of the word, historian Jack D. Warren observes that happiness "was not as vague a goal as it now seems. Happiness did not mean pleasure, though 18th-century thinkers held that happiness ought to be pleasant. For thinkers like Mason, a person achieved happiness when his condition fit his character, talents and abilities."

In other words, for the founders, happiness was synonymous with the dark horse definition of fulfillment.

4.

Jefferson could have promised equal fulfillment to all. But he did not. Instead, the equality he vouchsafed was the *pursuit* of fulfillment. This was a deliberate and informed choice resulting from a chain of reasoning characteristic of the Enlightenment.

Enlightenment thinkers venerated science. One of Jefferson's greatest heroes was Isaac Newton, who demonstrated the existence of inviolable scientific laws governing the operation of nature. For Jefferson and other founders, the pursuit of happiness was viewed as a scientific law of human nature, akin to Newton's law of universal gravitation.

The Scottish philosopher John Locke wrote a penetrating analysis of "the pursuit of happiness" in which he emphasizes the "constancy" of the pursuit of happiness within human nature, writing that "God Almighty himself is under the necessity of being happy." Francis Hutcheson, whom Jefferson studied, wrote, "Men are necessarily determined to pursue their own happiness." The author Laurence Sterne, whom Jefferson admired, wrote, "The great pursuit of man is after happiness; it is the first and strongest desire of his nature." Garry Wills, an emeritus professor of history at Northwestern University who spent a portion of his career studying what Jefferson meant by "the pursuit of Happiness," sums up these thinkers' influence on Jefferson: "Thus Jefferson talks of man as 'following after' happiness by more than vague yearning—indeed, by a uniform necessity of his nature, something as regular as a magnetic needle's turn to the North. This is a law that is normative, one that man can steer by."

According to Enlightenment thought, if something was a law of human nature, it was therefore necessarily a moral law. It was a *right*. In other words, since everyone was designed by nature to pursue happiness—to seek those circumstances that fit them best—this quest was a fundamental individual freedom that must be protected. "When they found what they must pursue," Wills explains, "they knew they had a right to pursue it."

In the final step in the Enlightenment chain of reasoning, if something was a moral law—an individual right—then that right must be protected by the government. It must become a *political* principle. Eight years before he signed the Declaration of Independence, founder James Wilson wrote, "the happiness of the society is the first law of every government." In one of the most influential treatises of the early Enlightenment, *A System of Moral Philosophy*, Hutcheson asserts, "The general happiness is the supreme end of all political union."

Thus, Jefferson believed that by proceeding through the logical steps of scientific law, moral law, and political principle, the pursuit of fulfillment was an individual right that must be guaranteed by any just social contract.

Most of the founders were in complete agreement that an independent American system of government must have as one of its paramount aims the protection and nurturing of its citizens' fulfillment. This is what they likely believed they were affirming when they signed the Declaration.

But Jefferson privately intended something more.

Jefferson is famous for his blue-sky thinking, for visionary ideas about how to improve the world that were often far ahead of his time. The pursuit of happiness was one of them. There is evidence that Jefferson intended "the pursuit of Happiness" not merely as a general avowal of the individual right to pursue fulfillment, but as a *solution* to the problem of how to provide fulfillment for everyone.

5.

Though they never would have used such modern language, many of Jefferson's Enlightenment idols believed in the existence of a positive feedback loop between the individual pursuit of fulfillment and the collective fulfillment of all members of society. According to this thinking, an individual's pursuit of fulfillment inevitably benefits her neighbors, while the act of increasing her neighbors' fulfillment elevates that individual's own experience of fulfillment.

Henry Home, Lord Kames, a Scottish philosopher who mentored David Hume and Adam Smith, may have been the first to express a rudimentary form of this notion when he wrote, "There is a principle of benevolence in man which prompts him to an equal pursuit of the happiness of all." Hutcheson then closed the loop between the individual pursuit of happiness and the collective happiness, writing: "That each Agent may discover it to be the surest way to promote his private Happiness, to do publickly useful Actions. . . . In the like manner, a publickly useful Action may diffuse some small Advantage to every Observer, whence he may approve it, and love the Agent."

Adam Ferguson, another Scottish Enlightenment philosopher whom Jefferson read, also believed there was a reciprocity between individual and collective fulfillment in society: "It is likewise true that the happiness of individuals is the great end of civil society: for in what sense can a public enjoy any good, if its members, considered apart, be unhappy? The interests of society, however, and of its members, are easily reconciled. If the individual owes every degree of consideration to the public, he receives, in paying that very consideration, the greatest happiness of which his nature is capable."

Jefferson imbibed these Enlightenment ideas about the social dynamics of fulfillment and concluded that the individual pursuit of fulfillment was not only a right, but a duty—a duty that served as the essential mechanism for increasing the collective fulfillment of society. In his 2006 book *Wealth in Families,* Charles Collier—a thought leader in charitable strategy—encourages would-be philanthropists to heed Jefferson's conclusion: "According to Thomas Jefferson, the 'pursuit of happiness' has to do with an internal journey of learning to know ourselves and an external journey of service to others."

In this light, Jefferson's most famous and perplexing phrase in the Declaration of Independence is a compact rendering of the Dark Horse Covenant, affirming both Equal Fit (your right to pursue fulfillment) and Personal Accountability (your duty to pursue fulfillment).

6.

Jefferson was a deeply flawed man. Though he believed that slavery was wrong, and made several attempts to limit or abolish it in his home state of Virginia, at the end of the day he was a slave owner who held more than six hundred human beings in bondage during his lifetime. Though some of his slaveholding peers eventually found the courage upon their deathbeds to free their slaves, including fellow Virginian George Washington, Jefferson did not. The record clearly shows that in his private life, Jefferson failed to live up to the principles he so passionately advocated in public. Like every one of us, Thomas Jefferson should be held to account for his sins.

But it is possible and necessary for us to separate the man from the message. We can condemn the inventor while praising his inventions. Newton's law of universal gravitation is beautiful and true regardless of any moral failings of Newton himself. And Jefferson's conception of fulfillment as both a right and a duty deserves to be viewed outside of any shadow cast by the author, for it holds the key to constructing a truly democratic meritocracy.

Any society that obliges its institutions to provide for the individual pursuit of fulfillment by all citizens while simultaneously obliging its citizens to pursue fulfillment as an essential duty will thereby institute a positive-sum game of both excellence and fulfillment—as long as one crucial assumption holds: that anyone who achieves personal fulfillment will feel a natural obligation to give back to the society that supported his or her right to pursue it.

As we've seen, the notion that the pursuit of personal fulfillment drives individuals to contribute to the fulfillment of others was a matter of faith among Enlightenment thinkers. More than two centuries later, we find that their faith was well-placed. Time and time again in the Dark Horse Project, we found that experts who attained personal fulfillment experienced a sincere desire to contribute to the happiness and welfare of others.

Even dark horses who achieved excellence in professions that don't seem particularly conducive to a charitable mindset feel a robust urge to give back. Annie Duke was a model PhD student in cognitive linguistics at an Ivy League school who, despite her formidable academic achievements, felt like things were going in the wrong direction in her life. She abruptly quit her doctoral program with just months to go before finishing her dissertation, moved to Montana, and found unexpected fulfillment playing poker in the smoky, rowdy back rooms of rural casinos. Driven by her newfound micro-motives for gambling, she spent seven years hustling and honing her bluffing and tell-reading skills in poker rooms from Las Vegas to Atlantic City until she was competing against the best players of her generation in the Texas Hold 'Em Tournament of Champions—the sole woman at the final table staring down names like Daniel Negreanu, Phil Hellmuth, and Phil Ivey. She beat them all and claimed the two-million-dollar prize.

And yet, despite her devotion to a field predicated upon doing whatever it takes to empty your opponents' wallets, Annie is one of the most decent and kind-hearted people you could meet. In 2012 she quit her poker career to devote herself full time to charity work. Her special interest is early education—trying to provide Equal Opportunity to all youth. She cofounded a nonprofit, How I Decide, to help underprivileged middle school students understand how to make decisions. She also serves on the board of multiple education-related nonprofits.

"As I understood my motivations and interests better, I became more purposeful, until now I've reached the point where I'm able to direct my charity in a way that fits who I am and where I can make my best effort," Annie says. "One thing that helped me so much was ignoring the destination and being open to new choices, and that's what I try to impress upon young people: if you stick to the straight and narrow, you will miss the opportunities that fit you even better."

Most remarkably, dark horses who came from humble beginnings, who endured every kind of hardship and degradation before finally attaining a fulfilling life—whom nobody would blame for wanting to insulate themselves and bask in their hard-earned prosperity—still made service central to their lives. One such individual is Thomas Price. Thomas is the son of an African American man and a Caucasian woman. The problem was, at the time, his mother was married to a Caucasian man, who was shocked and outraged to discover at Thomas's birth that, beyond a shadow of a doubt, his presumed son was not his own. A few years later, Thomas's mother killed herself. Thomas's abusive "stepfather" took Thomas with him to Alaska and moved in with a woman in Anchorage. Then his stepfather left, never to be seen again.

At age fourteen, Thomas was alone with a woman who had no ties to him at all—and no real interest in caring for him. She demanded that he earn money to pay for room and board. He got a job in a burger joint and began working forty-hour weeks while doing his best to stick with high school. She kept all his wages. Finally, at the age of fifteen, Thomas had enough. He moved out and took up residence in a trailer with a drug-dealing teenager. He had never known a loving or stable caregiver and would never have an adult guardian again.

Under the Standardization Covenant, there was little hope for Thomas to develop excellence, and that might be putting it mildly. Yet Thomas pursued fulfillment on his own terms. He found that he greatly enjoyed cooking and the camaraderie of the kitchen and became a leader at his restaurant. He began working at restaurants around the world, spending time in Mexico, Texas, Thailand, and Indonesia, before landing in Seattle, where he discovered the democratic meritocracy of sommeliers.

It was a perfect fit.

In 2012, at the age of forty-seven, he passed the Master Sommelier Diploma exam, and was anointed as one of the world's most talented sommeliers.

Thomas was cast aside by his guardians and forced to find his own path with little in the way of education, support, or human kindness. Yet today he makes it a point of pride to provide service to others, first as an elite hospitality professional, but also as Education Committee chairman for the Court of Master Sommeliers and as director of scholarships for the nonprofit Guild of Sommeliers Education Foundation (SommFoundation), roles that enable him to help needy students interested in pursuing careers in wine. "It's a wonderful feeling to be able to fund someone working toward any aspirational goal. When I think about the look on people's faces when they receive a scholarship check, I get choked up," Thomas says. "Considering how financially challenged I was when I was young, getting to give back to others has been immensely fulfilling."

There is a Yiddish proverb, *A moshel iz nit kain rai'eh*, which means *An example is not proof.* Some might argue that not everyone who finds fulfillment will feel obliged to help others. You might even contend that our dark horse interviews suffer from self-selection bias—that the kind of people who agree to open up to scientists about their lives for no tangible remuneration might be exactly the kind of people biased toward helping others. That's a fair critique. At the same time, if so many dark horses, from so many diverse backgrounds, who traveled such different journeys, all have ended up in a place where they are earnestly trying to improve the lives of others, it's a piece of evidence difficult to ignore.

But in the final analysis, whether or not we can prove that fulfillment inevitably leads every individual to want to contribute to society misses the point. It really comes down to a very simple question, a question that only you can answer:

Which system of opportunity do *you* want to support? A quotacracy? Or a democratic meritocracy?

Do you want to bet on your fellow citizens feeling charitable toward others under the Standardization Covenant? Do you want to bet on a majority of the populace, prevented from attaining society's best opportunities by quotas and equants, feeling the urge to give back to a society that sacrificed their own fulfillment for that of a privileged minority?

Or do you want to bet on your fellow citizens feeling charitable toward others in a society devoted to Equal Fit, where anyone and everyone feels supported to pursue fulfillment on their own terms?

Our institutions are charged with maintaining our quotacracy and preserving the Standardization Covenant. In contrast, the Dark Horse Covenant must be ratified and upheld by every one of us. In a society that values both Equal Fit and Personal Accountability, your own force of will always makes a difference. A democratic meritocracy will only function as a positive-sum game of fulfillment if we each feel a strong obligation to help one another, an obligation that must be supported by a social contract that ensures that individuality matters.

This was Jefferson's blue-sky vision of the pursuit of happiness. It was an idea ahead of its time.

Now, it is an idea whose time has come.

This staggering opportunity was birthed at the dawning of an epoch when the most luminous minds in the American colonies put aside their differences to fight shoulder to shoulder for the ultimate victory: an independent nation that—one day—could secure life, liberty, and, yes, the pursuit of fulfillment for all. It is an opportunity that can be realized only if you make the commitment to harness your individuality in the pursuit of fulfillment to attain excellence. It is an opportunity that can be realized only if you recognize that your own freedom to pursue fulfillment ultimately depends on you supporting the freedom of others to follow their own winding path.

This is what we were always supposed to be.

Let's finish what we started.

acknowledgments

Joint Acknowledgments

We were able to write the book we wanted to write, how we wanted to write it. To ascend our winding path to such a peak required the support of many wonderful individuals.

This book simply would not exist without the enthusiasm and faith of Gideon Weil, our marvelous editor, who supplied us with enough room for our ideas to take flight and enough guidance to land them. Howard Yoon, our incomparable agent, let us be ourselves and figured out the rest.

If there's a hall of fame for lawyers, then we'd nominate our attorney Chris Betke, who consistently goes above and beyond the call of duty to guide us, instruct us, and nurture our dreams.

Suzanne Quist might be the most hospitable and responsive production editor you've never met, as well as the most lucid and forthright. We hope you edit all our books. Jessie Dolch is a crackerjack copy editor whose keen eye and steady poise prevented us from toppling into the sinkholes and chasms. Bruno Gazzoni has a peculiar genius for seeing in three dimensions, a wondrous talent that we are lucky to have benefited from.

The team at Populace has been a constant source of inspiration and spiritual support. Thank you to Bill and Dewey Rosetti, Debbie Newhouse, Walter Haas, Brian Daly, Parisa Rouhani, Lorry Henderson, Lizza Vachon, Tanya Gonzalez, and Teresa Kalinowsky.

We owe a singular debt of gratitude to Jim Ryan, former dean of the Harvard Graduate School of Education, for supporting the Laboratory for the Science of Individuality and the Dark Horse Project.

Stella Kafka, executive officer of the American Association of Variable Star Observers, answered our questions about the heavens and helped us unearth astronomers who followed a winding path.

We also warmly thank Mandy Roberts of the Association of Professional Dog Trainers, Kenneth Kero-Mentz of the American Foreign Service Association, Tanya Khemet of the National Association of Certified Professional Midwives, Francie Likis at the *Journal of Midwifery & Women's Health*, Matthew Rice of the Cartography and Geographic Information Society, Grey Stafford of the International Marine Animal Trainer's Association, Rick Fienberg of the American Astronomical Society, Polly Carpenter of the Boston Society of Architects, Ted Floyd of *Birding* magazine, and Eryl Wentworth of the American Institute for Conservation.

We have nothing but respect, admiration, and love for the amazing folks at the National Association of Productivity and Organizing Professionals, especially the exceedingly productive and organized Jessica Kennedy. Special thanks are also due to Sue Pine, Lori Vande Krol, and Stephanie McGrath.

Southern New Hampshire University is a glimpse of what the future holds. Paul LeBlanc is an incandescent visionary, academic sorcerer, and human dynamo. Chrystina Russell and Libby May are wizard lieutenants.

We continue to be dazzled by the achievements of Summit Public Schools. We'd like to thank Diane Tavenner for showing us what education could—and should—be, and Mira Browne for her assistance.

A few men and women from the Dark Horse Project also merit particular mention for their generosity and warmth of spirit. Michael Meagher is our choice as sommelier at our next meal. Janice Carte is an extraordinary soul who slipped from the pages of this book at the last possible moment; as did Lars Winther, unsung hero of the Marvel movie empire, who slipped from the main text to pages 267–70. You can bet that both of these outstanding dark horses will appear soon in a future Rose/Ogas production. David Tanzer, thank you for introducing us to the balloon pilots of America, and we still hope that one day you will carry us aloft. Michelle Carter is an American heroine and model human being. Lawrence Millman is a lovely soul whose iconoclastic spirit infuses this book. We're sure you will hear more about him from us shortly. Matthew Applegate belongs in this book, too, but his time will come. And Annie Duke—we hope we never find you sitting to our left at the poker table, but we want to extend a royal flush of gratitude for your support and for inspiring us to expand the Dark Horse Project.

We must also thank our researchers: Jordan Harrod, Rosca Razvan, Milos Vidakovic, Radu Radu, Sarah Schmidt, Oleg Taganov, Jamie Miller, Emily Curtin, Artur Kolpakov, Henry Marcos, Nick Willows, and Tanya Goldmakher. And three astronomers who helped us understand the lay of the cosmological land: David Hogg, Scott Gaudi, and David Charbonneau. And two coaches who helped us learn the basics of track and field: Coach Darcy Wilson and Coach Brenner Abbott.

A few people assisted us with the manuscript in ways big and small, including Jennipher Murphy, Driss Zoukhri, Ron Tanner, Kalim Saliba, Dara Kaye, Kaylin Rose, Sandy Ogas, and Heiko Spalle.

Three scientists laid the intellectual groundwork for our research—courageous pioneers who saw dimensions of human-kind that others did not: Peter Molenaar, Kurt Fischer, and Richard Lerner.

Finally, and certainly most importantly, there is one astonishing assortment of self-starters whom we can never thank enough: the dark horses of the Dark Horse Project. This book is ultimately dedicated to them.

Personal Acknowledgments

Kaylin, Austin, and Nathan—thank you for being on this journey with me through the good times and the bad. Your love and support have meant everything to me. To be married to someone writing a book like this requires the patience of Job, and I am undeservedly blessed with such a spouse. SLB.

I thank my parents Larry and Lyda for being the perfect role models for the dark horse life. Kim, Doug, Kevin, Missy—you are the best siblings a guy could ask for.

Special thanks to Parisa Rouhani, my cofounder and partner-in-crime at Populace—what an adventure! None of this would be possible without your vision, dedication, and overall ability to get things done.

To my godchildren, Audrey and Emily Rouhani-Sadafi—you always put a smile on my face.

—TR

A bluebird for my long-suffering parents, who were always there at every step of my long and winding road. The prodigious intellect of my oldest collaborator and confidante, Sai Chaitanya, helped steer this book in profitable directions. I'm excited to see Meera grow up. Basil, Zaher, and Jeremy, my brothers, nurtured this book through thick and thin. Reem is a quiet marvel who will be writing her own books before long.

But priority of place goes to the only person in this universe who sees what I see. Without you, I would still be languishing at the bottom of the mountain. Without you, I would still be shoveling words into the obliterating fire. Without you, Tofool, *Dark Horse* would be a moon-faced chimera, and not this.

—OO

notes

introduction: breaking the mold

1   *"Behind it all is surely an idea so simple . . .":* John Archibald Wheeler, "How Come the Quantum?" *Annals of the New York Academy of Sciences* 480 (1986): 304–16.

2   *took a job cleaning out horse stables:* Jennie wanted to be a horse-racing jockey. She trained as the only girl among boys, until an accident with a horse broke her jaw and put an end to her racing aspirations.

3   *the first amateur to discover a new planet since 1781 . . .:* Jennie collaborated with other team members in the discovery of the planet, including another amateur astronomer (a gentleman with a PhD in bioengineering) who used the fourteen-inch telescope at the publicly funded Auckland observatory. Jennie was the only collaborator with her own backyard telescope.

6   *The expression "dark horse" first entered common parlance . . .: The Young Duke: A Moral Tale, Though Gay* was written by Benjamin Disraeli, the future British prime minister, in 1830 in order to finance his impending Grand Tour of Europe.

9   *"The better way is by making yourself so useful and efficient . . .":* Napoleon Hill, *The Law of Success in Sixteen Lessons* (Lexington, KY: Tribeca, [1928] 2012), front matter.

10   *most of us will switch jobs twelve or more times . . .:* Bureau of Labor Statistics, "Number of Jobs, Labor Market Experience, and Earnings Growth Among Americans at 50: Results from a Longitudinal Survey," August

24, 2017. Also, Claire Schooley from Forrester Research predicts that millennials will hold twelve to fifteen jobs in their lifetime: quoted in Alison Overholt, "Creating a Gem of a Career," *Fast Company*, March 1, 2006, https://www.fastcompany.com/55827/creating-gem-career.

11   *will outlive most of the organizations we work for:* Peter Drucker concludes in *Managing Oneself* (Cambridge, MA: Harvard Business Press, 2008), 55.

11   *the first university to jettison grades and credit hours . . .:* From SNHU president Paul LeBlanc email, January 30, 2018.

chapter 1: the standardization covenant

28   *and the Ford Motor Company . . . .:* Henry Ford himself wrote the first entry on "Mass Production" for the *Encyclopædia Britannica*, perhaps not surprisingly citing Ford Motor Company as the leading example of "more intelligent management" and the principles of efficiency.

30   *"We have found out as you have that we cannot trust some people . . .":* Ray Kroc quoted in John F. Love, *McDonald's: Behind the Arches* (New York: Bantam, 1986), 144.

30   *"to obey the orders we give them . . .":* Robert Kanigel, *The One Best Way: Frederick Winslow Taylor and the Enigma of Efficiency* (Cambridge, MA: MIT Press, 2005), 169: "In our scheme, we do not ask the initiative of our men. We do not want any initiative. All we want of them is to obey the orders we give them, do what we say, and do it quick."

31   *it marked the complete standardization of a human life:* Ironically, in the Age of Personalization we have been reducing the standardization of products before we reduce the standardization of people. We are more likely to demand a customized phone or pair of shoes than a customized education.

35   *Even though most parents know in their heart . . . .:* When young people hear their parents, educators, and employers all endorsing the conviction that the pursuit of excellence leads to fulfillment, they inevitably internalize these values, too—occasionally with fatal consequences. We personally knew several students who committed suicide at least in part because of the perception that their academic performance was substandard. During the 1960s, sticking to the straight path in college was often a life or death proposition, as the American Standardization Covenant was temporarily amended to *Be the same as everyone else, only better—or go to Vietnam.* One of the dark horses we interviewed, social worker–turned–astronomer Bill Goff, recalls taking a tough physics final in 1968. He knew if he failed, he would flunk out of college and be

drafted into the army. He failed. He flunked out. He was drafted. And for one harrowing year, he served honorably in the jungle battlefields of Southeast Asia.

45 *known, appropriately enough, as the science of individuality:* The science of individuality rejects averages, correlations, and other group-focused methods of nineteenth-century statistics in favor of the contextual, dynamic, and multidimensional methods of twenty-first-century dynamical systems theory—methods that prioritize the individual over the group. Research in the burgeoning fields of personalized medicine, personalized nutrition, personal genomics, personal training, and personalized learning all draw upon the science of individuality.

chapter 2: know your Micro-Motives

49 *"I think it all comes down to motivation . . .":* We considered using a quotation from Samuel Gompers as the epigraph for Chapter 2. It is from his testimony in 1911 at the first congressional hearings on the "Taylorization" (standardization) of industry at the dawn of the Age of Standardization: "If this Taylor system is put into operation . . . it will mean great production in goods and things, but in so far as man is concerned it means destruction. . . . It is producing wealth but grinding man, and, while I think we all agree that production is one of the essentials of life and that while greater productions must go on in order to satisfy our growing needs, there are other considerations of a primary and more important character, and that is the intelligence, that the physique, that the spirit, the mind, hopes, and aspirations of man shall be also cultivated and given an opportunity for higher achievements."

55 *A 2016 Gallup study found that while only 26 percent of fifth-graders . . .:* Valerie J. Calderon and Daniela Yu, "Student Enthusiasm Falls as High School Graduation Nears," June 1, 2017, Gallup, http://news.gallup .com/topic/gallup_student_poll.aspx.

55 *but Gallup found that a staggering 67 percent . . .:* "State of the American Workplace Report," http://news.gallup.com/reports/199961/state -american-workplace-report-2017.aspx.

55 *A 2014 survey by Education Week . . .:* Education Week Research Center, "Engaging Students for Success: Findings from a National Survey," https://www.edweek.org/media/ewrc_engagingstudents_2014.pdf.

55 *motivate kids by "encouraging healthy competition. . . .":* Scott Turansky, "10 Ways to Motivate Your Child," iMOM, http://www.imom .com/10-ways-to-motivate-your-child/#.WrULEmaZN-g.

55   *"Set your room in a U-shape . . .":* "Twenty Tips on Motivating Students," University of Nebraska–Lincoln, Office of Graduate Studies, https://www.unl.edu/gradstudies/current/teaching/motivating.

56   *"Kids really like to eat. . . .":* Stephanie Jankowski, "Light a Fire! 10 Unconventional Ways to Motivate Students," We Are Teachers, June 29, 2015, https://www.weareteachers.com/light-a-fire-10-unconventional -ways-to-motivate-students/.

58   *the remarkable specificity of micro-motives:* There are two reasons we employ the term "micro-motive" to differentiate standardized conceptions of motivation from the dark horse conception. First, micro-motives are incredibly fine-grained. The personalized success attained by dark horses reveals that any generic or supposedly universal personal motive (such as the desire for order) can usually be narrowed to a motive of much greater specificity (such as the desire to align physical objects). Thus, a micro-motive reflects the unappreciated *depth* of personal motivation. Second, each person's motivational profile consists of a multitude of distinct motives. Thus, a micro-motive also reflects the unappreciated *breadth* of personal motivation.

chapter 3: know your Choices

79   *"Destiny is not a matter of chance . . .":* Speech delivered February 22, 1899, at the Washington Day Banquet given by the Virginia Democratic Association in Washington, DC, published in Arthur Charles Fox Davies, ed., *The Book of Public Speaking*, 3 vols. (London: Caxton Pub., 1913), 2:120.

82   *Amazon alone offers more than five hundred million products...:* "How Many Products Does Amazon Sell?—January 2018," ScrapeHero, https://www.scrapehero.com/many-products-amazon-sell-january-2018.

86   *a concept from the science of individuality known as* fit *. . . :* This notion of fit is similar to the biological concept of norms of reaction. From Scott Barry Kaufman, *The Complexity of Greatness: Beyond Talent or Practice* (New York: Oxford Univ. Press, 2013), 7: "First, every person has some distribution of possible expressions of intelligence and ability in any area. The level that the person actually expresses is not the only level the person might have expressed, and the different possibilities depend on environmental circumstances. In the literature of evolutionary biology, these distributions are called norms of reaction. They express the ranges of trait observations that are possible in different environmental circumstances for given genotypes."

92   *"I still remember the month—October 1978 . . .":* Susan Rogers also tells us: "I was keeping track of my progress because in 1978 I escaped on

Elvis's birthday (I walked out on my husband on January 8) and had my first day of freedom on Jimmy Page's birthday (January 9)!"

94 *But no dark horse is average . . .:* The book *The End of Average: How We Succeed in a World That Values Sameness* (New York: HarperOne, 2015), by Todd Rose, explores the science and mathematical proofs behind the finding that there is no such thing as average body size, average talent, average intelligence, or average character: "Every one of these familiar notions is a figment of a misguided scientific imagination. Our modern conception of the average person is not a mathematical truth but a human invention, created a century and a half ago by two European scientists to solve the social problems of their era. . . . Today we face very different problems—and we possess science and math far better than what was available in the nineteenth century" (pages 11–12). "It is not that the average is never useful. Averages have their place. If you're comparing two different *groups* of people, like comparing the performance of Chilean pilots with French pilots—as opposed to comparing two *individuals* from each of those groups—then the average can be useful. But the moment you need *a* pilot, or *a* plumber, or *a* doctor, the moment you need to teach *this* child or decide whether to hire *that* employee—the moment you need to make a decision about an individual—the average is useless. Worse than useless, in fact, because it creates the illusion of knowledge" (page 11).

96 *the gap between your individuality and the institutional mold represents pure, unadulterated risk:* In fact, this is the primary way that institutions shift their institutional risk off of their own shoulders and onto yours. By compelling you to pick from the limited range of options they exert complete control over, the burden is on you to conform to the institutional demands for the option. If you don't like the required textbook, if you don't like the teacher, or if you don't like one of the required courses—too bad. The institution won't pay the price of the poor fit. You will.

The difference between an institution and you is the difference between a fox and a hare. The fox is running for its dinner. The hare is running for its life. The fox needs to get it right only once in a while to survive. But the stakes are much, much higher for you.

103 *was rewarded with his very best life:* When you become the person you want to be, it makes you want to give back to the community that made such an achievement possible. Two years ago, Alan was approached by a board member of the Courageous Faces Foundation, a charity devoted to changing the public's perception of people with disabilities. The woman told Alan about one of her charity's ambassadors, a man

named Reggie Bibbs. Reggie suffered from neurofibromatosis, a genetic disorder that produced large, inoperable tumors on the left side of his face and his left leg. The deformity caused people to stare and grimace, driving Reggie to seclusion. The board member told Alan that the Courageous Faces Foundation had hired a New York designer to make pants for Reggie, something of a challenge since Reggie's lower leg was the same size as his waist, but that the result was a disaster. Alan offered to make Reggie a better pair of pants.

Alan met with Reggie and took his measurements, but instead of simply making pants, Alan designed an entire $10,000 wardrobe for him, including a suit, sport coat, dress shirts, casual shirts, ties, belts, and jeans. It was another opportunity for Alan to push himself into new territory. He made use of all his hard-earned technical skills—including one essential component of Alan's design process, understanding the client on his own terms. Alan spent time with Reggie, getting to know him and what he aspired to be. He recognized that Reggie's greatest struggle was to *not* stand out from the crowd, while at the same time establishing an identity of his own apart from his physical imperfections. Alan designed the wardrobe around a man with a canny sense of humor and a natural exuberance that had so often been stifled.

The day came when Alan surprised Reggie with his new ensemble. "It was one of the most moving things I have ever experienced," Alan recounts. "I heard a fifty-one-year-old man tell me that it was the first time in his life that he felt like he fit in, that he was just like anybody else. He cried and I cried. It was this simple thing we all take for granted—being able to put on a decent-fitting set of clothes—but he had never been able to experience that before. I was completely humbled by the experience and I'm going to keep on doing it for as long as I'm standing."

In 2016, Alan received a World Humanitarian Award from the Courageous Faces Foundation, in part for restoring dignity and self-worth to those who are marginalized by their appearance. Alan has customized wardrobes for amputees, little people, victims of stroke and paralysis, and for individuals with congenital defects such as spina bifida and ALS—in other words, for men and women who need Alan's skills more than just about anyone.

104   *Seemingly small differences in fit can lead . . .:* This is because of a basic nonlinear principle from dynamic systems theory (and complexity theory) known, in mathematical parlance, as "sensitive dependence on initial conditions," but which is more commonly known as "the butterfly effect."

chapter 4: know your Strategies

113   *"In general, we're least aware of what our minds do best":* Marvin Minsky,
       The Society of Mind (Simon and Schuster: New York, 1988), 29.

114   *there are at least twelve well-established strategies . . . .:* "3x3x3 speed-
       solving methods," Speed Solving, https://www.speedsolving.com/wiki
       /index.php/3x3x3_speedsolving_methods. It has been mathematically
       proven that any starting position can be solved in twenty moves or
       less—known by cubers as God's number—but existing strategies aren't
       nearly as efficient, so there's still plenty of room for improvement in
       speed cubing.

116   *they anoint a single strategy for everyone to follow—a One Best Way:* Pro-
       fessions that are highly standardized, like medicine, law, and science,
       are especially likely to impose the One Best Way on its practitioners. In
       these fields, it is difficult to discover the best strategy for you because
       the Standardization Covenant's authority is so all-encompassing—even
       when the institutional strategy is manifestly flawed. If you want to get
       licensed as a dentist in Massachusetts, for instance, you must demon-
       strate knowledge of a cavity-filling strategy that was developed in the
       1890s—G. V. Black's "balanced amalgam formula"—even though the
       Black Method has been superseded by much better methods of filling
       cavities that employ new composite materials. Virtually every student
       who graduates from dental school today can expect to go through their
       entire career without ever needing to resort to the Black Method. Yet,
       the Massachusetts licensing exam still tests knowledge of this anti-
       quated strategy simply because every previous iteration of the licensing
       exam required knowledge of it, and because many of the administrators
       in charge of the exam were trained on Black's method in the 1960s and
       1970s. This would be like demanding that every computer program-
       mer's ability to get hired is dependent on demonstrating facility with
       COBOL, an obsolete programming language, just in case they get hired
       to work on a legacy project from the 1980s. Standardizing medical pro-
       cedures is often touted by institutions as a means of ensuring patient
       safety. But often, these standardized strategies merely serve to protect
       the financial and reputational security of the institutions themselves. If
       a hospital or physician can demonstrate that they followed all the steps
       of a standardized procedure in the standard manner, then a malpractice
       lawsuit becomes immeasurably difficult to prosecute. Black's cavity-
       filling technique does work pretty well most of the time, but there is a
       sizable minority of individuals who experience pain, infection, and even
       tooth cracking with the archaic method; dentists officially place the

blame for such undesirable outcomes on patients' "anomalous dental structure" rather than on dentists for sticking to a strategy that works well on average, but not so well for individuals.

121   *A strength is a fundamentally different kettle of fish . . .:* The Standard-
ization Covenant doesn't care much about your personal motives. But it cares a great deal about knowing your personal strengths. Institutions are constantly evaluating your purported strengths using an endless battery of standardized tests, grades, and head-to-head competitions. Schools declare that you evince better than average ability in analytical reasoning, or that your skill on the viola is below average, or that your vocabulary ranks near the top for your age. Such assessments seem sensible and scientific. But they all represent the covenant's self-serving and mathematically invalid assessments of your strengths and often have little to do with the true nature of your abilities and potential.

123   *The brains of many people who have trouble . . .:* Matthew H. Schneps, J. R. Brockmole, L. T. Rose, et al., "Dyslexia Linked to Visual Strengths Useful in Astronomy," *Bulletin of the American Astronomical Society* 43 (2011),
http://adsabs.harvard.edu/abs/2011AAS . . . 21821508S (abstract).

123   *Since strengths are fundamentally different from motives . . .:* The Stan-
dardization Covenant encourages you to construct your identity around your strengths. It wants you to see yourself as a gifted pianist, a tal-
ented chef, a math whiz. These are fine for your résumé, but building your self-concept upon your fuzzy strengths is like building a house upon sand. What if one of your strengths disappears overnight? This is not an uncommon event. An accident can cause a pianist to lose the use of his hands, a chef to lose her sense of taste, or an accountant to lose the ability to perform complex arithmetic. If you've anchored your self-image in your fuzzy strengths, then such a loss can be devastating. It doesn't need to be. It's always your micro-motives, and the passion and purpose that you engineer with them, that anchor your true self. Your motives endure through life's vicissitudes, even the most drastic of events. As long as you are committed to engineering your passion rather than following your passion, you can always find a new strategy for getting better at the things you care about most. Do you want to run in the Olympics, but lost your legs? That's been done (Oscar Pistorius). Do you want to compose symphonies, but lost your hearing? Also been done (Beethoven). Want to be the executive chef at a three-
Michelin-star restaurant, but lost your sense of taste from tongue can-
cer? Done, too (Grant Achatz). But these examples, though remarkable, are all instances of someone finding a new strategy to continue doing the same thing they were doing before. The dark horse mindset opens

up an infinite variety of other ways to find fulfillment—and new forms of excellence. If you lose the ability to be a competitive runner, you can become a coach, the editor of a running website, or a scientist studying the biomechanics of running—or take up stock car racing, dog sled racing, rowing, or the design of radio-controlled cars. Even if you don't lose your abilities, the Age of Personalization moves so fast and changes so quickly that what was a professional strength yesterday might be considered obsolete tomorrow. Video rental store managers, data-entry clerks, newspaper prepress operators, and switchboard operators were all thriving professions in the 1980s but have vanished today.

134   *It's easier to become a NASA rocket scientist . . . .:* "Rocket science" is usually employed as a colloquial term for aerospace engineering, though NASA actually does have "Rocket Scientist" as an official job title.

chapter 5: ignore the Destination

143   *"most of us discover where we are headed when we arrive . . . ."*: From Watterson's commencement address at Kenyon College, May 20, 1990. Walt Whitman puts it more elegantly in "Song of Myself," writing: "Not I, not any one else can travel that road for you, / You must travel it for yourself. / It is not far, it is within reach, / Perhaps you have been on it since you were born and did not know."

145   *Deep Blue prevailed:* Deep Blue may also have benefited from an overlooked bug in its programming: in one game, Deep Blue purportedly made an accidentally random move that unnerved Kasparov, who could not make sense of the computer's logic and feared that he was facing an opponent with unfathomable intelligence. If true, this underscores the fact that succeeding at chess is not simply a matter of looking as many moves ahead as possible.

146   *you get infinite winding paths . . . :* One of the most common refrains that dark horses reported hearing from a teacher, counselor, or coach was, "You don't have what it takes." Few phrases are so disheartening. It is a naked assertion that your individuality is incompatible with excellence, because your apparent set of strengths don't resemble the standard form of excellence. Such an assertion is always a pretense that strengths are not fuzzy at all but accessible, universal, and fixed. Former squash player Elizabeth Ricker told us that the key turning point in her development as an athlete occurred when her high school squash coach told her, "You don't have what it takes for this sport." He went so far as to suggest that she quit the team to make room for players with more promise. "I'll tell you the truth, before he said that, I was more interested in playing

soccer than squash," Elizabeth told us. "But after that, I was so angry that I worked very hard to prove I could play. Keep in mind, he didn't say that as some kind of tactic to motivate me—he said it to get rid of me." She sought out a new coach, one who focused on Elizabeth's individuality. "I was still lacking confidence, and I kept asking him to tell me if I had talent or not. He refused to answer. He just focused on developing the things I could do well, maximizing what I had to work with. It was a much better approach for me, since I stopped asking the pointless question—do I have what it takes or not—and just moved forward, trying different things, trying to find something that worked for me." Elizabeth ended up as the best player on the team and eventually became one of the top-ranked female players in the country.

146   either *compelling characters* or *a compelling plot:* Surely every field requires at least *one* mandatory ability in its practitioners? To play the trumpet, you might argue, every aspiring musician must learn basic embouchure technique—the proper way to shape your lips to the mouthpiece, which every student is taught during their first year. To succeed at the pole vault, which requires that you firmly plant a heavy fifteen-foot pole into the ground and thrust yourself up and over a bar, you must have superior upper body strength. Except trumpeter Louis Armstrong became one of the most inventive jazz musicians in history without ever learning proper embouchure. And the relatively short Renaud Lavillenie set the world's record for pole vaulting at the 2012 Olympics despite having weaker upper body strength than most competitors.

147   *the spectacular variety of individual expertise:* We might call the variety of excellence the "*Mario Kart* Theory of Talent." In Nintendo's racing video game *Mario Kart*, each vehicle has its own unique set of performance traits, such as size, top speed, rate of acceleration, steadiness on curves, armor, and attack capability. Princess Peach is slow but has fast acceleration, for instance, while Toad handles sharp curves with quick bursts of speed. Yet, despite their differences, every vehicle has a chance of winning the race—*as long as you operate the vehicle according to its unique characteristics.* The *Mario Kart* Theory of Talent applies to all video games that allow you to select from a collection of avatars with variable traits, including *Civilization, Diablo,* and *Warcraft.*

163   *the dark horse mindset function as a gradient ascent algorithm:* To be more specific, the dark horse mindset is equivalent to a simulated annealing algorithm (bold moves) with stochastic gradient ascent (trial and error strategy selection, since your optimal strategy can never be known).

163   *Here's how gradient ascent works . . . .:* Nature already figured out how to harness the process of gradient ascent to improve the excellence of biolog-

ical life. It's called evolution by natural selection. Charles Darwin showed that even though amazing things like wings, claws, and human minds *seem* like predetermined biological destinations designed according to some long-term plan, in fact evolution proceeds by exclusively making near-term choices—by situational decision-making. Those organisms that manage to survive in the environment they face *right now*, and manage to reproduce *right now*, will pass on their traits to their offspring, who will repeat the process anew in whatever landscape they will face. Step by step, peak by peak, in an entirely unpredictable fashion, an amoeba can evolve into a monkey.

164   *you jump to an entirely new mountain . . . :* Bold moves (e.g., choosing a new opportunity or a new endeavor) are the counter to the local maximum problem, enabling you to jump to a new region of your landscape of excellence. You may continue to get stuck in local maxima, but what's wrong with that, as long as you're experiencing fulfillment along with each ascent to a local peak of excellence? The question isn't whether you will ever find your global maximum, but how the dark horse mindset's gradient ascent compares with what the standardization mindset offers you: a fixed, immobile ladder.

It's also worth pointing out that in reality your landscape of excellence will not be three-dimensional, as represented here, but highly multidimensional—and perhaps even infinite-dimensional. Regardless of the dimensionality of your excellence landscape, everything about the dark horse gradient ascent algorithm still holds and will still enable you to ascend to a local maximum with the possibility of jumping to other maxima.

167   *It just won't ever be straight:* Sometimes you have no alternative but to aim for a destination. Sometimes you need a diploma or other standardized credential to qualify for an opportunity that you believe will be a great fit for your individuality. As long as you've done the work of Knowing Your Micro-Motives and Knowing Your Choices, there's nothing wrong with making a destination your goal. When that happens, go right ahead and ride your well-engineered sense of purpose down the straight path. That's what Lars Winther did.

When he was young, Lars nursed vague hopes of one day playing professional hockey or perhaps getting a business degree. He enrolled in St. Lawrence College. "I played some football and some hockey, I joined a fraternity. I did not put academics as my first priority. I fell behind and then spent the year struggling to catch up." During the summer after his freshman year, Lars's brother Peter invited him to do a summer internship with him. Peter worked for the HBO series *1st & Ten*, featuring

O. J. Simpson in a starring role. It sounded interesting, so Lars headed to Los Angeles and began working as an office production assistant.

"Basically, you do things like take a stack of checks to the set for the producer to sign and then bring them back to the office," Lars says. "But the great thing was that twice a day I got to go to the set where all the action's at." As the end of the summer approached, Lars fully expected to return to college. "That was my plan. The internship was just something that seemed fun to try out. But the people who worked in the office, the production coordinator and production secretary, they really liked me. They got a new job on a new show, and they said, come join us."

That's when Lars experienced his turning point. He wasn't very happy studying in college, and he knew that sports wasn't a realistic path for him. On the other hand, he had enjoyed working on the show immensely—to his surprise, it felt like a terrific fit. But the idea of abandoning his education seemed like too drastic a decision. At first, he considered transferring to USC or UCLA and maybe majoring in film. "But on one of the sets there was another production assistant who was four years older than me, and he had just graduated from UCLA film school and here he's doing the same thing that I'm doing. And I'm like, *Why go to film school?* So there was a big mental shift where I made the decision—*Why don't I just start working and see where it takes me?*"

Lars abandoned the straight path of college for the winding path of exploring a career in Hollywood. The first step was to figure out what, exactly, he might like to do. He had no interest in being an actor—that much he knew from the start. He didn't want to be an agent or a manager, either. The idea of being a producer held some appeal, but to do that you needed a lot of money, which he certainly didn't have. After his experience working as an office PA, he knew he didn't want to work in an office—he wanted to be around the set, where all the action was. So he got a job as a set PA. "You're the low man on the totem pole, and you work long hours, but the great thing is you get to see a little bit of everything—the lighting guys, the wardrobe people, the makeup and hair people, the camera people. You get to work under the assistant director. It gives you the opportunity to go, *Wow, I like this!* Or, *Oh, there's no way I want that job!*"

At first he thought he might want to be a cinematographer. So he got a job as a camera PA. "It was hauling boxes and loading film, and I wasn't good at it and I got yelled at a lot. It wasn't what I thought it would be."

Next, he got a job as a special effects PA. "You're just a laborer, and that's some hard, dirty work. You're wetting down streets, putting down fake snow. I didn't see myself doing it."

Eventually he realized that the position that seemed to hold the most interest for him was working as an assistant director. "That job gave you a little bit of everything, which I liked. You work with actors, you work with the producer and the director, you're on the set all the time. You get to control people and things, which really appealed to me, because I like being a boss. There's a creative element, because you set up the crowd and you work hand in hand with the director and cinematographer. It's always something new and different, and I knew I needed constant change or I would get bored and lose interest. So I decided to take that route and try to become an assistant director on big-budget movies."

But there is one and only path to becoming an assistant director (AD) in the movie industry: a rigidly standardized professional ladder controlled by the Directors Guild of America. To reach his desired goal, Lars needed to work a certain number of hours as a "second second" AD, then a certain number of hours as a key second AD, after which he would finally be eligible to be hired as a first AD. Though Lars spent the next seven years of his life marching toward an institutional destination he had selected when he was in his early twenties, he had first done the necessary work to confidently judge that it would be a great fit for his micro-motives, and he expected to enjoy every step of his journey.

He was right.

"I loved almost every one of my jobs," Lars explained. "There's always a few busts, when a movie's funding falls through or the producer loses his mind, but even those were learning experiences. I don't regret a moment of it."

His first jobs as a second second AD were on two movies shot in Canada, *Dolores Claiborne* and *The Scarlet Letter*. He was quickly recognized for his enthusiasm for the job and caught an early break when Roland Emmerich (the eventual director of the *Independence Day* movies) hired him as the second second AD on *Universal Soldier*. Not long after that, he worked as the second second AD on *The Lost World: Jurassic Park*, directed by Steven Spielberg. After moving up to key second AD on a few movies, he was in the running to be the key second AD on Steven Spielberg's *A.I.* but turned it down in order to work his very first movie as a first AD, on *Eight Legged Freaks*, executive produced by Roland Emmerich.

Lars had followed the straight path to his destination.

Now that he was a working first AD, he had the freedom to do exactly what he wanted to do. After that, he worked as the first AD on *S.W.A.T.*, which was produced by a man named Louis D'Esposito. Louis became copresident of Marvel Studios and the executive producer of the first *Avengers* movie and hired Lars to be the first AD. Lars went on a run as the first AD on ten Marvel movies, including some of the most successful movies in recent years, such as *Spider-Man: Homecoming* and *Doctor Strange.*

Today, Lars still works as a first AD, but he also works as a producer for his own production company, Winther Bros. Entertainment, with multiple movie projects in the pipeline with budgets around twenty million dollars.

interlude: the battle for the Soul of human potential

175   *The conflict between these two mindsets . . . :* You might wonder: How can scientists, educators, and policymakers working in good faith arrive at such drastically different interpretations of talent? Because each side relies upon drastically different mathematics.

The math supporting the standardization mindset is fixed and rigid—it is *static*, hence its name, "statistics." It is a mathematics of averages, correlations, stereotypes, and ranking. The standardization mindset ignores the inevitability of change and therefore does not often consider the role of time, but when it does, its mathematics usually considers time as linear and absolute—as an independent variable that *causes* excellence.

There is a good reason that most working social scientists embrace the average-based statistics of the Standardization Covenant: it's much more convenient to conduct research on talent, education, and expertise using nineteenth-century statistics than the more complex methods of the twenty-first–century science of individuality. One consequence of this fact is that scientists who study excellence largely limit themselves to domains where it is easy to assign a one-dimensional score to talent. A prime example is chess.

Chess players are assigned a numerical rating (called an Elo score) that rises or falls with one's wins and losses in sanctioned competition. Thus, defining a player's level of talent in chess becomes a simple mathematical statement. You are a master if you have attained an Elo score of 2,300, for instance; a grandmaster, meanwhile, is someone whose score exceeds 2,700. This one-dimensional simplicity is one reason that chess has long served the same role in success research as the guinea pig in biology research or the *Drosophila* fruit fly in genetics research. It is a consensus "model organism" used in study after study.

Scientists who adopt the standardization mindset are always looking for similar one-dimensional measures of excellence that they can plug into their linear equations: studies of tennis excellence rely on the ATP

Rankings of player ability; studies of the excellence of scientists often use the number of citations a scientist's publications have received as a measure of their talent; studies of cooking excellence often rely on the average ratings of a group of tasters, another one-dimensional metric; studies of intelligence, of course, rely on IQ scores. In the standardization mindset, all of the jaggedness of chess talent, tennis talent, scientific talent, and cooking talent is boiled down into a single number that can easily be inserted into calculations of rankings and correlations.

The math supporting the dark horse mindset fully embraces change—it is *dynamic*, hence its name, "dynamical systems theory." It is a mathematics of multiple (and possibly infinite) dimensions where time is treated as a dependent variable that is nonlinear and relative. The mathematics of the dark horse mindset views individuals as complex and dynamic and interacting with an environment that is complex and dynamic, creating multidimensional nonlinear feedback loops that are often intractable. It views individuals as capable of dramatic change in ways that are difficult to predict, rendering it nearly impossible to make assertions about an individual's potential with any confidence. The mathematics of dynamical systems is the basis for gradient ascent. By expanding the number of dimensions and expanding our conception of time, the dark horse mindset is literally a more expansive conception of what it means to be human.

It is messier to study excellence through the lens of the science of individuality, and even more daunting, its results are often nuanced, nongeneralizable, and resistant to neat summation. It doesn't take much effort to crisply declare, "Student A is smarter than Student B because A has an IQ that is ten points higher than B." It's far more onerous to declare, "If it's night, summer, indoors, and the task is doing algebra problems with a group of peers, Student A will perform better than Student B. If it's day, autumn, outdoors, and the task is doing algebra problems alone, Student B will perform better than Student A."

chapter 6: tricking the Eye, cheating the Soul

177   *"Somebody once observed to the eminent . . .":* James Burke, *The Day the Universe Changed* (Little, Brown: New York, 2009), 11.

180   *Americans justifiably viewed themselves as the underdog . . . .:* The 1985 movie *Rocky IV*, released just before the end of the Cold War, features the American pugilist Rocky fighting the Soviets' top boxer, Ivan Drago. Rocky, of course, is portrayed as the underdog. What is amusing in retrospect is that Ivan is portrayed as benefiting from highly advanced So-

viet science and technology, while Rocky must rely upon more mundane training practices like chopping wood and jogging through the snow. The American wins in the end through superior heart, not superior talent. It's difficult to imagine any movie today portraying the USA as technologically inferior to another country.

180   *the same talent development system as everyone else, only better:* In both democracies and dictatorships, the reason the *authorities* endorsed the Standardization Covenant was straightforward: they believed that a standardized system of talent development guarantees that society will always have a predictable, reliable stream of world-class experts.

This conjecture happens to be true.

The reason the covenant was endorsed by the *people* in each society was also simple: they believed it was a fair and equitable meritocracy where anyone with talent can succeed.

This conjecture happens to be false.

191   *the answer is the same:* it depends: What kind of talent mold would you use to demonstrate that you had the necessary aptitude to become an orthodontist *and* a medieval Japanese history scholar *and* an urban planner? You might think that such a mold does not exist. But American universities would disagree. They believe they've found the perfect mold for all occasions, an all-purpose equant known as the GRE.

The Graduate Record Examination is a standardized test required as part of the admissions application at most graduate programs in *every* field. The test comes in two formats: the general GRE and the GRE subject tests. The general GRE is the more peculiar of the two. It contains abstract questions about trigonometry, logic, and vocabulary. The subject GREs are field-specific and contain questions evaluating your knowledge of the basic subject matter in that field, such as psychology, English literature, or chemistry.

If you were applying to a graduate program in psychology, you might expect that a test of your understanding of psychological methods, findings, and theories would be a more appropriate metric than a test of your ability to complete random sentences with fancy words. But that's not how standardized meritocracies work. American schools don't particularly care about the subject GREs. Precious few use them, and over the years most subject GREs have been eliminated. Instead, graduate programs want to know your score on the general GRE since that makes it easier for the gatekeepers to fudge their way to the results they want.

194   *Heidi Krieger was broad-shouldered . . . :* There is a sad coda to the story of Heidi Krieger, one that further illuminates the dark side of relying upon institution-dictated molds. Since institutions under the Standard-

ization Covenant have the power to decide what talent looks like for any given field, the authorities often used underhanded attempts to fit candidates to the desired mold. The Soviets initiated a secret doping program as early as the 1960s—a program that was never fully discontinued, as witnessed by the ban of Russian athletes at the 2016 Olympics. The tragedy is that the Soviet athletes themselves often didn't know they were getting drugged. The Soviets doped Heidi with anabolic steroids without her awareness or consent starting when she was sixteen, after she came in second at the Spartakiad, telling her the pills were "vitamins" or "supportive drugs." She ended up having a sex change and now lives as Andreas Krieger. Though he is happy with who he is now, his memories of what happened are still very painful. Andreas is married to a former East German swimmer who was also a doping victim. Together, they remain very involved in antidoping activism.

194   *a contestant in a beauty pageant, pleading, "Pick me! . . .":* Author Seth Godin refers to this as the "tyranny of being picked."

198   *The jagged profile:* For more about jagged profiles, see Todd Rose, *The End of Average.*

204   *a uniquely jagged profile of talent:* To put a finer point on the *Mario Kart* Theory of Talent: every vehicle has a chance of winning the race, as long as you operate the vehicle according to its jagged talent profile.

204   *the conceptual basis for the variety of human excellence:* As the pioneer of the science of individuality Peter Molenaar puts it, "An individual is a high-dimensional system evolving over place and time."

204   *a logical formalism that explains . . .:* The jagged profile also explains why your own potential for excellence is utterly unique. To see how, let's pretend that intelligence comprises thirteen dimensions of mental ability, with low correlations between dimensions. To simplify further, imagine that each of these dimensions is either high or low or average (you have either a large vocabulary or a small vocabulary or an average-size vocabulary, for instance). Under these very simple conditions, there will be more than 1.5 million different potential patterns of intelligence. If we double the number of dimensions of intelligence to twenty-six, we already have more patterns of intelligence than there are stars in the Milky Way, more than 2 trillion.

In reality, there is a nearly limitless number of potential dimensions of mental ability, each on a continuum. (Your ability to discern shades of blue is distinct from your ability to discern shades of red. Your ability to remember melodies is distinct from your ability to remember lyrics. Your ability to quickly generate a list of verbs is distinct from your ability to quickly generate a list of names.) Thus, the potential number of individ-

ual patterns of intelligence is for all intents and purposes infinite—and
your own jagged talent profile is far more unique than your fingerprint.

206   *all* you *need to do—is make a choice:* Fortunately, in the United States,
education is controlled by state and local governments, making it much
easier to change through voting and political processes than the central-
ized educational system of the Soviet Union. And it's even possible to
take matters into your own hands, as witnessed by the Opt Out Movement, consisting of parents who are refusing to let their children take
standardized tests.

chapter 7: the Dark Horse Covenant

207   *"It is also possible that the explosion . . .":* Thomas Piketty, *Capital in the
Twenty-First Century* (Cambridge: Belknap Press, 2014), 334.

208   *the term "meritocracy":* "Meritocracy" is a hobgoblin of a word, squash-
ing together the Latin *mereō,* "earn," and the Greek *kratos,* "power."

208   *his derisive label was co-opted . . .:* This also happened with other dispar-
aging terms from history like "impressionists," "suffragettes," and "big
bang theory."

209   *It is a quotacracy:* Aristocracies and quotacracies share one important
thing in common: they both always involve a roll of the dice. In an aristocracy, the roll of the dice happened before you were born: Were you
lucky enough to have a baroness or count as your parent? Under the Standardization Covenant, the roll of the dice happens after you are born,
once your "talent" is measured and ranked by the system to determine
whether you are special. No wonder people prefer the covenant—it gives
parents hope that their child's roll of the dice might still turn up sixes.

210   *the opportunities of the many are sacrificed . . .:* In a quotacracy, only a
small fraction of the population will ever fit the institutional mold for
standardized excellence, whether that mold is in a communist or capi-
talist nation. The Soviet Union, a totalitarian and individual-repressing
state, was able to maintain talent parity with the United States, a free and
individual-celebrating state, because of the mathematics of negative-
sum games. It was a straightforward arithmetical consequence of implementing a quotacracy in two nations with similarly sized populations
and similar notions of what excellence looks like.

When you pit one quotacracy against another, the winner—the
producer of more top-shelf excellence—is ultimately determined by
who has more candidates to choose from. If the number of spots at the
top of the talent ladder is fixed—say, Olympics team, or Mathematical
Olympiad team, or astronauts, or ballet team—then whoever has the

greater population has a greater chance to fit the mold of standardized excellence.

In 1980, the population of the two adversaries was very similar, with an edge to the Soviets: 226 million in the United States and 265 million in the USSR. Even today, with the Soviet Union gone, Americans still evaluate their nation's educational success by comparing their students to other nations' students using the same international standard molds of excellence, such as the PISA (Programme for International Student Assessment) test. But as long as our notion of talent involves a fixed template, and as long as we maintain a standardized meritocracy, we will eventually be doomed to "losing" to other nations using standardized meritocracies that have larger populations—such as China, and perhaps one day India and Brazil. We're all playing the same negative-sum game, which places strict limits on the number of elite talents who will be manufactured by the system.

The United States didn't win the Cold War because of our superior system of talent development or our superior elite talent. Both were the same as the USSR's. But the United States always had an overlooked talent advantage, one hiding in the shadows but that made all the difference. This talent advantage was hidden inside our divergent economic systems.

The United States has what economists call a "market economy." In a market economy, every economic agent, whether an individual or an enterprise, is free to independently produce or consume products as they see fit. Since every agent is free to make choices according to their individual needs and wants, the forces of supply and demand help distribute resources where they are needed most and raise the standard of living for everyone. A market economy is a positive-sum game of production.

The Soviet Union, in contrast, had what economists call a "command economy." It is inflexible, highly inefficient, and has tremendous difficulty growing. In theory, a command economy is a zero-sum game at best, though in practice the Soviet system operated as a negative-sum game of production.

In a command economy, a "central planning committee" arbitrarily decides how many products to manufacture, regardless of demand, and without individual profit in mind. In the USSR, the State Planning Committee (or Gosplan) decided how many automobiles, apples, and shoes the country's factories would produce every five years. In other words, the State Planning Committee set a fixed production quota.

Where else do we find a fixed production quota? In our system of higher education. Every quotacracy functions as a command economy. Every standardized university imposes a talent quota decided by a cen-

tral planning committee—the university administrators—regardless of
the actual demand for talent in society. Just as Soviet factories didn't
care whether they produced enough (or too many) shoes to meet the
demands of its citizens, American educational institutions don't care
whether they produce enough (or too many) engineers, doctors, or play-
wrights. It overproduces talent in fields with low demand and underpro-
duces talent in fields with high demand; even more disastrously—and
just like the Soviet command economy system—it manufactures narrow forms of standardized excellence instead of opening itself up to the
production of an unlimited and unpredictable variety of excellence, like
the American market economy.

And not surprisingly, the Soviet command economy was rife with
corruption, just like our own quotacracy. Since there were never enough
products to meet the demand, high-level Soviet officials skimmed the
best items for themselves directly from the top of the production chain.
Everywhere else down the line, bribery and backdoor access were the
norms. And in our educational quotacracy, the wealthy and privileged
get special access to spots in the limited quota.

Yet, even though the USA and USSR remained locked in talent parity at the elite levels, the overall breadth of talent produced by the USA
was much greater. How did this happen? The USA did not win the
Cold War because of our quotacracy. We won *despite* our quotacracy.
We won the competition for the greatest variety of human excellence.
*We won the Cold War because our market economy gave individuals the
freedom to follow a winding path.*

In the USSR, if you were booted from the talent ladder, there was no
alternate path to success. But in the USA, even if you fail to make it into
a talent quota, you still have a chance to succeed, because our market
economy provides opportunity to everyone, regardless of whether you fit
a talent equant or not. The United States won the Cold War because of
the dropouts, burnouts, rebels, and misfits, working in the margins, unsung and unappreciated. We won because of the Doug Hoerrs and Ingrid
Carozzis and Saul Shapiros and Alan Rouleaus and Susan Rogerses.

210   *Far more than half the population will never even get the chance . . .:* What
happens if you try to climb to the top of the ladder but are outcompeted
by the other candidates grappling on your rung? In the Soviet Union,
out of the hundreds of thousands of students who ardently desired to
develop excellence in electrical engineering, opera singing, or water polo,
only a handful were ever admitted to the supreme rung. Many more
hopefuls who were just as passionate and purposeful were left behind. In
the USSR, the reality for these also-rans was almost never a career of ex-

cellence, nor even a career of near-excellence. Once cut, these castaways received no further support from the state—at least, no support different from that due any Soviet citizen. As one former Soviet-bloc athlete told us: "In East Germany, all the lifeguards at the community swimming pools had been cut from the national swimming program. These were elite swimmers, and many of them had fallen one level short of making the national squad. Even though they did not have any money or status as lifeguards, they were still the lucky ones—most swimmers who did not make the national team ended up working in a factory."

211 *But that's not the only way . . .:* Even if you aren't lucky enough to fit the institutional mold, there are other ways to game a quotacracy. Just *pretend* to fit the mold. Fabricate extracurricular activities, lie on your college essay, forge letters of recommendation. Another common mold-fitting technique is cheating on standardized tests, a practice that is common throughout the world but that has been elevated to an art form in China, where tests are the most important component of the country's rigid academic mold.

In a democratic meritocracy, the opportunities for cheating are drastically reduced, since there are no standardized tests, no quotas, no institutional molds. You are not trying to be better than everyone else; you're trying to be your best self.

212 *"gave favorable admissions treatment . . .":* Stephanie Saul, "Public Colleges Chase Out-of-State Students, and Tuition," *New York Times*, July 7, 2016, https://www.nytimes.com/2016/07/08/us/public-colleges-chase-out-of-state-students-and-tuition.html.

212 *the wealthy and the privileged will always have an advantage . . .:* The aristocracy that existed at the dawn of the Age of Standardization *loved* the rise of the meritocracy. It was like a moral laundry machine. At a time when the commoners were beginning to foment rebellion against the moneyed class (and even succeeding, in Russia and parts of South America), along came a system of opportunity that billed itself as a system of merit. The lower and middle classes loved the Standardization Covenant, because it promised that everyone willing to work hard and follow the straight path could rise to the top of society's ladder and enjoy the privileges previously reserved for the aristocracy. And a great many did indeed make the climb. But the aristocracy liked it, too, since they could still buy their way into the quota, but now instead of worrying about getting tagged with an attack-inviting label like "plutocrat," "robber baron," or "oligarch," they could wave a diploma with the name of a fancy university on it—the same kind of diploma that now seemed open to anyone with talent. In a meritocracy, they became mer-

itorious rather than predacious. The old-school aristocracy never went away. They just learned to hide themselves behind Harvard MBAs and Stanford Law degrees.

213   *Over the past century, many people . . . :* We shouldn't disparage standard-ization too much, though. There are no villains here. We needed the Age of Standardization to create the conditions so that we could have a new social contract enabling the formation of a democratic meritoc-racy. We needed the Age of Standardization to invent the sciences and technologies that made the Age of Personalization possible, just as the Age of Feudalism made the Age of Mercantilism possible. Standardized industry gave us a robust, diverse economy. Standardized businesses gave us personalized technologies. Standardized science gave us the necessary data, insights, and information to leave it behind. We needed Ptolemy's *Almagest* before we could have Newton's *Principia Mathematica*.

215   *We have the right economy for a democratic meritocracy:* "Every existing society, even the most individualistic one, takes two things for granted, if only subconsciously: that organizations outlive workers, and that most people stay put. But today the opposite is true. Knowledge workers outlive organizations, and they are mobile. The need to manage oneself is therefore creating a revolution in human affairs," Peter Drucker con-cludes in *Managing Oneself* (page 55).

217   *one thing that each of us . . . :* Self-correction is an American trait. It's wired into our political system (the amendments to the US Constitu-tion). It's wired into our economic system (the free market principles of capitalism). But it never got wired into our educational system.

217   *inextricably linked with a society's perception of merit and its system of op-portunity:* We didn't agree to every little detail that we now have under the Standardization Covenant. We never agreed to career ladders, talent equants, or standardized tests. Those were outcomes of the basic so-cial truths that we bought into—namely, that only special people have talent and deserve the best opportunities, and that those who sacrifice personal fulfillment for the pursuit of professional excellence deserve society's rewards.

218   *the opportunity to pursue fulfillment, and you are accountable for your own fulfillment:* The terms of this Dark Horse Covenant are staunchly nonpartisan, or perhaps more accurately postpartisan, because they fuse into a seamless unity what is often considered a bedrock liberal principle (equal opportunity) and what is often considered a bedrock conservative principle (individual responsibility). However, under the Dark Horse Covenant, each principle takes on a different meaning than we're accustomed to.

218   *These two obligations—when conjoined together . . .:* To understand why
a system based upon Equal Fit and Personal Accountability unleashes
excellence instead of artificially limiting it, just consider this question:
What if every student in a school graduated with a perfect 4.0 GPA? In
other words, what if every single student attained excellence?

    In a standardized meritocracy, if every student in a school graduated
with a perfect 4.0 GPA, we would react with severe and justified skepti-
cism. We might assume there was grade inflation, widespread cheating,
or some other corruption of the system. No other conclusion is possible
if we believe that talent is rare and rankable. We might even instinctively feel derision toward the idea that every child is an A student,
mocking the guilty school for treating everyone like special snowflakes
and declaring everyone a winner. Most likely, the school would apply a
bell curve or other arbitrary differentiator, as the SAT does, to figure out
who "truly" possessed merit and who was merely mediocre.

    In a democratic meritocracy, however, since every student is free to
get better at the things they care about most—since they can choose
their own winding educational path, learn at their own pace, and select strategies that fit their jagged talent profile—every student can and
should excel at their chosen program of study. Democratic meritocracies
reject the use of grades, of course, but we would expect every single student to pass their chosen competency-based evaluation, as long as they
are provided with genuine choice.

221   *But to implement a working democratic meritocracy . . . .:* Every society
faces a fundamental question regarding its form of social organization:
Who has the obligation to conform to the other, the institutions or
the people? Under the Standardization Covenant, the institution reigns
supreme. This doctrine was stated right up front in 1911 by Frederick
Taylor when he declared, "In the past the man has been first; in the
future the system must be first." But under the Dark Horse Covenant,
it is the institutions that must conform to the people.

222   *the real challenge for providing Equal Fit . . . .:* But we must stay vigilant
in making sure that everyone has access to personalization technologies
and that the best systems are not hoarded by a privileged few. So far, the
leading developers of personalized education technologies have managed to offer them to all sectors of the populace, but we should never
take this for granted. Personalization and choice must be universally
available to make our democratic meritocracy a positive-sum game for
everyone.

224   *Why would an institution ever want . . . .:* There are two big advantages
institutions that provide personalization and choice will have over

standardized institutions: increased growth and increased productivity. By getting rid of quotas, personalized institutions can adopt business models based on growth, as opposed to the static models employed by standardized institutions. We see this remarkable growth potential in both Summit Learning and Southern New Hampshire University. Also, personalized institutions get greater productivity out of their employees because they value personal fulfillment. Fulfilled employees are more engaged and more productive.

conclusion: the pursuit of Happiness

235   *"He who receives an idea from me . . .":* Thomas Jefferson, letter to Isaac McPherson, August 13, 1813. We also considered as an epigraph this quotation from Robert Louis Stevenson: "There is no duty we so much underrate as the duty of being happy."

235   *The most influential sentence in Western political history:* Though this chapter draws from many sources, we are most heavily indebted to Garry Wills's *Inventing America: Jefferson's Declaration of Independence* (1978) for introducing us to its central theme. *Inventing America* was, for us, the most useful and informative text we have yet encountered about the Declaration. We highly recommend it.

    For a summary of the latest scholarly thinking about the inclusion of "the pursuit of Happiness" in the Declaration—including a critique of Garry Wills's arguments—we recommend reading the highly informative entry on "The Pursuit of Happiness" in *The Bloomsbury Encyclopedia of Utilitarianism*, edited by James Crimmins.

236   *appeared in an Edinburgh magazine: The Scots Magazine,* August 1776.

237   *the preferred version:* See "Jefferson's Draft of the Declaration of Independence, 28 June, 1776," American History, http://www.let.rug.nl /usa/documents/1776-1785/jeffersons-draft-of-the-declaration-of -independence.php.

239   *"as a father, to his enlightened . . .":* Letter from Thomas Jefferson to Louis H. Girardin, January 15, 1815.

240   *historian Jack D. Warren observes that happiness:* Jack D. Warren, "George Mason, the Thoughtful Revolutionary," *Gunston Gazette* 6, no. 1 (2001): 6–8: http://www.gunstonhall.org/georgemason/essays/warren _essay.html#jdw.

241   *John Locke wrote a penetrating analysis . . . :* "As therefore the highest perfection of intellectual nature lies in a careful and constant pursuit of true and solid happiness; so the care of ourselves, that we mistake not imaginary for real happiness, is the necessary foundation of our

liberty. The stronger ties we have to an unalterable pursuit of happiness in general, which is our greatest good, and which, as such, our desires always follow, the more are we free from any necessary determination of our will to any particular action, and from a necessary compliance with our desire, set upon any particular, and then appearing preferable good, till we have duly examined whether it has a tendency to, or be inconsistent with, our real happiness: and therefore, till we are as much informed upon this inquiry as the weight of the matter, and the nature of the case demands, we are, by the necessity of preferring and pursuing true happiness as our greatest good, obliged to suspend the satisfaction of our desires in particular cases." In John Locke, *An Essay Concerning Human Understanding* (T. Tegg and Son, 1836), 171.

241 *"Men are necessarily determined to pursue . . .":* Francis Hutcheson, *An Essay on the Nature and Conduct of the Passions and Affections* (R. and A. Foulis, 1769), 31.

241 *"The great pursuit of man is after happiness . . .":* Laurence Sterne, *The Complete Works: With a Life of the Author Written by Himself* (Edinburgh: Nimmo, 1882), 251.

242 *"the happiness of the society is the first law . . .":* "All men are, by nature, equal and free: no one has a right to any authority over another without his consent: all lawful government is founded on the consent of those who are subject to it: such consent was given with a view to ensure and to increase the happiness of the governed, above what they could enjoy in an independent and unconnected state of nature. The consequence is, that the happiness of the society is the first law of every government." Written by American founding father James Wilson in 1768 in "Considerations on the Nature and Extent of the Legislative Authority of the British Parliament," as referenced in James Wilson, *The Works of the Honourable James Wilson*, ed. Bird Wilson (Philadelphia: Lorenzo Press, 1804), 206.

242 *"The general happiness is the supreme end . . .":* Francis Hutcheson and William Leechman, *A System of Moral Philosophy*, 3 vol. (London: Millar, 1755), 1:226.

243 *"There is a principle of benevolence . . .":* Henry Home, Lord Kames, *Essays on the Principles of Morality and Natural Religion: In Two Parts* (C. Hitch and L. Hawes, R. and J. Dodsley, J. Rivington and J. Fletcher, and J. Richardson, 1758), 57.

243 *"That each Agent may discover . . .":* Francis Hutcheson, *An Essay on the Nature and Conduct of the Passions and Affections* (London: A. Ward, V. and P. Knapton, and T. Longman, 1756), 210–11.

243   *"It is likewise true that the happiness of individuals . . .":* Adam Fergu-
       son, *An Essay on the History of Civil Society* (Dublin: Boulter Grierson,
       1767), 85.

244   *"the 'pursuit of happiness' has to do with an internal journey . . .":* A sim-
       ilar idea is expressed by Linda Bolton in *Facing the Other: Ethical Dis-
       ruption and the American Mind* (Baton Rouge: Louisiana State Univ.
       Press, 2004), 101: "We must read this tenet of the Declaration as one
       that prioritizes and, at least in theory, ensures the responsibility of the
       individual to the whole. Jefferson's ideal citizen, in the pursuit of his
       particular happiness, discovers that happiness is dependent upon the
       well-being and happiness of those with whom he is associated through
       the 'silken bands' of government and society."

245   *a natural obligation to give back to the society . . . :* Fulfillment is the only
       possible mechanism for ensuring this, since any other metric results in
       winners and losers. Fulfillment is the only way we can all win, since—
       like Jefferson's comparison of ideas to a candle flame—your fulfillment
       can increase without diminishing mine.

       One reason for this is the fact that almost all our interactions with
       institutions of opportunity under the Standardization Covenant are
       transactional. I pay you tuition, and in return I expect a diploma (rather
       than an education). I am paying you for a precious slot in the talent
       quota, and in return you damn well better help me climb the talent
       ladder. But this means that those who don't get a spot in the quota,
       those who are booted off the ladder, feel no obligation toward anyone.
       My educational transactions did not benefit me, so why in the world
       should I give back?

       In contrast, almost all our interactions under the Dark Horse Cov-
       enant are *relational.* You are getting better at the things that matter
       most to you. You are attaining fulfillment and excellence on your own
       terms. Now you must give something back to the system that wel-
       comed you, warts and all, and gave you so much—a system that re-
       spected and nurtured your individuality, instead of compelling you to
       fit the mold to climb the ladder.

index

about the authors

Todd Rose is the author of the bestselling *The End of Average*. He is the director of the Mind, Brain, and Education program at the Harvard Graduate School of Education (HGSE), where he leads the Laboratory for the Science of Individuality. He completed his graduate work at HGSE, where he was mentored by Kurt Fischer, one of the pioneers of the science of individuality. Dr. Rose was a postdoctoral researcher at the Harvard-Smithsonian Center for Astrophysics. He is the cofounder of Populace, a nonprofit organization dedicated to transforming how we learn, work, and live so that all people have the opportunity to live a fulfilling life.

Ogi Ogas is the director of the Dark Horse Project in the Laboratory for the Science of Individuality at the Harvard Graduate School of Education. He received his PhD in computational neuroscience from Boston University and was a Department of Homeland Security fellow. Dr. Ogas attended the Massachusetts Institute of Technology on an AT&T science and engineering scholarship.